Rhetorical Women

Rhetorical Women

Roles and Representations

Edited by
Hildy Miller and Lillian Bridwell-Bowles

The University of Alabama Press
Tuscaloosa

∞
The paper on which this book is printed meets the minimum requirements of American National Standard for Information Science—Permanence of Paper for Printed Library Materials, ANSI Z39.48–1984.

Typeface: Minion

Library of Congress Cataloging-in-Publication Data

Rhetorical women : roles and representations / edited by Hildy Miller and Lillian Bridwell-Bowles.
p. cm.
Includes bibliographical references and index.
ISBN 0-8173-1458-X (alk. paper) — ISBN 0-8173-5183-3 (pbk. : alk. paper)
1. English literature—Women authors—History and criticism. 2. American literature—Women authors—History and criticism. 3. Feminism and literature—English-speaking countries. 4. Women and literature—English-speaking countries. 5. Authorship—Sex differences. 6. English language—Rhetoric. 7. Feminism in literature. 8. Sex role in literature. 9. Women in literature. I. Miller, Hildy, 1950– II. Bridwell-Bowles, Lillian.
PR111.R48 2005
820.9′9287—dc22

2004025899

Contents

Acknowledgments

In the richest sense of feminist collaboration, this collection is the result of contributions from our colleagues at many universities. Our work has been enriched by exchanges with women scholars around the world, and we hope that readers new to this constellation of fields that is "feminist rhetoric" will find ways to connect with others doing pioneering work at the intersections.

We begin with our thanks to Lisa Ede and Cheryl Glenn, the founders of the Feminism(s) and Rhetoric(s) Conference, first held at Oregon State University in 1997. They planted the seeds for an international gathering of women interested in roles and representations of women as rhetors and rhetoricians.

In 1999 we reunited many of these same women and added more from around the world at the Second Biennial Feminism(s) and Rhetoric(s) Conference at the University of Minnesota in Minneapolis, a conference we cochaired. Our work at Minnesota was enriched by colleagues such as Ann Browning, Erika Rivers, Mary Strunk, Terri Klegin, Linda Tetzlaff, Karlyn Kohrs Campbell, Lisa Albrecht, Mary Lay, Laura Gurak, and many others who added their expertise and care to our efforts.

The exchanges and intellectual stimulation at these biennial gatherings have flourished at each new venue (Millikin University, chaired by Nancy

DeJoy in 2001; Ohio State University, chaired by Nan Johnson in 2003), and we look forward to many more collaborations to come (including the 2005 conference at Michigan Technological University, chaired by Elizabeth Flynn).

The Coalition of Women Scholars in the History of Rhetoric and Composition, which meets annually at the Conference on College Composition and Communication, has also provided an organizational structure that is crucial to scholars in rhetoric, composition, and gender studies. For this we thank its founding members and ongoing leaders such as those mentioned above, as well as Andrea Lunsford, Shirley Logan, Jacqueline Jones Royster, Joy Ritchie, Kate Ronald, Susan Jarratt, and many others. Without these opportunities to learn from feminist scholars, we would not have had the vision for this book.

Our current colleagues at Portland State University and Louisiana State University continue to support us. Michelle Masse, Katrina Powell, Jim Catano, and Tiffany Walter in particular, provided support for our work in women's and gender studies, as well as critical readings that made our work better. We are also grateful to Cheryl Glenn for her helpful advice on our manuscript. And, finally, special thanks goes to the University of Alabama Press, including the anonymous reviewers who sharpened our focus, and our excellent editor, Daniel Waterman, for his steady encouragement of the project.

We also wish to thank the following publishers for granting permission to reprint the following essays either in part or in their entirety:

University of Chicago Press for Lois Cucullu's essay, "Exceptional Women, Expert Culture, and the Academy," which appeared in *Signs* 29.1 (Autumn 2003), 27–54.

Composition Studies for Cindy Moore's essay, "Why Feminists Can't Stop Talking about Voice," part of which appeared in *Composition Studies* 30.2 (Fall 2002), 11–25.

The National Council of Teachers of English for Malea Powell's essay, "Princess Sarah, the Civilized Indian: The Rhetoric of Cultural Literacies in Sara Winnemucca Hopkins's *Life among the Piutes.*" Parts of this essay appeared as "Rhetorics of Survivors: How American Indians Use Writing," in *College Composition and Communication* 53.3 (Feb. 2002), 396–434.

Duke University Press and Taylor and Francis Books for Jane Gallop's essay, "Econstructing Sisterhood," which appeared both in *Anecdotal Theory* by Jane Gallop, Duke University Press, 2002, 135–54, and in *Time and the Literary,* edited by Karen Newman et al., Routledge, 2002, 101–18.

Rhetorical Women

Introduction

Whenever writers, rhetors, historians, critics, or artists attempt to represent "woman," or even "a woman," they inevitably risk being accused of missing the mark—either deliberately or unintentionally—out of misogyny or ignorance of a range of possible vantage points and interpretations. This is true whether women or men are doing the representing. Nearly always someone can see the woman's role from a different perspective. Certainly, before the nineteenth century no culture had produced a literate audience diverse enough to recognize the social implications of consistently representing women from a male or patriarchal perspective. Since the middle of the last century, feminist theorists have outlined a number of different "feminisms" and feminist perspectives that prove helpful in trying to understand the contested rhetorical spaces women have occupied throughout recorded history.

In this collection of essays we hope to outline some of the major rhetorical patterns that are at work in this complicated business of representation—from describing the rhetorical perspective of self, to the positions of individual women rhetors, to whole groups of women in various periods. We know that our collection of essays does not capture all of these mechanisms, but we hope that the ones we have included will suggest many other patterns and individual cases yet to be examined.

From the beginnings of recorded history, as in the mythologies of foundational Western civilizations, the allowable spaces for women have been limited and therefore rhetorically complicated. For example, when Ariadne aided and abetted Theseus and provided the thread to help him find his way out of the labyrinth and escape the Minotaur, she functioned in the role of helpmate, a silent partner who made it possible for the hero to prevail. She provided him with the tools he needed to make sense of his ancient predicament. Some have even said that she was the real hero. And yet there are complex ambiguities in the ways the generations have interpreted her actions, both in art and in literature. At times she is portrayed as a helpless victim, a lover abandoned in her sleep by the ungrateful hero. At other times she is a powerful figure, exercising her own agency in the world. Sometimes, after giving all she has of herself, she is relegated to a celestial position, deified and fixed in the heavens as a constellation, an ornament. In Edmund Spenser's words, "Being now placed in the firmament, through the bright heaven doth her beams display, and is unto the starres an ornament" (*The Faerie Queen,* Book VI, Canto X, iii).

Such variety in representation is often the case with women who have succeeded in speaking to us from their historical positions. Too often their reputations and relationships to male figures, perceived to be more important, have overshadowed their own actions and words. Also, too often, even when their words have come down to us, they have been interpreted as mythological rather than possible, ideal rather than real, exceptional rather than expected, and—even more often—as inferior, eccentric, plagiarized, or derivative. Much recent work in feminist rhetorical studies has sought to rectify these distortions by focusing on three major strands of inquiry: (1) basic archeological work—simply digging out the literary, oratorical, and rhetorical legacies of women who wrote or spoke publicly; (2) reinterpreting the work of women whose reputations have not received their due or whose depictions now seem inadequate; and (3) cultural critique of the ways gender, class, race, religion, language, and other aspects illuminate the roles and representations of women writers and rhetors. Rapidly developing feminist theories, along with these rhetorical analyses, make this collection possible.

Women's rhetorical history is analogous to almost all other histories of cultural production. Similar themes can be found in histories of literature, music, and art. For example, Judy Chicago, in her recent anthology, *Women and Art: Contested Territory,* coedited with Edward Lucie-Smith, writes that "women have been involved in art for many centuries—often meeting obstacles in obtaining training and the right to professional opportunities, as well as having to face social disgrace at worst, extreme isolation at best" (15).

Her anthology is an attempt to depict "this struggle over representation, about who is to determine the nature of female identity and, of course, ultimately, who decides what constitutes great art." (15). Among the many roles Chicago and Lucie-Smith include in their collection are the woman as goddess, lesbian, visionary, virgin, crone, hero, saint, mother, laborer, domestic, shopper, musician, painter, traveler, seductress, whore, martyr, killer, rebel, body (or body part), child, narcissist, exotic "other," victim, patient, and libertarian. As we studied these images, we realized that so many of the rhetorical roles that have been available to women parallel their visual histories (as object) and artistic roles (as agent). If one were to take popular depictions of women at face value in much of Western history (and most rhetorical history is limited to Greco-Roman and Judeo-Christian heritage in the West), we would have a most distorted picture, written (or painted) from the perspective of mostly male authors who are unaware that there might be other perspectives. The archeological work necessary for our field must correct the distortion by finding the missing texts, reinterpreting those that have been read only from a hegemonic perspective, and creating new kinds of texts and interpretive theories.

Like Ariadne's traces in Greek mythology and the images of women in the history of art, the depictions of women in the history of rhetoric reveal women in a range of subject positions, sometimes enabling male heroes and at other times acting on their own, sometimes claiming their own authority to speak and at other times justifying themselves with visions, insanity, religion, collaborations, and associations with hegemonic ideas. Occasionally some rise to popularity and are deified and fixed in a canonical firmament because they are all we have found of women's presence at particular historical moments. Witness Aspasia and Mary Astell and Julian of Norwich, to name only a few of the larger-than-life heroines we often study in rhetorical history.

New Rhetorics and New Frameworks in Feminist Rhetorics

Much work in the last twenty years lays the groundwork for the material we present here. To name a few key book-length studies appearing in our field: Miriam Brody's *Manly Writing;* Andrea Lunsford's *Reclaiming Rhetorica;* Cheryl Glenn's *Rhetoric Retold;* Louise Phelps and Janet Emig's *Feminine Principles and American Experience in American Composition and Rhetoric;* Susan Jarratt and Lynn Worsham's *Feminism and Composition Studies;* Krista Ratcliffe's *Anglo-American Feminist Challenges to the Rhetorical Tradition;* Jacqueline Jones Royster's *Traces of a Stream* and *Southern Horrors and Other Writings;* and Christine Mason Sutherland and Rebecca Sutcliffe's *The Changing Tradition.* Most of these studies, through the processes of reclaiming rhetors and reinterpreting texts, contributed to the formation of possible new canons, even as they critiqued the process of canon formation and defined the existence of the field of feminist rhetorics.

For scholarly work in this group, an opening question was "Who, indeed, are the woman rhetors?" Lunsford, Glenn, Ratcliffe, Royster, and Sutherland and Sutcliffe all presented previously unknown, minor, or misinterpreted women rhetors, ranging from antiquity to the present. The classical figure of Aspasia, for example, was a shadowy minor character in our histories of rhetoric, thought of mainly as a consort of Pericles in fifth-century Athens, until her name and influence became known through Lunsford's book and through others in this group. Historical and contemporary figures as varied as Julian of Norwich, Mary Astell, Margaret Fell, Julia Kristeva, and Susanne Langer also appeared for the first time as rhetoricians to widespread audiences in rhetoric and composition. Still other figures, known but not generally thought of as rhetors, were introduced: Glenn, for example, made the case that Elizabeth I was not just a monarch but a skillful rhetorician; Ratcliffe claimed rhetorical theorist status for Adrienne Rich and Virginia Woolf, more often thought of strictly as literary figures, and for Mary Daly, usually thought of as a theologian. Royster uncovered African American women rhetors, including Ida B. Wells and lesser-known figures such as Mary Jane Patterson. Collections of critical essays by Molly Meijer Wertheimer and by Sutherland and Sutcliffe ranged across history from classical to contemporary rhetors. And Lunsford's book, in particular, was a bellwether, often singled out as the first volume of scholarly commentary on women in rhetoric.

Beyond recovering and reclaiming, these scholars provided new frameworks for conceptualizing the work of women rhetors; they wrestled with the question of how to validate and enrich the representations of these figures through analysis and how to write appropriately revisionist histories that would take into consideration their richer accounts. Glenn, for example, presented the overarching metaphor of a rhetorical map as a scheme for including women in rhetoric. She encouraged us to envision this process as one of veering off the usual well-worn paths not only onto side roads but also into wholly uncharted territory. Patricia Bizzell (in an essay appearing in Phelps and Emig's volume) suggested the metaphorical figure of Erasmus's Folly to depict the rhetorical authority of women trying to speak from the margins. Since, as often as not, women were denied access to formal education, these works also began the process of suggesting where to look for women rhetors—in cloisters, at salons, on abolition and temperance platforms, in private homes, and elsewhere.

We find too in these books some of the first rereadings of women in rhetorical history. Essays by Shirley Logan and by Joy Ritchie and Kate Ronald (appearing in Jarratt and Worsham's collection) represented these efforts, with Logan's being one of the first to consider gender in relation to other axes of difference, such as race, and with both essays seeking connections between present-day practices and their historical precedents. Brody's book sweepingly critiqued the gendered nature of what we previously thought of as the rhetorical tradition, showing not only how most contributors were male but also how masculinist values (argument, persuasive ethos, etc.) permeated our conventional readings of rhetorical history. These studies, then, are chief among those that identified women rhetors, justified rereadings of rhetorical history, and modeled the kinds of research—namely, the examination of archival materials—that later became commonplace in the field.

Socially Situated Analyses of Women Rhetors

As the field of feminist rhetorics began to achieve identity and status, and as it tested more valid methodologies, another layer of outstanding work focused on a more specific level of cultural critique: Shirley Logan's *"We Are Coming"*; Carol Mattingly's *Well-Tempered Women* and *Appropriate[ing] Dress;* Susan Miller's *Assuming the Positions;* Anne Ruggles Gere's *Intimate Practices;* Molly Meijer Wertheimer's *Listening to Their Voices;* Danielle Clarke and Elizabeth Clarke's *"This Double Voice";* Janet Carey Eldred and Peter Mortensen's *Imagining Rhetoric;* Gwendolyn Audrey Foster's *Troping the Body;* Cinthia Gannett's *Gender and the Journal;* and Nan Johnson's *Nineteenth-Century Rhetoric in North America* and *Gender and Rhetorical Space in American Life, 1866–1910.* In this recent work we see a focus on particular issues, figures, groups, or contexts that suggests not only the socially "situatedness" of rhetoric but also a flowering of responses to the question "What are the sites of women's rhetoric?"

In the domestic sphere Gannett looked at private journal keeping; Foster, at etiquette texts and conduct literature; and Johnson (*Gender and Rhetorical Space*), at elocution manuals and letter-writing handbooks. Others examined particular locations of women's literacy, such as Mattingly, who considered the women who wrote and spoke as part of the nineteenth-century temperance movement; Gere, who looked at the literacy practices of women's clubs (including Jewish, African American, and white women) from 1880 to 1920; Logan, who examined the public discourse of African American club- and churchwomen from 1880 to 1900; and Miller, who exhaustively examined the writing of upper-class Virginians, including many women, from 1650 to 1880, as they produced diaries, letters, recipes, and commonplace books. Some works covered wider-ranging studies of women in historical periods, including Clarke and Clarke, who considered gendered writing in early modern England; Eldred and Mortensen, who looked at American women's civic rhetoric between the American Revolution and the Civil War; and Johnson, who critiqued nineteenth-century rhetorical practices (*Nineteenth-Century Rhetoric*). In all of these studies we see the varied rhetorical locations of women rhetors and how they managed to make themselves heard, though from outside the conventional sites and genres to which most male rhetors had access.

New and Revised Canons

And finally we find, as an important sign of growth of the field, a third group consisting of the collected works of an individual rhetor, more inclusive anthologies, and new anthologies of women rhetors. The canons that we saw forming in the first wave of scholarship about women rhetors are indeed coming to fruition. This grouping speaks to the related questions "How can adding women create revised rhetorical canons?" and "What are possible canons of women rhetoricians?" Among this group are JoAnn Campbell's *Toward a Feminist Rhetoric;* Patricia Bizzell and Bruce Herzberg's *The Rhetorical Tradition;* Michael G. Moran and Michelle Ballif's *Twentieth-Century Rhetorics and Rhetoricians;* Karlyn Kohrs Campbell's *Man Cannot Speak for Her;* Joy Ritchie and Kate Ronald's *Available Means;* Karen Foss, Sonja Foss, and Cindy Griffin's *Feminist Rhetorical Theories and Readings in Feminist Rhetorical Theory;* and Jane Donawerth's *Rhetorical Theory by Women before 1900.*

JoAnn Campbell's critical edition of the works of Gertrude Buck, a pivotal figure in women's rhetorical history—actively trained as a rhetorician and teacher of writing, and intentionally producing rhetorical theory—stands as perhaps one of the first widely distributed critical editions of a single figure in our field. Meanwhile, anthologies also began to change. Early on, Bizzell and Herzberg produced a relatively more inclusive anthology of rhetors than we had seen before, with their first edition of *The Rhetorical Tradition,* which included a small number of women and rhetors of color;

their second edition continued to add significantly to this number. More recently, we have seen *Twentieth-Century Rhetorics and Rhetoricians,* an anthology of contemporary rhetoricians, including not only the usual male figures such as Kenneth Burke but also contemporary female rhetors such as Andrea Lunsford. New anthologies consisting exclusively of women rhetors have also proliferated. Early on, Campbell collected excerpts from nineteenth-century American women participants in the suffrage movement into an influential anthology. More recently we have seen Foss, Foss, and Griffin's anthology of contemporary rhetors; Donawerth's anthology of women writing between the fifth and nineteenth centuries, notable for its effort to be truly global rather than exclusively Anglo-American; and most especially, Ritchie and Ronald's admirably comprehensive anthology of women rhetors. In all of these books we find both well-known and new figures; a sense of continuity in women writing and speaking across time, though not in a linear tradition; and a sense of the variety of rhetorical locations and genres, along with a diversity of rhetors in whom gender crosses other social axes such as class, sexuality, and race.

Our contribution to this textual tapestry is to focus on analyzing the roles and representations of women rhetors across a range of historical moments and across a range of subject positions. We have endeavored to take a key rhetorical issue and to criss-cross time, place, and rhetor, juxtaposing rhetorical contexts in order for the subject positions of the women to stand out in relief. Yet, like our predecessors, we also identify a variety of rhetorical figures, some now practically canonical (Julian of Norwich) and some possible newcomers to canons (Jane Gallop). And we, too, focus on the cultural contexts in which women rhetors work(ed) and the interrelations of their many axes of identity, including not only gender but also race, ethnicity, class, and other markers.

Representations and Rhetorics of Woman/Women?

Throughout this project we have struggled with our own questions: Why "woman" or why "women"? We are well aware that these are highly contested terms to use. The category "woman" is often seen as problematic for two reasons. First, for many scholars, it is an axis of identity that always mingles with other axes such as race, class, and sexuality. Each axis has its own characteristics, history, and agenda, yet when entangled with the others it is difficult to say which one predominates or which forms of oppression issue from what axis. For some scholars one social marker overrides another to such an extent as to render a single marker such as "woman" meaningless. One feminist historian, for example, goes so far as to say that black women and white women have absolutely nothing in common in their respective experiences of oppression, with any notion of commonality a "feminist fantasy" (Bordo 133). Secondly, many scholars are not persuaded that "woman" is even a discrete or valid category anymore. If, as Judith Butler argues, "gender" is a fluid category found along a continuum of gender possibilities rather than located in a binary of "woman" and "man," then the category "woman" itself can be inferred to be, in the most extreme view, a meaningless designation, or in the least extreme, an outdated conceptual relic of second-generation feminism. Even as a biological category, "woman" appears no longer hard and fast but instead likely positioned along a "male"/ "female" continuum.

We agree, generally, that "woman" is indeed a problematic category. However, with that said, we still think that the term is nonetheless crucial to feminist rhetorical studies. The principle of identity politics still applies, even if it is now seen as imposed by interpellations based on the perception of the rhetor as a woman rather than on any innate qualities of women. "Woman," in fact, is such a highly visible marker that it may overshadow interpellations based on more ambiguous markers such as sexuality. "Woman" is also a legal category still, and women were and are legally silenced and disabled in a variety of ways across the globe. Moreover, many women mirror this external repression with an internal repression—creating the "Angel in the House" who continues to haunt and silence many women rhetors and writers. How, then, we must ask, do women perform gender rhetorically when it is already internally and externally problematized for them? Women *must* establish alternative subject positions when they cannot identify with a universal (i.e., male) subjectivity.

As Susan Bordo, Linda Alcoff, and others have said, we must continue to use the category of "woman" and the principle of identity politics, epistemologically suspect as they may be, in order to acknowledge sociopolitical realities of oppression and to further social agendas for change. Similarly, we would argue that in order to conduct postmodern feminist analysis of historical and contemporary rhetors and their rhetorics, we must hold at least one term constant—and that term we select as "woman." With this one provisional constant, we can make sense of the "dizzying accumulation of narratives" (Bordo 134) associated with postmodern critique. We can give the "view from nowhere" (143) some perspective and shape. Therefore, our intent is neither to legitimate nor to deconstruct the idea of essential female subjectivity. Instead, our assumption is that there probably is no *one* such thing, but that "woman" nonetheless still serves as a pivotal construct for feminist rhetorics.

Roles and Representations?

Why our focus on "roles" and "representations"? For feminist rhetorics perhaps no issue is more important than the contentious postmodern debate about the terms "ethos," "persona," and "voice." As Roger Cherry (90–92) points out, the terms are often conflated with one another yet actually originate in different eras and have different shades of rhetorical meaning. "Ethos" dates back to classical rhetoric and refers to a rhetor's moral character, which was a powerful means of persuasion. "Persona" dates back to Roman rhetoric and drama, in which it served as a device for transformation, later coming into use in the 1940s to distinguish between the actual author and the author as presented in literary works. The term "voice" came into use much later, in the 1960s and 1970s, commonplace in early Expressivist approaches, which stressed its key role in writing processes (Elbow xix). Though the three terms have different origins and different rhetorical shadings, since the postmodern turn all three have been troubled by their entanglement with modernist assumptions and inferences. "Voice," in particular, has suffered from the most vitriolic attacks from deconstructionists who declared the death of the author, positions that continued throughout the reactionary anti-Expressivist period in the mid-1990s. The modernist characteristics in which these terms are entwined include, of course, the idea that the self is a unitary entity, quite possibly essentialist rather than constructed, and that this self possesses the agency to express its inherent ethos, choose its persona, or speak in its authentic voice.

Whether we can or should recover *any* of these terms is at the crux of the debate. To name a few key contributors to these discussions: Darsie Bowden maintains that voice, in particular, is so hopelessly enmeshed in modernism that we need to invent a new term. Cindy Moore (in this collection) claims that it is we, who made the shift from modernism to postmodernism, who are unduly troubled by the modernist "taint." Our students, a generation coming of age since the postmodern turn, not only tolerate but also take for granted the ambiguity of "voice"—that it implies both multiple selves and a unitary self, or both cultural agency and individual agency simultaneously. In the fields of feminist rhetoric(s) and composition, the fact that most scholars blend the worlds of scholarship and pedagogy, theory and praxis—thus resolving the conflicts around "voice"—seems crucial to us. Randy Freisinger (197) argues for reconceiving such terms in ways that mediate or include both modernist and postmodernist constructions, also seeking a pluralistic solution. It would seem, in short, as Peter Elbow once observed, ". . . [v]oice is a lightning rod that attracts ideological dispute . . ." (xlvii).

Lightning rod, indeed. When we began this project our dearest hope was to avoid entering this fray. We too had been struck by the sheer vehemence of postmodern objections to anything remotely suggesting essentialism or difference. As Susan Bordo once commented, she was appalled at the "raw hostility" of some feminists, the kind of "visceral reaction to theorists of gender difference" (149). However, when it became clear to us that for women rhetors, "coming to voice" (hooks 58) was still pivotal, we reluctantly entered the fray. Along with Susan Jarratt and Nedra Reynolds, we have rejected the most radical postmodern theories that would entirely deny rhetorical agency, instead adopting Jarratt and Reynolds's concept of "situated agency." After all, deconstructing "gender" and "voice" for women would render the analyses in this book theoretically untenable. As we see it, these terms are both "real" (in social contexts) and "unreal" (in old-fashioned semantic terms and in new-fashioned postmodern terms). Instead, we prefer the terms "roles and representations," with "roles" suggesting not only the pre-postmodern adoption and adaptation of personas but also the postmodern performance of a multiplicity of selves by any rhetor; and with "representations" suggesting not only the pre-postmodern "voice" or "voices" but also a host of other animating rhetorical choices, including a rhetor's relationship to authorities and to audiences, along with strategies and techniques for performing self that sometimes transform the very shape of traditional rhetorical texts. In foregrounding roles and representations at different moments in time, we come to see not only which are effective or ineffective but also how different cultural and linguistic contexts contribute to this process of subject formation.

Intersections

Our contributors highlight what we see as the pivotal rhetorical activity of women rhetors by examining the intersections between "woman" and "roles and representations." Yet we, along with other scholars, have grappled with the thorny question of just what should supersede those pre-postmodern conceptions of ethos, voice, or persona. For Kristie Fleckenstein, "material identity" must be distinguished from "rhetorical identity." In our collection too we see the value of this distinction, for it encompasses both voice and persona in terms less burdened by modernist associations. Our term "woman" refers to the varied "material identity(ies)" of the rhetors under consideration, while our terms "roles" and "representations" refer to the rhetorical identity(ies) these rhetors craft. However, beyond this important distinction, we like Johanna Schmertz's more animating notion of ethos recast as "the ever-shifting points of convergence in the subject's ongoing intersection with language" (86). Still, it seems to us that the cultural context is omitted from her definition, for to be truly comprehensive the intersection is really one of rhetor, language, and culture. That is, a rhetorical act occurs not through the rhetor's agency alone but also through the point in language and the place in the cultural context that the utterance occurs. To rephrase and supplement James Britton's famous phrase in postmodern terms, it is "shaping at the point *and place and medium* of utterance" that appears as the primary generative act for many women rhetors beset by challenges from without and within. For that matter, we believe that the complexity of this act obtains for *all* rhetors and rhetoric(s), even though our focus here is on feminist rhetoric(s) and women rhetors. Britton's original term "utterance," potentially problematic nowadays, we alter into the term "medium of utterance" so that it can stand for both oral and written expression of all kinds.

Whereas postmodernists tend to credit language and culture for that shaping, modernists tend to credit the rhetor. For us, however, this rhetorical shaping and meaning making is interactive, a synergy of these three components—rhetor, language, and culture—as they manifest in a particular location. Furthermore, all the components themselves must be understood to be pluralistic. The term "rhetor," in particular, includes, at the very least, "material identity(ies)" and "rhetorical identity(ies)." It is also understood that these synergies are animate and constantly changing. As Schmertz describes the process: "When we attend to our own ethos in a postmodern rhetoric, we are both constructing a subjectivity for ourselves and retroactively reconstructing or recuperating that subjectivity in a process that is never finished because it is already shaping its own critique, shifting to a new position or location. And as this subject we have made, moves, it pulls upon the rest of the rhetorical situation, creating new points of convergence among its elements" (86).

If the essays in this collection highlight this pivotal moment of "shaping at the point—and place and medium—of utterance," we have achieved our goal, for it is in this fashion that our women rhetors "come to voice." By criss-crossing time and exploring the tensions between women rhetors and their roles and representations, we see that ethos, voice, or persona, once considered primary to women writers and rhetors, have not been lost in postmodern analysis. Rather, they have changed their shapes.

And, finally, what is the outcome of "situating woman"? Do we read the patterns that sometimes emerge from the kinds of rhetorical strategies employed by women as constituting a kind of "women's rhetoric"? In a word, no. Though it may be rhetoric by women, it is not necessarily indicative of a woman's or women's rhetoric. After all, there has been no "women's tradition" into which women are writing. We agree with Ritchie and Ronald when they observe that many historical texts written by women "read as if a particular woman is writing or claiming the right to speak for the first time, without a history of writing behind her; too often it feels eerily as if she is writing alone" (xvii). We recall an analogous situation: the reclamation of rhetoric by women was preceded by the reclamation of literature by women. Elaine Showalter, a pioneer in that project, also observed of women writing literature that it was as if they were each writing alone. There has been no women's tradition per se, no visible, continuous development like the one that allows us to read T. S. Eliot against John Donne or Richard Whately against Aristotle. But as Showalter found, patterns and themes do emerge when reading from one female isolee to another. She too was drawn early on to the authorial ethos, persona, or voice of these literary women and their ways of negotiating their subject positions as women authors—whether they wrote as women or as men, whether they validated literary tradition or created new literary forms entirely. Of course, Showalter was pilloried for declaring that these patterns constituted a women's literary tradition. Learning from the missteps of our literary predecessor in her archeological dig, we refuse to step into that particular postmodern trap.

Instead, we attempt to counteract the perceived isolation of women by offering a range of studies "situating women" across both historical and contemporary moments. In these selections, when read against one another, we see variations of that shaping pivotal moment in which women "come to voice." We also see familiar patterns and themes such as, for example, collaborative strategies—Margaret Fell, bolstering her assertions by reference to other respected writers, or Frances Wright, inviting a dialog with her readers. Such patterns point not to a tradition and certainly not to any essentialist women's rhetoric. Rather, they hauntingly suggest what might have been, what a larger rhetorical tradition, more inclusive of women, might have been. And they also suggest what may yet be, as contemporary rhetors wrestle with situating themselves and being rhetorically situated. "What *is* women's rhetoric?" one of us asked her seminar in the History of Women in Rhetoric. One student answered: "I know it doesn't exist and I can't explain it. But I know it when I see it." We would add that if there *is* a women's rhetoric, it is as elusive, contradictory, and fragmentary as the footprints of Ariadne.

Conclusions

Throughout the essays included in this text, we see rich depictions of women rhetors' roles and representations, the tactics they employ in their rhetorics, and new ways many women rhetors are experimenting with "coming to voice." As we have said, we see this process of "shaping at the point—and place and medium—of utterance" as perhaps the primary generative task for women rhetors. The familiar terms "ethos," "persona," and "voice," traditionally at the center of studies of women's rhetoric and writing, have not lost their primacy. However, they are refigured in these essays as the synergy of rhetor, language, and culture—as complex processes of subject formation by women for whom rhetorical expression is both externally and internally problematized. Their stories weave a complex tapestry showing some of the choices women make when they represent themselves as rhetors, how their cultural and linguistic contexts contribute to their identity construction, and the forms and features of the rhetorics they produce. Our contributors link past practices with present ones to highlight correspondences and to offer critiques that suggest how these practices succeed, fail, and vary in their applications. In their representations of women and their rhetorics, these essays highlight both common traces and important differences in the ways women imagine their speaking and writing roles.

We have by no means included all of the facets of women's rhetorical roles and representations in this collection. We expect that other historical studies will unearth yet more women rhetors and offer yet more intensive studies of these women and their ways of making themselves heard. For example, the range of examinations of women's literacy in particular cultural contexts, from women's clubs to the temperance movement and beyond, will continue to expand as new rhetorical sites are identified. Our contemporary essays take up issues of women's representations head-on. But we do not include, for example, the possibilities for gender construction and gender-bending illuminated by such theorists as Judith Butler and Judith Halberstam. Neither have we moved into literary arenas where fictional constructions of female identities are exploring exciting new roles and representations. And, of course, we look forward to studies of women's subject formations outside the Anglo-American sphere in truly global women's rhetorics. Nevertheless, it is our hope that the sampling we have provided here—varied in space, time, ethnicity, spirituality, race, and class—illuminates the pivotal processes of representation, "coming to voice," and interpretation for an even broader spectrum of women rhetors and writers.

Works Cited

Alcoff, Linda. "Cultural Feminism vs. Poststructuralism: The Identity Crisis in Feminist Theory." *Signs: Journal of Women in Culture and Society* 13 (1988): 405–36.

Alcoff, Linda Martin, and Eduardo Mendieta, eds. *Identities: Race, Class, Gender, and Nationality.* Malden, MA: Blackwell, 2003.

Bizzell, Patricia, and Bruce Herzberg, eds. *The Rhetorical Tradition: Readings from Classical Times to the Present.* 2nd edition. New York: Bedford/St. Martin's. 2001.

Bordo, Susan. "Feminism, Postmodernism, and Gender-Skepticism." *Feminism/Postmodernism.* Ed. Linda J. Nicholson. New York: Routledge, 1990.

Bowden, Darsie. *The Mythology of Voice.* Portsmouth, NH: Boynton/Cook, 1999.

Britton, James. "Shaping at the Point of Utterance." *Reinventing the Rhetorical Tradition.* Ed. Aviva Freedman and Ian Pringle. Conway, AK: L&S Books, 1980. 61–65.

Brody, Miriam. *Manly Writing: Gender, Rhetoric, and the Rise of Composition.* Carbondale: Southern Illinois UP, 1993.

Butler, Judith. *Gender Trouble: Feminism and the Subversion of Identity.* New York: Routledge, 1990.

Campbell, JoAnn. *Toward a Feminist Rhetoric: The Writing of Gertrude Buck.* Pittsburgh: U of Pittsburgh P, 1996.

Campbell, Karlyn Kohrs. *Man Cannot Speak for Her.* Vols. I and II. New York: Praeger, 1989.

Cherry, Roger. "Ethos Versus Persona: Self-Representation in Written Discourse." Elbow 85–103.

Chicago, Judy, and Edward Lucie-Smith. *Women and Art: Contested Territory.* New York: Watson-Guptill, 1999.

Clarke, Danielle, and Elizabeth Clarke, eds. *This Double Voice: Gendered Writing in Early Modern England.* New York: St. Martin's, 2000.

Donawerth, Jane. *Rhetorical Theory by Women before 1900.* Lanham, MD: Rowman and Littlefield, 2002.

Elbow, Peter, ed. *Landmark Essays on Voice and Writing.* Davis, CA: Hermagoras, 1994.

———. "Introduction." Elbow xi–xlvii.

Eldred, Janet Carey, and Peter Mortensen. *Imagining Rhetoric: Composing Women of the Early United States.* Pittsburgh: U of Pittsburgh P, 2002.

Fleckenstein, Kristie. "Resistance, Women, and Dismissing the 'I'." *Rhetoric Review* 17 (1998): 107–25.

Foss, Karen A., Sonja K. Foss, and Cindy L. Griffin. *Feminist Rhetorical Theories.* Thousand Oaks, CA: Sage, 1999.

———. *Readings in Feminist Rhetorical Theory.* Thousand Oaks, CA: Sage, 2004.

Foster, Gwendolyn Audrey. *Troping the Body: Gender, Etiquette, and Performance.* Carbondale: Southern Illinois UP, 2000.

Freisinger, Randall. "Voicing the Self: Toward a Pedagogy of Resistance in a Postmodern Age." Elbow 187–212.

Gannett, Cinthia. *Gender and the Journal: Diaries and Academic Discourse.* Albany: SUNY Press, 1992.

Gere, Anne Ruggles. *Intimate Practices: Literary and Cultural Work in U.S. Women's Clubs, 1880–1920.* Urbana: U of Illinois P, 1997.

Glenn, Cheryl. *Rhetoric Retold: Regendering the Tradition from Antiquity through the Renaissance.* Carbondale: Southern Illinois UP, 1997.

Heilbrun, Carolyn G. *Writing a Woman's Life.* New York: Norton, 1988.

hooks, bell. "'When I Was a Young Soldier for the Revolution': Coming to Voice." Elbow 51–58.

Jarratt, Susan C., and Lynn Worsham, eds. *Feminism and Composition Studies: In Other Words.* New York: Modern Language Association, 1998.

Jarratt, Susan, and Nedra Reynolds. "The Splitting Image: Contemporary Feminisms and the Ethics of Ethos." *Ethos: New Essays in Rhetorical and Critical Theory.* Ed. James S. Baumlin and Tita French Baumlin. Dallas: Southern Methodist UP, 1994. 37–63.

Johnson, Nan. *Gender and Rhetorical Space in American Life, 1866–1910.* Carbondale: Southern Illinois UP, 2002.

———. *Nineteenth-Century Rhetoric in North America.* Carbondale: Southern Illinois UP, 1991.

Logan, Shirley W. *"We Are Coming": The Persuasive Discourse of Nineteenth-Century Black Women.* Carbondale: Southern Illinois UP, 1999.

Lunsford, Andrea A., ed. *Reclaiming Rhetorica: Women in the Rhetorical Tradition.* Pittsburgh: U of Pittsburgh P, 1995.

Mattingly, Carol. *Appropriate[ing] Dress: Women's Rhetorical Style in Nineteenth-Century America.* Carbondale: Southern Illinois UP, 2002.

———. *Well-Tempered Women: Nineteenth-Century Temperance Rhetoric.* Carbondale: Southern Illinois UP, 1998.

Miller, Susan. *Assuming the Positions: Cultural Pedagogy and the Politics of Commonplace Writing.* Pittsburgh: U of Pittsburgh P, 1998.

Moran, Michael G., and Michelle Ballif, eds. *Twentieth-Century Rhetorics and Rhetoricians: Critical Studies and Sources.* Westport, CT: Greenwood, 2000.

Phelps, Louise Wetherbee, and Janet Emig, eds. *Feminine Principles and Women's Experience in American Composition and Rhetoric.* Pittsburgh: U of Pittsburgh P, 1995.

Ratcliffe, Krista. *Anglo-American Feminist Challenges to the Rhetorical Traditions: Virginia Woolf, Mary Daly, Adrienne Rich.* Carbondale: Southern Illinois UP, 1996.

Ritchie, Joy, and Kate Ronald, eds. *Available Means: An Anthology of Women's Rhetoric(s).* Pittsburgh: U of Pittsburgh P, 2001.

Royster, Jacqueline Jones. *Southern Horrors and Other Writings: The Anti-Lynching Campaign of Ida B. Wells, 1892–1900.* Boston: Bedford Books, 1997.

———. *Traces of a Stream: Literacy and Social Change among African American Women.* Pittsburgh: U of Pittsburgh P, 2000.

Schmertz, Johanna. "Constructing Essences: Ethos and the Postmodern Subject of Feminism." *Rhetoric Review* 18 (1999): 82–91.

Showalter, Elaine. *A Literature of Their Own: British Women Novelists from Brontë to Lessing.* Princeton, NJ: Princeton UP, 1999.

Spenser, Edmund. *The Faerie Queene, 1596.* Vol. 1. Intro. by Graham Hough. London: Scolar Press, 1976.

Sutherland, Christine Mason, and Rebecca Sutcliffe, eds. *The Changing Tradition: Women in the History of Rhetoric.* Calgary: U of Calgary P, 1999.

Wertheimer, Molly Meijer, ed. *Listening to Their Voices: The Rhetorical Activities of Historical Women.* Columbia: U of South Carolina P, 1997.

Part 1

Representing Women Rhetors: Complications, Misrepresentations, Occasional Successes

In this section our contributors consider how women at various historical moments found ways to speak and write and make their influence felt, negotiating their various rhetorical positions with respect not only to gender but also to race, class, ethnicity, and spirituality. In authorizing themselves to speak, the subjects of these essays represented themselves as complicated and contradictory subjects. Their pluralistic positions were often oxymoronic in their times and in ours: female prophet, female writer, civilized Indian, and black feminist. Their representations yielded both intended and unintended consequences, which both enabled and disabled them. Some of these rhetors were actually taken seriously, while others were dismissed. And there were also troubling complications and misrepresentations in their positions that made their contemporaries (and ourselves) vastly uneasy.

Our collection begins in the late Middle Ages rather than with an investigation of representations in the rhetoric of mythology, with shadowy figures such as Aspasia or Diotima, or with a number of other women represented entirely by male rhetoricians, poets, and playwrights. Nor have we included theories about the rhetorical roles that Sappho and others may have chosen for themselves or had chosen for them. We have left this work to others who are conducting the painstaking archeological work involved in constructing these histories from the fragments available. This section instead focuses on varied historical figures who cast more substantial shadows and whose pluralistic positions, when read against one another and their own circumstances, allow us to foreground the conundrums into which women spoke and wrote.

In "Women and Authority in the Rhetorical Economy of the Late Middle Ages," Julia Dietrich describes the rhetorical context of the late Middle Ages and examines the body of writing available from Julian of Norwich and Angela Merici, women who successfully claimed rhetorical authority by basing their assertions on their personal experiences of divine revelation. In the late Middle Ages the power of scholastic rhetorical authority was receding, and the possibility of lay authority through empirical knowledge and individual experience began to emerge. Although this shift seemingly opened up possibilities for women to speak publicly, cultural prohibitions against women assuming public authority were still pervasive. Using the texts available from Julian of Norwich and Angela Merici, Dietrich describes how they managed to authorize themselves not only to speak but also to advance innovative ideas still scorned by their cultures. Julian, for example, put forward the theological idea of the motherhood of God, and Angela proposed a lay educational model in which unmarried women would educate young girls. Both dared to claim rhetorical authority as "female prophets," a paradox given their subject positions and personal lives built around self-denial of all sorts.

In "The Role of Language in the Construction of Mary Wortley Montagu's Rhetorical Identity," Yvonne Merrill describes a familiar story: how Mary Wortley Montagu flawlessly mimicked her eighteenth-century male peers in order to conform to the rhetorical standards of her time. The artist Judy Chicago refers to her own attempts to paint like men as her period of "male drag." This role is unmistakably present throughout rhetorical history, but it is not always one that is successful for the woman rhetor. Montagu's rhetorical identity was crafted in response to the classically trained intellectuals and stylists of dominant Enlightenment discourse. Her mentors and models established standards for public rhetoric, rules of taste and decorum, that by and large excluded all public discourse except that informed by classical criteria. This was the very style, of course, that privileged their own voices. Most male writers assumed that female writers could not be educated in the Western cultural tradition. In fact, the very notion of a "female writer" was virtually an oxymoron. Significantly influenced by these attitudes, Montagu's rhetorical strategy was emulation—of such important figures as Jonathan Swift and Alexander Pope. Yet, even though she acquired a classical education and a rhetorical voice indistinguishable from that of her male peers, her work was discounted as that of an uninformed woman—a literary slattern. The patent authority of her voice was thus undone by her publicly known gender.

Malea Powell, in "Princess Sarah, the Civilized Indian: The Rhetoric of Cultural Literacies in Sarah Winnemucca Hopkins's *Life among the Piutes,*" examines the work of a nineteenth-century Native woman who represented herself as both Paiute and Euro-American. This is the oxymoronic hybrid role—another familiar strategy—in which the rhetor tries to move between two cultural and rhetorical worlds. Though successful with her immediate audience, the implications of her way of being a "civilized Indian" are troubling to us today. As far as we know, Sarah Winnemucca was the only Native woman in tribal history to represent herself textually as a literate practitioner of both Euro-American and Paiute cultural discourses. She thus authenticated herself as that most contradictory of subjects—a civilized Indian—in the eyes of late-nineteenth-century reformists and politicians, an audience with the power to shape policy that could have greatly aided Winnemucca's Northern Paiute peoples. Though she gestured toward new possibilities for representing Native peoples as something other than a victimized group, her bifurcated ethos both compromised and complicated her project.

Elizabeth West, in "Cooper and Crummell: Dialogics of Race and Womanhood," analyzes another role that women often play: the respectful female rhetor trying to assert herself with ideas slightly different from those of her male mentor. Both nineteenth-century African American activists, Anna Julia Cooper and Alexander Crummell, struggled to define themselves as black intellectuals by accommodating to the values of the dominant culture but at the same time rejecting its views of race. Both shared an ideological commitment to the idea of "racial uplift," but they complicated their representation of "black femininity" by infusing it with middle-class, Euro-American ideals. This paradox demonstrates the complicated relationship between the rhetorics of civilized society and black femininity during a period when the roles and representations of black women were highly debated among blacks, particularly among the "talented tenth." Cooper also attempted to correct some of Crummell's shortcomings on the subject of "woman," but she ultimately employed arguments very similar to his. Cooper's and Crummell's writings provide a site for exploring the dynamics of black female and male attitudes toward gender, as well as the sometimes paradoxical ideologies of "racial uplift." These complicated views would survive well into the twentieth century.

1

Women and Authority in the Rhetorical Economy of the Late Middle Ages

Julia Dietrich

An anthologist of rhetoric seeking to represent the late medieval period in Western Europe has no obvious choice. No single text or theorist speaks to the broad questions of meaning and communication that modern rhetoricians see as central to their discipline. The *ars dictamini* and *ars praedicandi* offer instruction in the arts of letter writing and of preaching, respectively, and from them we can glean some assumptions about persuasion and instruction and the ethical construction of the writer or preacher.[1] Geoffrey de Vinsauf (ca. 1210), in the *Poetria Nova,* and Matthew of Vendome (ca. 1175), in *Ars Versificatoria,* tell us about poetics and literary style. Dante Alighieri (1265–1321), in his letter to Can Grande della Scala, takes on the multiple ways in which texts mean and offers a concise explanation of allegorical modes of interpretation. But we can point to no rhetor's theory or practical manual that represented the culture's voice or even its debate on questions central to argument: What constitutes "proof"? How can a claim be supported? What counts as evidence for different assertions? What are legitimate sources of warrants? Such questions were not irrelevant to the late medieval period. Indeed, they were vitally important then, as they are in any period of significant cultural change. But they were being worked out not in rhetoric but in the allied field of metaphysics and in the complicated, conflicted arena of public discourse.

The Limits of Reason

The thirteenth century had been an era of synthesis, integrating Aristotelian logic, newly recovered along with a wealth of Arabian commentary, and theological tenets of scripture and tradition.[2] Thomas Aquinas (1225–1274), whose *Summa Theologica* stands as the monument to this synthesizing impulse, took as his guiding assumption the belief that faith never contradicts reason. Using Aristotelian dialectic, he integrated philosophy (concerned with the nature of being) with theology (concerned with the nature of God). To maintain that we can know God through the medium of reason, he argued the connectedness of the realm of the necessary (God) and the realm of the contingent (creation). As reason can understand the contingent, it can then also know God.

The price to be paid, in theological terms, for this ability to know and describe God seemed a very heavy one by the last decades of the thirteenth century and certainly into the fourteenth century: if reason can know God, then God must be constrained by reason. To be knowable, describable, or predictable is to have limits, to be compelled to act in certain ways. To constrain the divine in this way was unacceptable to the most influential thinkers after Aquinas, and John Duns Scotus (ca. 1270–1308) is only the most famous of the thinkers who worked to reclaim free will for the divine.[3] Commentaries on the *Sentences* of Peter Lombard are the main vehicle through which the Scholastics elucidated their theories, and in Duns's two commentaries, *Opus Oxoniense* and *Reportata Parisiensia,* he rejected any analogy between the necessary and the contingent, the creator and the creation. Reason could know God as being but could not offer any guidance about his mercy, his justice, or his dealings with humankind. Peter Auriole (d. 1322), the Franciscan Archbishop of Aix-en-Provence, argued that the mind knows natures, not universals, which Aquinas understood to be mediators between the mind of God and the individual. Durandus of Pourcain (ca. 1270–1332)—a Dominican, like Aquinas—likewise rejected such a role for universals.

William of Ockham (ca. 1285–1349), an English Franciscan, has been regarded, at least since the nineteenth century, as the primary agent in the destruction of synthetic Scholastic thinking. Not only does he argue that universals are products of the human mind, not indwellings of divine ideas, but his epistemology distinguishes between intuitive knowledge, by which we know that a thing exists, as when we see it before us, and abstractive knowledge, by which we then think about the thing. Only intuitive knowledge is verifiable. Abstractive knowledge must always remain speculative, because we can think about things without knowing that they do in fact exist. Ockham was an influential teacher, studying and teaching at Oxford, lecturing on the *Sentences* from 1317 to 1319, then writing and debating in London. His career suggests that his order was grooming him for the influential post of regent master at Oxford. Although he was effectively "acquitted" of heresy after being summoned to Avignon and questioned about the views expressed in his *Sentences* commentary, he did finally run afoul of the papacy and took refuge with the emperor until his death, reputedly of the plague, in 1349.

The extent and nature of Ockham's influence is currently a subject of some debate. Traditionally, the empiricism implicit in his epistemology—granting verifiability only to intuitive knowledge—has been credited with fostering experimental science; and his refusal, following Duns, to allow reason to encompass theology has been seen as the death blow to the Scholastic synthesis of philosophy and theology, of faith and reason. Reason, no longer tethered to the tenets of scripture and ecclesiastical authority, could roam where she would, laying the foundation for a secular culture, with secular knowledge. Recent scholarship has complicated this narrative a bit with evidence that in both Oxford and Paris, theologians in the decades after Ockham's departure, men like Adam Wodeham and Gregory of Rimini, who were working on optics and cognition, believed it sounder to build their epistemology on a theory of mediating species between the object and the perceiver, the very mediation that Ockham's razor had cut away (Tachau 243–74, 316–52).

But even if Ockham is shown to be less dominatingly influential than he was once thought to be, the effects with which he is associated remain undeniable: throughout the fourteenth century, the scope of reason was gradually reduced, philosophy and theology became more separate, empiricism gained credibility, and the Aristotelian dialectic that had dominated intellectual life since the mid-twelfth century was no longer hegemonic.[4]

It is not surprising that the extent of Ockham's influence has been questioned in recent years. As scholars have been increasingly willing to look at changes in society as affecting modes of thought, Ockham and his brother philosophers have had less weight to bear. Dom David Knowles's classic exposition of medieval philosophy, *The Evolution of Medieval Thought,* regarded fourteenth-century mysticism as rushing in to fill the gap that arose when reason was discredited as a means to know God, but we might now argue that mysticism was no mere reaction but rather a product of a culture that needed—and possessed—roads to knowledge other than that of dialectic. Although any summary of the major social and cultural changes affecting Western Europe from the fourteenth to the sixteenth century is bound to oversimplify, we should take note of the fact that commercialism was creating a sphere of influence and expertise for a segment of the population that had formerly lacked these. Empiricism was the basis of trial-and-error technological development, and such knowledge was demonstrably valuable because it could be commodified, as when one bought a more accurate map to find a better trade route.[5] Townspeople, from merchant capitalists to artisans, recognized themselves as creators and consumers of practical, empirical knowledge, which gave them power. Likewise, the political separation of the nation-state from ecclesiastical dominance, paralleling the separation of philosophy and theology, recognized and legitimated the power of the laity in their own sphere.[6]

In this milieu, wherein empirical knowledge, individual experience, and lay authority are increasing in value and competing with Scholastic dialectic as epistemic, we might well expect a new rhetorical paradigm for argument, and we might also expect greater opportunities for women to enter into argument. Barred from university admission and seldom able to get equivalent education privately, all but the most exceptional women were cut off from the intellectual debates of consequence to their societies as long as dialectic and philosophical discourse held sway.[7] Whereas Hildegard of Bingen (1098–1179) could write and preach with some authority, using divine revelation as her warrant (Dietrich 1999), the arrival of the "New Aristotle" into universities in the middle of the twelfth century so transformed methods of thinking and arguing that Chaucer's clerk's matriculation to the university is described as going "to logic," and women were largely cut out of public discourse.

The citing of authorities, another traditional, nonphilosophical method of warranting an argument, seems to have survived into the late medieval era, if literary depictions are a reliable guide, but its power seems diminished. Chaucer's Wyf of Bath will engage important debates of her time, announcing, "Experience, though no authority, is in this world right enough for me." She finds Jankyn's book of authorities on marriage to be an agent of her oppression and so tears out three leaves and tosses them into the fire. And Chaucer's own *Tale of Melibee*, replete with proverbial wisdom, has resisted definitive modern interpretation; perhaps our own inability to decide if it is a serious tract of traditional wisdom or a parody of such tracts reflects the same ambivalence of Chaucer's audience toward the authority of tradition and the strategy of quotation to ground an assertion. Chaucer's characters are, of course, simply characters, with no need to worry about argumentation, but it is interesting and probably telling that Chaucer, himself a product of the upper middle class, should represent them as voicing skepticism about traditional ways of making arguments.

Women and Argument Making

Because rhetoric itself is always grounded in both epistemology and cultural practice, we should not be surprised to find that the breakdown of the Scholastic synthesis did not soon result in a new method of argument. Cultural forms hold authority just by virtue of holding authority. Thomas Bradwardine (ca. 1290–1349), proctor of Oxford University and Archbishop of Canterbury, was an accomplished mathematician who argued that Ockham had given too much importance to natural, earthly experience and discounted the role of grace. As Gordon Leff has noted, the effect of Bradwardine's reassertion of traditional doctrines of faith was, ironically, to endorse Ockham's separation of reason and faith, differing only in preferring faith to reason. Equally ironic was Bradwardine's choice of argument strategy: "Bradwardine employed the full weight of dialectic and Aristotle to make faith independent of metaphysics or philosophy" (Leff, *Medieval Thought* 299). He opposed Aristotelianism and chose Aristotelian method to argue against it. Argument forms are culturally located, and we should not be surprised that Aristotelian method outlasted Scholasticism. Rather, we would be very surprised if we found that schoolmen of the late Middle Ages adopted the crude empiricism of Chaucer's miller. Allegiance to cultural forms often outlasts belief in their efficacy. And arguments from experience were socially suspect.

Empirical arguments, especially as they depend on individual experience, call attention to social location. Whereas dialectic may appear to be simply a tool, empiricism is always someone's tool, depending for its authority either on striking a sympathetic chord in the audience ("yes, that's my experience too") or on the status of the arguer ("he's smarter, or richer, or more socially prominent than I am, so he might know something that I don't know, or at least it's his version of things that will count"). Although it seems likely that further study of the understanding of experience in the late Middle Ages will reveal a more nuanced picture than we are currently able to draw, it is fair to say that experience was regarded not as a cultural construct but as an encounter with "what is," and thus yielding not merely a personal insight but rather a more general truth. In spite of this, not everyone's experience is regarded as equally authoritative. Thus does the ethical construction of the writer assume great importance.

Women, therefore, enjoyed in the late Middle Ages a new opportunity to enter into public discourse, in that the culture was open to the authority of argument forms other than dialectic. But they still faced the cultural prohibition against women assuming public authority in any form, even in the realm of religious experience. Such a prohibition must have created an internal inhibition that most women found difficult to overcome. This chapter will examine the arguments made by two women, Julian of Norwich and Angela Merici, from the period of cultural transition during which Western Europe was both medieval and early modern. We will ask what rhetorical support they offered for the assertions they made and speculate about the ways in which gender influenced these choices. We cannot, of course, recover their thinking about those choices. We cannot know whether they consciously constructed personae and chose particular lines of argument for their rhetorical power or whether they were unconscious of rhetorical choice and thought of themselves as just "telling the truth." In fact, the dichotomy in itself is probably misleading, because they likely had to convince themselves first. To challenge a cultural expectation and to dare to write, they had first to justify the actions to themselves. Before putting forth ideas like the motherhood of God or the need for a company of uncloistered women to teach young girls, they had first to work through for themselves the very objections that other readers of their culture were likely to raise. We would be wrong to assume that women who dared to make public arguments took for granted their right to do so (Petroff 3–5). The first audience is always the self. We cannot know how much of the rhetorical work of making the radical acceptable was done to convince themselves and how much was consciously chosen for another audience.

Julian of Norwich and the *Showings*

The history of church attitudes toward women who claimed a personal and individual relationship with God is a complex and ambiguous one. On the continent, where the Cathar heresy was an immediate threat, women in the twelfth and thirteenth centuries wielded considerable power as they used their visions and their heroic mortifications as weapons in defense of orthodoxy.[8] Jo Ann McNamara has shown that an alliance of sorts existed between priests of the Dominican order and women whose visions confirmed Dominican preaching and whose prayers, fasts, and mortifications demonstrated that the flesh could be purified, contravening the Cathar view of it as corrupt (12). Their devotion was particularly, and pointedly, directed toward the body of Christ in the Eucharist, and the communion with God through that sacrament was so intense as to give them direct revelations. In many cases a priest who served as spiritual director could temper these revelations and appropriate them through interpretation, but in spite of this, women of devotion came to be perceived as threatening enough to warrant restraint. By the middle of the fourteenth century, a reaction had set in, exemplified by the pronouncement of Jean Gerson, the chancellor of the University of Paris, to the effect that we should be suspicious in a time of too many visions and too many visionaries, as God was not inclined to repeat himself and so did not need so many spokespersons—in effect, taking Ockham's razor to the search for truth (McNamara 25).

English women seem to have come to mysticism later than their continental sisters. Nicholas Watson has argued that by 1390 attitudes in the English church were beginning to be more accepting of female visionaries, and the writings of Bridget of Sweden, Catherine of Siena, and Mechtild of Hackeborn began to appear in English (653), but English women mystics still faced considerable suspicion. Indeed, Gerson's theory of an economy of revelation has a corollary: if God spoke directly to laymen and women, then the message was not likely to be one that could have been expected to arise naturally from the discourses of the theologians. By its very nature, then, a visionary message is a disruption of natural process, a corrective, implicitly a challenge.[9] The fourteenth-century church admitted the validity of visionary revelation but examined very carefully any claim to such experience, looking for heretical ideas, fakery, self-promotion, or individual psychosis.

We should not be surprised, then, that we know so little about the life of Julian of Norwich. Self-abnegation offered some haven.[10] One might wish to be simply the vessel for revelation, the messenger who was in no way the author of the message, absolved by humility from any possible charge of self-promotion, offering no personal detail that might be used to connect one to the message. Indeed, as Hildegard of Bingen had argued, women's outsider status was a plus in that it proved that their hands were clean: women did not write theology, so the theology must be from God.[11]

Julian tells us that in May of 1373, in her thirty-first year, she became ill unto death. Her mother, some friends, and the parish priest were with her. She began experiencing paralysis and assumed that her death was very near. In that condition, she received sixteen revelations from Christ crucified. She then recovered her health. We know from a bequest to her in a will of 1416 that she lived to old age, and contemporary sources speak of her as an anchoress. We do not know when she entered her anchorhold or whether she was a member of the Benedictine community to whose church it was attached.[12] She lived in times of social upheaval, when periodic revisitations of the bubonic plague compounded its original devastation, and she appears to have given spiritual counsel to those who visited her. Margery Kempe records such a visit, in which Julian advises her about how to know if a vision is truly from God: "The Holy Ghost never moves contrary to charity, for if He did, He would be going contrary to His own nature, for He is all charity. Also He moves a soul to all chastity, for those who lead chaste lives are called the Temple of the Holy Ghost, and the Holy Ghost makes a soul stable and steadfast in the true faith and the true belief. . . . And much more, when God visiteth a creature with tears of contrition, devotion, or compassion, he may and ought to believe that the Holy Ghost is in his soul" (Windeatt 120–21, translation mine).

The test that Julian offers to Margery is, no doubt, the test she applied to her own visionary experience: if the vision teaches charity, chastity, firm faith, and genuine devotion, then the vision must be from God. In rhetorical terms, Julian is grounding authority in the ethical construction of the writer: the life testifies to the truth of the text.[13] "The life" for women writers of the fourteenth and early fifteenth centuries seems to have meant the life of the writer outside the text as well as the writer constructed within the text. Julian warranted her assertions, therefore, by her exemplary charity, chastity, faith, and devotion. Within the text, she presents a self of similar virtues. But we also have reason to think that she saw her rhetorical project in more sophisticated terms than simply the transparent representation of self in text.

The "*Showings*" that Julian reported emphasize the "vision" aspect of visionary experience; that is, they are grounded in seeing as a privileged way of knowing.[14] Indeed, the result of sin is "spiritual blindness" (chapter 23). In chapter 1 she writes: "I wished that I had been at that time with Mary Magdalen and with the others who were Christ's lovers, so that I might have seen with my own eyes our Lord's Passion which he suffered for me, so that I might have suffered with him as others did who loved him, even though I believed firmly in all Christ's pains, . . . But despite all my true faith I desired a bodily sight, through which I might have more knowledge of our Lord and saviour's bodily pains."[15] The rationale for wanting to see for oneself is not to discover or test a truth but rather to come to a fuller, more affecting knowledge. Thus is interpretation folded into seeing in Julian's hermeneutic: seeing leads us to know in a more than intellectual way, and that additional dimension of knowledge is most often expressed in metaphor. In the opening of chapter 4, for example, she explains: "And at the same time as I saw this corporeal sight, our Lord showed me a spiritual sight of his familiar love. I saw that he is everything that is good and comforting for our help." This explanation introduces the famous incident in which Julian sees a hazelnut in the palm of her hand and "is given to understand" that it represents everything that exists and that its existence is proof of God's great love. The link between what is seen—in other words, the hazelnut—and the assertion of God's love is the existence of the hazelnut itself. The idea that the created world tells of the love of God for humankind is as old as the psalms; it becomes revelatory only in the context of Julian's optimistic theology, emphasizing divine love and the belief that "all shall be well." The force of the "showing" is in its homely accessibility, the dependence of the interpretation not on a complicated or debatable allegoresis but on the simple, undeniable existence of the hazelnut. Seeing and empirical verification are central to Julian's rhetoric.[16]

Nicholas Watson has argued convincingly that the immediacy we feel especially in the short text of the *Showings* has misled scholars into accepting too early a date for its composition (657–71). Julian writes as if the experience is fresh, taking the reader back to the scene of the visions, including details of the scene that are not strictly germane (e.g., her mother and the parish priest and his acolyte were present), and describing first what she saw and then her coming to an understanding of it. The opening of chapter 8 offers an example of the usual rhetorical method:

> And after this I saw God in an instant of time, that is, in my understanding, and by this vision I saw that he is present in all things. I contemplated it carefully, knowing and perceiving through it that he does everything which is done. I marveled at this vision with a gentle fear, and I thought, What is sin? For I saw truly that God does everything, however small it may be, and that nothing is done by chance, but it is of endless providence of God's wisdom. Therefore I was compelled to admit that everything which is done is done well, and I was certain that God does not sin. Therefore it seemed to me that sin is nothing, for in all this sin was not shown to me. And I did not wish to go on feeling surprise at this, but I contemplated our Lord and waited for what he would show me.

Typically, Julian does not situate herself as one who tries to convince us but instead re-creates the process by which she was herself convinced.[17]

Julian's theology included such ideas as the motherhood of God and an optimism about the likelihood of salvation that ran counter to the theological tenor of the times.[18] She prefaces her writing about such doctrines with assertions that she wishes in no way to go against the true teaching of the church. How did she overcome all the internal and external obstacles and make her voice heard? Rhetorically, she reduced her presence in the text to the role of humble and faithful believer; she used her own ethical credentials to bolster the claim of divine origin for her ideas; she reported the showings with an immediacy that suggests experience unsullied by interpretation; she relied on the empirical authority of seeing; and she relied on the common-sense authority of "everyday argument," as in the syllogistic treatment of sin in the passage above. Although she occasionally refers to apostolic writing, her *Showings* are notable for their lack of appeal to traditional authorities. She appears to have been writing for an audience who shared her desire to see for themselves.

Angela Merici and the Problem of Innovation

A child of the burgher class, Angela Merici was born in 1474 in Desenzano in the Italian lake country. After her parents' deaths, she was raised in the household of an uncle in nearby Salo. Early on she chose piety and asceticism, and as a young woman she returned alone to her childhood home in Desenzano, engaging in charitable work and joining the Third Order of Saint Francis but never expressing any desire to enter the cloister. She did not write but could apparently read both Latin and Italian. She appears to have been at a loss for a direction in life and prayed for guidance, which she believed to have been granted when she stopped on a journey to pray at a remote spot called Brudazzo. There she was granted a vision in which she was told that she would found a company of dedicated women. Decades passed before she acted on this information, and we can only speculate about the mixture of practical difficulties and sheer mystification that delayed her. Religious orders for women were, by definition, cloistered at this time, and her interests were in practical charitable work in the cities and towns around Lake Garda, a region that suffered much as Venice and France contested for control of it.

Too little evidence remains for us to understand fully Angela's response to the intellectual controversies of her time. One of her twentieth-century biographers believes that she disliked the neo-Platonism of her time, finding it neither practical nor useful (Maginnis 76). She was widely known for her ascetic practices, and in her *Fifth Counsel* she wrote of the "traitor world, where there is no repose nor content, nothing but empty dreams, hard labor, and things unhappy and harmful."[19] In these things, she seems to have been fully in sympathy with the renunciatory tradition of the Middle Ages. She was living in Brescia in 1520 when news of Luther's protest reached the area and religious conflict compounded political warfare. Angela conferred regularly with the confessor who was her spiritual director in the Third Order, and on pilgrimage to Rome in 1525 she met with Pope Clement VII. In sum, she appears to have taken pains to receive and follow clerical advice.

Finally, in 1532, after Francisco Cornaro had been appointed to Brescia, she put forward the idea of a company of unmarried women who would continue to live in their own homes but would devote themselves to charitable work, most particularly to the teaching of young girls. A dozen women were ready to join her in the company. In November of 1535 the Company of Saint Ursula was formally established with the permission of church authorities. When Angela died in January of 1540, her written legacy consisted of the *Rule,*[20] an appendix of Counsels, and a *Testament.* These were penned by her secretary, Gabriel Cozzano, who attests that he added nothing but rather wrote down exactly what she dictated to him. The benefit of having a male as secretary, to give an implicit "imprimatur" to a document from its very beginning, seems to have been widely recognized by women writers in this period. If respected male authority was a benefit of this arrangement, then Cozzano constituted an early audience for the writing (Lunsford). As we consider Angela's rhetorical choices, it is well to keep this in mind.

Before we turn to look more closely at Angela's written works, we should pause to note how radical a project she had begun. Her aim—to educate young girls, especially in matters of religion—served the very conservative effort of countering Reformation inroads into the area around Lake Garda, but the attention to the education of girls as a primary goal was new indeed. Monastic women had long offered education to girls who were sent to them, but never before had there been a Company that took education as its main mission and worked in the cities and towns, from their own homes, meeting only monthly at their oratory for a shared liturgy. Clare of Assisi had wanted her sisters to be uncloistered and to do charitable work in the cities, but she had lost that struggle with the papacy and the order had been cloistered (Petroff 231–34). Indeed, in later years the Rule of the Company of Saint Ursula would be rewritten to conform more closely to that of a traditional cloistered order.[21]

The late Middle Ages and the early years of the Reformation were particularly damning of innovation in thinking. Elisabeth Schonau, the twelfth-century mystic, had explained that she did not reveal her visions because she did not want to appear arrogant or as the creator of novel ideas ("*ut arrogantiam evitarem, et ne auctrix novitatum viderer,*" Ferrante 25–26). Luther, in the 1518 preface to the *German Theology,* felt the need to assert that the ideas were not innovative but grounded in tradition (Ozment 240).

Indeed, the most fundamental objection leveled at Reformation theologians was that they were innovators. Tradition, along with scripture, was the repository of truth, and change was acceptable only to effect a return to original intention or custom. As Giles of Viterbo had reminded the Fifth Lateran Council (1512–1517), "It is proper that people be changed by religion and not religion changed by people" ("*homines per sacra immutari fas est, non sacra per hominess,*" qtd. in Ozment 401). The condemnation of "new things" extended not only to doctrinal matters but also to the ways religious beliefs gave rise to action in the world.

The particular form of Angela's innovation—education of girls by an order of uncloistered women—constituted a potential red flag,[22] because the role of women in the northern Italian territories was a source of contentious debate in the sixteenth century. As Virginia Cox has pointed out, declining revenue from trade had decreased incomes, and "dowry inflation" was serious enough to create something of a social crisis. Many women could not marry, because their families would have been bankrupted by the dowry they would have to provide. What, then, was the role of this growing group of single women within the society? Could the traditional connection between women's nature and the roles of wife and mother be so confidently asserted when so many women were cut off from these roles? Could wives be expected to be submissive to their husbands when their dowries had been so important in maintaining the household and its status? Those who successfully promoted the sumptuary laws in this period argued that women's spending on costume was in need of legal restraint, because husbands were not successful in curbing their wives' spending (Cox 551). Agostino Valier, in *Modo di vivere proposto alle vergini che si chiman dimesse* (1577), proposed that the single women find a role in charity and domestic usefulness, combined with rigid self-discipline, and both Lucrezia Marinella and Moderata Fonte wrote in praise of the freedom of self-definition and action that came with the single life (Cox 513ff). Though these writers were Venetian, Brescia was under control of Venice for much of the period, and the cultural ties were many. Angela's Company, offering a new role for single, celibate women, is clearly an early response to the contemporary dowry crisis, and, as the later written responses make explicit, the possibility of a social role outside of marriage or cloister provoked a great deal of cultural anxiety (Zarri 404).

The immediate audience for the Counsels was the group of *colonelli,* or leaders of the order in each neighborhood of Brescia. Their superiors, the governors of the Company, were the primary audience for the Testament, and the Rule was addressed to all members of the Company, literate and illiterate. Such documents, however, required approval of ecclesiastical authorities, who constituted an unaddressed but critically important audience. In the first two documents, Angela is giving advice to leaders of the Company on fostering the development of all the members. As such, the documents themselves are about persuasion: how to encourage the members to persevere in the work, how to discourage them from bad habits. Several times she tells the leaders that good conduct must be freely chosen, so their task is to persuade, not to force. In the documents, then, she is modeling the persuasion she is also advising.

Angela confesses her own unworthiness, but not at great length. Indeed, whereas Hildegard of Bingen in the twelfth century had repeatedly to argue that the times were so corrupt that God had chosen a lowly woman as spokesperson so as to shame the churchmen, Angela's demur seems more a ritual nod or an expression of personal modesty rather than a rhetorical strategy to legitimate a woman writing. Like Hildegard, however, she claims authority for her pronouncements on the grounds that they are from God. But to this, then, she links a new claim to authority: the respect and affection that her "sisters and daughters" have for her personally. In the *Third Counsel* she urges her daughters to be obedient to their superiors in the Company: "for by obeying them, you will be obeying me; and in obeying me, you will be obeying Jesus Christ, who, in His great goodness, chose me to be the mother in life and in death of this noble Company, although I for my part was most unworthy,—but having chosen me, He gave me the grace to govern it in accordance with His will" (11). And in the *Fourth Counsel* she urges them to be forceful in making the superiors recognize the needs of the members they represent: "Insist, if you see that they are slow to make provision, and in this matter you may use my name and be persistent and exacting" (12). And in the *Last Legacy* she concludes: "Hold it for certain that this Rule has been planted directly by His holy hand and that He will never abandon this Company till the end of time. If it was He who planted it in the first place, who is there that can uproot it? Believe this: do not doubt but have firm faith that this will be so. I know what I am talking about" (28). Angela herself, a woman of ascetic life and charitable work, a woman known personally to the members of her Company, vouches for the salvific nature of the advice she gives, and that is enough.

But because Angela also believed that God intended for her Company to last until the end of time, she would have yet another audience, later members who had not known her personally. These, and the ecclesiastical readers, might require grounds for assent that went beyond her personal ethical appeal. Thus it is characteristic for the Counsels and the Legacies to include quotations from scripture and examples for the life of Christ or the lives of the saints. The *First Counsel,* for example, urging humility on the leaders of the Company, includes the Latin quotation of the words of Christ, "*Ego fui in vobis non tamquam qui recumbit, set ut qui ministrat,*" and translates them into the Italian as "I am among you, not as one seated at table, but as one who serves" (9). Then follows the example of Saint Gregory, who, though a pope, regarded himself as the "Servant of the Servants of God." Angela then explains that this means one who "strives to suppress all feelings for self, all self-satisfaction at his own renown, because he hopes for and expects from God a very different satisfaction and a more enduring honour and glory." Thus she appropriates the authority of the scripture and the papacy as support and in the process interprets them to support her vision of sanctity. We see this again in the *Third Legacy,* where she strongly urges kindness and love as hallmarks of the educational process. Several quotations from scripture buttress this tenet, and the last of these is interpreted: "And above all, be careful not to use force, because God has given free will to everybody and wants to force nobody, but only points out, invites and counsels, as He does through the mouth of St. John, saying: 'Suadeo tibi emere coronam immarcescibilem': which means, 'I counsel you to buy the crown that cannot waste away.' 'I counsel you,' he says, not 'I compel you.'" Thus scripture lends its authority to Angela's point and is interpreted in such a way as to support one of the ideals that she wished to characterize her Company.

The scriptural references and the examples also help to anchor the writings firmly within the honored genre of religious pattern-of-life writings, the formal and informal "rules" that founders of religious movements traditionally left for their followers since the time of Saint Benedict.[23] One could read Angela's work and never know that the role she is outlining for single women is entirely new or that her work could also be read as part of the discourse on women's roles in society. She has simply chosen not to acknowledge that aspect of her ideas. The only glimpse she gives of a woman acting outside a traditional role is the reference in the first chapter of the *Rule* to Judith cutting off the head of Holofernes, and it is allegorized as warrant to "cut short the deceits of the devil."[24] Indeed, she uses the earthly family and the roles of wife and mother as the analogical framework for her description of the Company. Its members are not single women but "spouses of Christ." This characterization runs throughout all of Angela's writings and is integral to her argument for maternal love as the wellspring for the care of the members by their superiors. The *Fourth Legacy* describes the care with which biological mothers prepare their daughters to be wives and mothers, and it concludes:

> How much more, then, must you try to act in this way for our spiritual daughters. They are the brides, not of earthly, mortal husbands, who will rot away after death, but of the immortal Son of the Eternal God. What an unheard of joy and privilege to be the guides and mothers of the brides of the King of kings and Lord of lords, and to be in a sense, mothers-in-law to the Son of God, and by means of your daughters to obtain the favour and love of the Most High. You will be overjoyed, if you are able to recognise and appreciate your new and singular vocation. (23)

Thus is the new and singular characterized as simply a spiritualization of the socially acceptable and traditional.

It is in the warning against heretical influences in the *Sixth Counsel* that Angela urges, "Keep to the traditional way and practice of the Church, established and confirmed by so many saints, under the guidance of the Holy Spirit. For your part, lead a new life" (16). Her Company is thus "new" in the sense that its members have put on a new—in effect, dedicated—life. This newness is carefully distinguished from any heterodox innovation. And again in the *Last Legacy* she directs her Company to follow the Rule in good faith but also to change it if they must to adapt to new circumstances. Thus she again distinguishes between the animating charism of the Company and the working out of that charism in any set of historical circumstances. To accept that distinction is to accept that women may take on new roles in society, the better to fulfill their roles as mothers and loyal Catholic daughters.

Finally, an examination of Angela's warrants and reasons reveals an engaging practicality, based in her personal experience and observation. This daughter of the urban middle class tells the leaders of her Company to guard the members against intimacy with men, even against an intense spiritual relationship with a man, because such relationships too seldom remain spiritual (*Sixth Counsel*). She tells them also to deal with disobedient members by simply leaving them alone and letting loneliness and lack of attention bring them back to the fold. Being left alone allows you to understand your sin, and it was for this reason that God sent Adam away from paradise (*Fifth Legacy*). (Here again we see Angela bringing in scriptural authority and interpreting it to support her point.) She repeatedly urges the leaders to get to know each of their daughters individually, just as a biological mother does. And, finally, in the *Ninth Legacy,* in discussing alms-giving, she explains the psychological connection between charity and obligation: "Just as, for example, after a young girl agrees to accept a present from some stranger she remains obliged to do that person's will and cannot very well say no; so, too, alms, in more or less the same way as gifts, draw people and in a way constrain them to do good, and to continue to do good while they remain so bound. Make use of these tried methods and you cannot go wrong" (26).

Rhetorically, Angela presents her Company as a bulwark of tradition against heresy, an extension of the mother role, a means for women to find mutual encouragement in a life of charitable work, duty, and penance. She grounds her arguments in her own personal authority, in visionary guidance from God, in experience, and in scripture. The importation of scripture allows her not only to borrow its authority but also to make it say what she wants it to say. Such a nonconfrontational rhetoric, based in allegory and appropriation, is not surprising from one who urged kindness, personal connection, and good example as the keys to influencing the behavior of others.

Conclusion

Skepticism about the power of reason and dialectic to know God; growing respect for empirical learning, common sense, and experience, especially among the ascendant middle class; an embattled institutional church, whose authority was compromised by its inability to carry out its own reform; the growth of lay piety and its cultural forms—all of these helped to open the door to women who wished to shape the religious culture of the late Middle Ages. Julian and Angela, like so many other women writers, derived their ethical authority from lives of self-denial; indeed, fasting could be regarded as part of the rhetorical practice of women writers in this era who wished to take part in religious discourse.

All rhetoric is local, and Julian and Angela were writing in different cultural settings, for different purposes, and for different audiences. What they share in the larger frame, however, is the experience of writing in the centuries when Western culture was making the gradual transition from the medieval to the early modern epoch, all the while scorning and denying innovation. In such a period we should not be surprised to find a rhetorical practice that claims the authority it denies, that appeals to experience but claims revelatory origins, and that elides the gendered social location that gave rise to both the structure and the message. And just as Julian and Angela derived authority from the rhetorical strategies they employed, so also did they give credibility to the strategies themselves. In so doing, they participated fully in the circulation of authority through the late medieval rhetorical economy.

Notes

1. The several works of James J. Murphy provide the best overview of medieval rhetoric: *Medieval Rhetoric: A Select Bibliography; Medieval Eloquence: Studies in the Theory and Practice of Medieval Rhetoric;* and *Rhetoric in the Middle Ages: A History of Rhetorical Theory from St. Augustine to the Renaissance.* Also helpful are Joseph M. Miller, Michael H. Prosser, and Thomas W. Benson, eds., *Readings in Medieval Rhetoric;* Rita Copeland, *Rhetoric, Hermeneutics, and Translation in the Middle Ages;* Martin Camargo, *Medieval Rhetorics of Prose Composition;* and Ruth Morse, *Truth and Convention in the Middle Ages.*

2. By the middle of the twelfth century, scholars began to have available the complete *organon* of Aristotle on logic, with the arrival of the *Analytica priora, Analytica posteriora, Topica,* and *De elenchis sophisticis.*

3. I follow Gordon Leff (*Medieval Thought, William of Ockham,* and *The Dissolution of the Medieval Outlook*) in regarding the tension between free will and the scope of reason as the central issue in late medieval philosophy, subsuming the controversy between nominalists and realists over the nature of universals. See also Marilyn McCord Adams, *William of Ockham;* Marsha L. Colish, *The Mirror of Language: A Study in the Medieval Theory of Knowledge;* William A. Frank and Allan B. Wolter, *Duns Scotus, Metaphysician;* Armand A. Maurer, "William of Ockham"; and Michael Haren, *Medieval Thought: The Western Intellectual Tradition from Antiquity to the Thirteenth Century.*

4. Edward Grant, in *God and Reason in the Middle Ages,* has demonstrated the extent to which dialectic remained central to medical and legal discourses and, indeed, to all facets of university education into the seventeenth century. Theological discourse also continued to use dialectic, but in the fourteenth century it could no longer convincingly claim access to certainty in so large a sphere, and alternative forms of theological discourse were available to compete with dialectic.

5. For an argument that the accumulation of wealth was central to the quest for knowledge in the transition from medieval to early modern culture, see Lisa Jardine, *Worldly Goods: A New History of the Renaissance.*

6. Sheila Delaney, in "Undoing Substantial Connection: The Late Medieval Attack on Analogical Thought," argues that the attack on the validity of analogical argument, gaining force in the late thirteenth and fourteenth centuries, had ramifications in many arenas, from literary allegory to political theory.

7. Joan Ferrante, in "The Education of Women in the Middle Ages in Theory, Fact, and Fantasy," provides a good overview of the types of access to education women had at various times and notes that the dominance of universities in the thirteenth century signaled a widening of the educational gap between men and women. She mentions Heloise (1101–1164) as an exception to the rule that women

did not receive training in dialectic—witness her *Problemata,* the forty-two theological questions she posed for Abelard.

8. Caroline Walker Bynum's *Holy Feast and Holy Fast: The Religious Significance of Food to Medieval Women* examines the relationship of eating to issues of control, power, and physicality for a wide range of medieval women. Bynum argues, using the example of Julian and the hazelnut, that women saw the physical world and flesh itself as redeemed and therefore had no need to transcend their femaleness in order to be saved. Jo Ann McNamara and others have argued that religious women had to become spiritual men.

9. H. P. Owen, in "Experience and Dogma in the English Mystics," takes the position that prior beliefs shape mystical experiences. He notes that Julian's *Showings* touch on such topical theological issues as the Trinity, the problem of evil, and the path to redemption and that she reconciles her visionary experience with accepted doctrine. His reading emphasizes the assertions of orthodoxy and downplays the struggle—which Julian's rhetoric preserves—to reconcile her vision to orthodox thinking.

10. Nicholas Watson believes that Julian was consciously writing with a view toward protecting herself from charges of Lollardy (e.g., from a Lollard disdain for graven images). For a reading of Julian as less motivated by defensiveness, see Felicity Riddy, "'Women Talking about the Things of God': A Late Medieval Subculture."

11. Lynn Staley Johnson explores Julian's relationship to her scribe to construct her own persona as a writer. She notes that theological writing was open to careful examination after the 1378 papal censure of Wycliffe and after the 1404 constraints put in place by Bishop Arundel. Staley argues that the short text is presented as a devotional text, but the longer text is more rhetorically assertive about the visionary experience.

12. For a valuable discussion of the nature of Julian's religious affiliation and the date at which she took up that life, see Benedicta Ward, "Julian the Solitary" and "Lady Julian and Her Audience: 'Mine Eve-Christian.'"

13. The idea that the life of the writer testifies to the truth of the work is basic to the Christian rhetoric of the Middle Ages. Martin Camargo traces the development of this key idea in the thinking of Augustine of Hippo and its formulation in his *De doctrina christiana.*

14. Katherine H. Tachau offers a substantial argument that vision and the study of optics were central to fourteenth-century epistemology. We have no reason to think that Julian knew these epistemological treatises, but she is likely to have known the theological arguments related to them (e.g., how human beings can know God). Her interest in vision as a way of knowing is most likely prompted by the empirical turn in the culture, a turn that seems to have both fostered philosophi-

cal speculations about the nature of vision and been given energy by them. See Jeffrey F. Hamburger for a discussion of the relationship of the face of Christ in the second Showing to the "Veronicas" that appear in German visual arts and visionary texts.

15. All quotations from the *Showings* are taken from the short text in the Colledge and Walsh translation. The weight of critical opinion still favors the view that the long text is a later expansion of the short text, a product of continued meditation on the *Showings.* The Watson article provides a good summary of the evidence for dating and for the relationship between the texts.

16. See Cynthea Masson for an argument that Julian's rhetoric, like her theology, is built on "a coincidence of opposites" (155). The tension between things shown and things hidden runs throughout Julian's text. Masson explores Julian's rhetorical strategies for writing about an experience of the ineffable.

17. Christopher Abbott, in *Julian of Norwich: Autobiography and Theology* (see 107–12), offers a helpful discussion of the relationship between the personal and the universal in the *Showings,* including the rhetorical effectiveness of familial references and metaphors.

18. Alexandra Barrett, in "Julian of Norwich and the Holy Spirit, 'Our Good Lord,'" cautions us to remember that Julian's characterization of Jesus as Mother is metaphoric and should not be treated as a reification. Given the metaphoric nature of much theology, however, the choice of this particular metaphoric vehicle seems highly significant. In contrast to Barratt, Liz Herbert McAvoy argues that Julian constructs a hermeneutic through the connection of the motherhood of God with discourses about the female body arising from the new commodity culture of the time.

19. Luciana Mariani, O.S.U., and Elisa Tarolli, in *S. Angela Merici, Regola, Ricordi, Legati, Testo Antico e Testo Moderno,* provide the texts in sixteenth-century Brescian dialect and modern Italian translations. English translations of Angela's writings are available in Sr. Monica Maginnis, *Angela Merici and Her Teaching Idea;* Teresa Neylan's *The Writings of St. Angela Merici;* and Anon., *The Spirit of St. Angela Merici.* Saint John's Monastery, in Collegeville, Minnesota, has also made available the *Spiritual Testament and Counsels.* Quotations in this text are from the Neylan translation. The definitive biography is Teresa Ledochowska's.

20. The *Primitive Rule* was edited in 1581 by Charles Borromeo, the Cardinal Archbishop of Milan, in the wake of the Council of Trent. Although that Council had confirmed *Periculosa,* the canon law of 1298 that made monastic enclosure irreversible, the Company was allowed to continue without solemn vows.

21. In 1610 a French branch of the Company, under the guidance of Mme. St. Beuve, accepted enclosure and adopted a form of the rule that is usually called the *Monastic Rule.*

22. Maginnis notes that Angela's intention that the Company extend to other

cities and other countries clearly marks it as a type of religious order and not a confraternity. Likewise, papal authority confirmed that the dowry rights of women who joined that Company would be the same as those who had joined cloistered orders.

23. Dorothy L. Latz argues for the importance of reading Angela in light of the Franciscan influences that she encountered through her membership in the Third Order. In particular, she argues that the word *specchio* is most often wrongly translated as "model" rather than the more accurate "mirror," with its intimations of neo-Platonic transcendence. Latz believes that Angela would have encountered the thinking of Marsilio Ficino while in Salo and would have been influenced by Duns Scotus's writings through the Franciscans in the region of Brescia. Such influences inform her hermeneutics and her imagery, including that of vision.

24. Judith's beheading of Holofernes furnished subject matter for a number of artworks in the fifteenth century, including those by Donatello and by Andrea Mantegna, suggesting anxiety about changes in women's roles.

Works Cited

Abbott, Christopher. *Julian of Norwich: Autobiography and Theology.* Rochester, NY: D. S. Brewer, 1999.

Adams, Marilyn McCord. *William Ockham.* Notre Dame, IN: U of Notre Dame P, 1987.

Barratt, Alexandra. "Julian of Norwich and the Holy Spirit, 'Our Good Lord.'" *Mystics Quarterly* 28.2 (2002): 78–84.

Bynum, Caroline Walker. *Holy Feast and Holy Fast: The Religious Significance of Food to Medieval Women.* Berkeley: U of California P, 1987.

Camargo, Martin. *Medieval Rhetorics of Prose Composition: Five English Artes Dictandi and Their Tradition.* Binghamton, NY: Binghamton UP, 1995.

———. "'Non Solum Sibi Sed Aliis Etiam': Neoplatonism and Rhetoric in Saint Augustine's De Doctrina Christiana." *Rhetorica* 16.4 (1998): 393–407.

Colish, Marcia L. *The Mirror of Language: A Study in the Medieval Theory of Knowledge.* New Haven, CT: Yale UP, 1968.

Copeland, Rita. *Rhetoric, Hermeneutics, and Translation in the Middle Ages: Academic Traditions and Vernacular Texts.* Cambridge: Cambridge UP, 1991.

Cox, Virginia. "The Single Self: Feminist Thought and the Marriage Market in Early Modern Venice." *Renaissance Quarterly* 48 (1995): 513–81.

Delany, Sheila. "Undoing Substantial Connection: The Late Medieval Attack on Analogical Thought." *Medieval Literary Politics: Shapes of Ideology.* Ed. Sheila Delany. Manchester: Manchester UP, 1990. 19–41.

Dietrich, Julia. "The Visionary Rhetoric of Hildegard of Bingen." *Listening to Their*

Voices: The Rhetorical Activities of Historical Women. Ed. Molly Meijer Wertheimer. Columbia: U of South Carolina P, 1997. 199–214.

Ferrante, Joan. "The Education of Women in the Middle Ages in Theory, Fact, and Fantasy." *Beyond Their Sex: Learned Women of the European Past.* Ed. Patricia H. Labalme. New York: New York UP, 1980. 9–42.

Frank, William A., and Allan B. Wolter. *Duns Scotus, Metaphysician.* West Lafayette, IN: Purdue UP, 1995.

Grant, Edward. *God and Reason in the Middle Ages.* Cambridge: Cambridge UP, 2001.

Hamburger, Jeffrey F. *The Visual and the Visionary: Art and Female Spirituality in Late Medieval Germany.* New York: Zone Books, 1998.

Haren, Michael. *Medieval Thought: The Western Intellectual Tradition from Antiquity to the Thirteenth Century.* 2nd ed. Toronto: U of Toronto P, 1992.

Jardine, Lisa. *Worldly Goods: A New History of the Renaissance.* New York: Nan A. Talese, 1996.

Johnson, Lynn Staley. "The Trope of the Scribe and the Question of Literary Authority in the Works of Julian of Norwich and Margery Kempe." *Speculum* 66.4 (1991): 820–38.

Julian of Norwich. *Julian of Norwich: Showings.* Ed. Edmund Colledge and James Walsh. New York: Paulist, 1978.

Kempe, Margery. *The Book of Margery Kempe.* Ed. Barry Windeatt. New York: Longman, 1999.

Knowles, David. *The Evolution of Medieval Thought.* New York: Knopf, 1962.

Latz, Dorothy L. "The Writings of St. Angela Merici in the Light of Bonaventuran Exemplarism: The Motherhood, Fatherhood, and Transcendence of God." *Mystics Quarterly* 10 (1984): 126–35.

Ledochowska, Teresa, O.S.U. *Angele Merici et la Compagnie de Ste. Ursule.* 2 Vols. Milan: Ancora, 1967.

Leff, Gordon. *The Dissolution of the Medieval Outlook: An Essay on Intellectual and Spiritual Change in the Fourteenth Century.* New York: New York UP, 1976.

———. *Medieval Thought: St. Augustine to Ockham.* Chicago: Quadrangle, 1958.

———. *William of Ockham: The Metamorphosis of Scholastic Discourse.* Manchester: Manchester UP, 1975.

Lunsford, Andrea. "Medieval Women as Collaborative Writers." Paper presented at the Conference on College Composition and Communication. Minneapolis, Minnesota. April 2000.

Maginnis, Sr. Monica. *Angela Merici and Her Teaching Idea, 1474–1540.* New York: Longmans Green, 1927.

Masson, Cynthea. "The Point of Coincidence: Rhetoric and Apophatic in Julian of

Norwich's Showings." *Julian of Norwich: A Book of Essays.* Ed. Sandra J. McEntire. New York: Garland, 1998. 153–81.

Maurer, Armand A. "William of Ockham." *Individuation in Scholasticism: The Later Middle Ages and the Counter-Reformation, 1150–1650.* Ed. Jorge J. E. Gracia. Albany: SUNY Press, 1994. 373–96.

McAvoy, Liz Herbert. "Julian of Norwich and a Trinity of the Feminine." *Mystics Quarterly* 28.2 (2002): 68–77.

McNamara, Jo Ann. "Rhetoric of Orthodoxy." *Maps of Flesh and Light: The Religious Experience of Medieval Women Mystics.* Ed. Ulrike Wiethaus. Syracuse, NY: Syracuse UP, 1993. 9–27.

Merici, Angela. *S. Angela Merici, Regola, Ricordi, Legati, Testo Antico e Testo Moderno.* Ed. Luciana Mariani, O.S.U., and Elisa Tarolli. Brescia: Queriniana, 1975.

———. *The Writings of St. Angela Merici.* Trans. Teresa Neylan. Rome: Ursulines of the Roman Union, 1968.

Miller, Joseph M., Michael H. Prosser, and Thomas W. Benson, eds. *Readings in Medieval Rhetoric.* Bloomington: Indiana UP, 1973.

Morse, Ruth. *Truth and Convention in the Middle Ages: Rhetoric, Representation, and Reality.* Cambridge: Cambridge UP, 1991.

Murphy, James J. *Medieval Eloquence: Studies in the Theory and Practice of Medieval Rhetoric.* Berkeley: U of California P, 1978.

———. *Medieval Rhetoric: A Select Bibliography.* Toronto: U of Toronto P, 1971.

———. *Rhetoric in the Middle Ages: A History of Rhetorical Theory from St. Augustine to the Renaissance.* Berkeley: U of California P, 1974.

Owen, H. P. "Experience and Dogma in the English Mystics." *Mysticism and Religious Traditions.* Ed. Steven T. Katz. Oxford: Oxford UP, 1983. 148–62.

Ozment, Stephen. *The Age of Reform, 1250–1550: An Intellectual and Religious History of Late Medieval and Reformation Europe.* New Haven, CT: Yale UP, 1980.

Petroff, Elizabeth Alvilda. "Introduction." *Medieval Women's Visionary Literature.* Ed. Elizabeth Alvilda Petroff. New York: Oxford UP, 1986. 3–59.

Riddy, Felicity. "'Women Talking about the Things of God': A Late Medieval Subculture." *Women and Literature in Britain, c. 1150–1500.* Ed. Carol M. Meale. Cambridge: Cambridge UP, 1993.

The Spirit of St. Angela Merici. St. Martin, OH: Ursulines of Brown County, 1907.

Tachau, Katherine H. *Vision and Certitude in the Age of Ockham: Optics, Epistemology, and the Foundations of Semantics, 1250–1345.* Leiden: E. J. Brill, 1988.

Ward, Benedicta. "Julian the Solitary." *Julian Reconsidered.* Eds. Kenneth Leech and Benedicta Ward. Oxford: Fairacres Press, 1988. 11–31.

———. "Lady Julian and Her Audience: 'Mine Even-Christian.'" *The English Religious Tradition and the Genius of Anglicanism.* Ed. Geoffrey Rowell. Oxford: Oxford UP, 1992. 47–63.

Watson, Nicholas. "The Composition of Julian of Norwich's Revelation of Love." *Speculum* 68 (1993): 637–83.

Zarri, Gabriella. "Monasteri Femminili e Citta (Secoli XV-XVIII)." *La Chiesa e Il Potere Politico Del Medioevo All'eta Contemporanea.* Eds. Giorgio Chittolini and Giovanni Miccoli. Turin: Giulio Einaudi, 1986. 357–429.

2

The Role of Language in the Construction of Mary Wortley Montagu's Rhetorical Identity

Yvonne Merrill

Postmodern, or "linguistic," feminism views public and private rhetorical contexts as the medium in which working social realities are constructed (Fraser 158). According to Kathy Ferguson in *The Man Question: Vision of Subjectivity in Feminist Theory* (1993), linguistic feminism opposes epistemologies that claim an inherent social and metaphysical order to existence. Female subjectivity, as with any other social phenomena, is constructed by the prevailing social conversation. In this chapter, I would like to show how British writer Mary Wortley Montagu's rhetorical identity was negatively influenced by the configuration of gender, class, and socioeconomic influences in her personal social milieu. I argue that this identity lacked ethos because prevailing Augustan neoclassicism provided no public rhetorical space for a female voice. Carrying out the theme of this volume, I will also argue that despite Montagu's fluency in eighteenth-century neoclassic and belletristic discourse resulting from her socioeconomic class, she still failed to achieve a credible public voice, simply because she was a woman.

Eighteenth-century male writers' attempts to establish standards for public discourse and rules of style, taste, and decorum by and large excluded all public uses of language, save those informed by the classical tradition for which they were exclusively groomed. Though women writers such as

Bathsua Makin and Mary Astell had called for improved women's education for nearly a hundred years, women received neither private classical instruction nor public education as a rule. And although education for both men and women had reached a nadir just prior to the 1688 Glorious Revolution (because widespread literacy threatened the privileges of the aristocracy), upper-class women such as Montagu suffered disproportionately (Graff 239; Lawson and Silver 207–8). Educational opportunities for women across classes would not increase appreciably until after mid-century and the establishment of a literate bourgeoisie.

No one assumed, in any case, that a female's education in Montagu's milieu would be equivalent to the classical education in the Western cultural tradition given to men (Jones 2–8). In men's formal schooling, Aristotelian-Ciceronian rhetoric was central and focused on the belles lettres—sociohistorical commentary, literary criticism, and political persuasion. It was intended to buttress political patriarchy, define social norms and mores, and stabilize class boundaries—an education for the public sphere, closed to women by definition. Sociopolitical developments in early-eighteenth-century England created simultaneously the distinctions both between sex and gender and between public and private spheres, resulting from the rise of a bourgeois middle class. Women, particularly married women of the upper classes, were becoming legally defined as nonpersons, even as more of them gained access to a literary education (McKeon 295–96; Baecker; Eger, Grant, O'Gallchoir, and Warburton 3–5; Skinner 91, 103).

Based on the principles of Aristotle, Cicero, Quintilian, and Horace, rhetoric was inherently public, intended to be persuasive, epideictic, and epistemic. Its topoi were those used for the social construction of cultural taste, nationalism, ethnocentrism, and morality for a public person. The popular genres—periodical essays, unpublished manuscripts, epigrams, travelogues, squibs, partisan pamphlets, and poetry—were widely circulated, even though often conventionally anonymous. Montagu was as prolific in her strategic use of these popular forms of publication as were her male peers (Looser 62). She was a recognized voice in the contemporary circulation of ideas, yet she did not enjoy the acceptance or authority of her male contemporaries for any apparent reason other than her gender, even though George Justice argues that women's choice of "unpublished" manuscripts was deliberate and had more influence than currently recognized (3–5). Her forays into political history, usually considered a male genre, were published without her name or after her death, gaining her little recognition from her contemporary society (Looser 1–2, 63). The voice of the privileged male elite *was* the public voice (McKeon 295–96). Discourse, however, was a social art, not a pragmatic craft, simply because those who practiced it eschewed the bourgeois ethic and monopolized its production.

The privileged rhetorical genres used by these male writers made little distinction between the *ars rhetorica* and the *ars poetica,* because all public discourse served a social end. The early part of the century had seen the canons of invention and arrangement reunited with Aristotle's other rhetorical canons—memory, style, and delivery—allowing rhetorical principles to be applied to all texts, both literary and nonliterary. The belletrists considered poetry, history, and essay all within their purview, and they became the primary arbiters of style and taste. But above all they were rhetoricians, because they subscribed to the humanistic ideal that the end of discourse was the advancement of mankind—a public, social mission.

In order to discover how Lady Mary Wortley Montagu attempted to construct an authorial subjectivity, we therefore have to examine the social influences on her and her male literary peers to determine whether she could compete successfully with them as a writer who happened to be a woman. The most significant disadvantage to Montagu's public identity was that "female author" was, for the most part, an oxymoron in her society. Women had no social or legal public identity, and for the neoclassic Augustans, authorship was inherently public, therefore dominated by men. I will refer to the public rhetorical style of the period as inherently *masculine* in the sense that only classically educated male writers employed it successfully. The access to this education was generally what distinguished the writing styles of men and women. For her ethos, then, the first task of a woman writer was to acquire an education equivalent to that of her male peers if she hoped to have a public audience. Those women who dared to write on public topics for public audiences, however, were castigated and likened to prostitutes (Rogers 21). Margaret Cavendish and Aphra Behn in the recent social past had suffered such censure. The triumvirate of female virtues—chastity, silence, and obedience—were still very much the ideal for early-eighteenth-century English women. When encouraged by Mary Astell to publish her literary letters describing Turkish society, written during her husband's ambassadorship to Turkey, Montagu steadfastly refused, giving instruction for them to be published only upon her death. The social opprobrium she would have suffered would not allow her to subject herself to such ego damage and public (read *male*) outrage.

The social, economic, and political circumstances that foster public roles for women did not obtain in Augustan society. Though complex, the reasons have recurred throughout Western history and essentially result from a thriving bourgeois class, creating economic competition between classes and genders. With wealthy merchants encroaching on the privileges of the landed gentry, domestication of women was a necessity for maintaining wealth in families and taking women out of the labor pool. Women merely conveyed wealth from one male patriarch to another. They lost the legal right to the wealth they carried, so they could not dissipate it or confer it of their own free will. Feminist cultural historians, such as Marylin Arthur, Susan Moller Okin, Renate Bridenthal, Claudia Koonz, and Eva Cantarella, have all shown that the conditions resulting in the removal of women from the public sphere and their domestication have regularly occurred in the West during times of bourgeois ascendancy. Early-eighteenth-century England experienced such a historic moment. Thus, most women were excluded from university or private educations that were the necessary preparation for action in the public sphere. Only as the result of her widowed father's unorthodox and casual upbringing, and the eclectic wealth of his personal library, was Montagu able to acquire a classical education on her own.

When just a teenager, she translated and wrote her own Latin and French verse, read Greek, and learned Italian, using only grammars and dictionaries to decipher the texts of entire classical and contemporary works, Ovid's being among her favorites. And when she was only eight years old, her father took her to the Kit-Cat Club to show off her wit to the fashionable Whig supporters of the Hanoverian succession; and her frequent contact with his friends Joseph Addison, Richard Steele, William Congreve, and Dr. Samuel Garth encouraged her intellectual precocity. As an adult she taught herself Turkish and German well enough to translate Turkish verse and converse with the new Hanoverian monarch. As an avid follower of politics, she was a knowledgeable supporter of her husband's political career. Like her male contemporaries, she wrote frequent and telling social commentary in biting verse, which Alexander Pope even praised in print before the two had a falling out. Given her social contacts, intelligence, and learning, she enjoyed all the advantages that leveraged her male counterparts into public rhetorical space.

But another negative influence on women's authorial position in the early eighteenth century was that when invention and arrangement were retrieved from the discipline of logic, rhetoric became more specifically the prerogative of men, because according to classic Aristotelian wisdom, women's logical faculty had no authority. Most of Montagu's detractors, for example, accused her of ignorance, stupidity, or illiteracy, for no other reason than that she was a woman. The cultural assumption was that she had an inferior capacity for logic or no sphere in which to display it, despite her broad knowledge and obvious command of classical conventions and popular genres.

Since no publicly sanctioned rhetorical space existed for a woman's necessarily private experience, Montagu's subjectivity assumed a masculine persona and was generally indistinguishable from that of her more successful male peers when her voice was anonymous. Vicarious public life was the only life Montagu knew, since all of her familiar conversants were men, classically trained for public social discourse. She was raised by an aristocratic father, haphazardly notwithstanding, and among her principal and familiar conversants were two of the most influential writers of her time—Alexander Pope and Joseph Addison. These were her only models, and they were the best. Being an apt student, she would easily have "passed for" a man in her writing had her gender been obscured. We can observe her replication of the prevailing style dictated by such male authorities in her public topics, even though she was *not* anonymous to these peers. Like them, her wit was recognizably individual and her insights those of a social insider.

Montagu's masculine rhetorical style can easily be seen in comparison to that of her male conversants. Though she assumed the same authority as they, her writing embodied many of her personal views, which made it highly recognizable. Because she was recognizable and competent, her work was known to the foremost style arbiters of her day, with the result that her literary endeavors were generally disparaged as indecorous, merely because they were a woman's. Pope implied she was a literary slattern and claimed she knew nothing of the subjects she discoursed upon. Horace Walpole had this to say about her public identity, even though she was many years his senior and well versed in the prevailing social conversation—not just in England, but in Europe as well: "Only figure the coalition of prudery, debauchery, sentiment, history, Greek, Latin, French, Italian, and metaphysics; all, except the second, understood by halves, by quarters, or not at all" (Halsband 200).

Ignorance was the principal libel leveled against female thinkers. Yet Addison's complimentary response to her editing of his *Cato* translation reveals her command of classical languages and literature, as does the fact that Henry Fielding and Voltaire also submitted their manuscripts for her approval (Halsband 32, 120, 128). Yet, she was a woman and therefore summarily discounted on the social *assumption* that she was unlettered and uninformed. Indicative of the dominant speakers' power and agenda to control public language and limit its speakers, Jonathan Swift was able to construct Montagu's peer Eliza Haywood, who *did* publish periodical essays under her own name, as a "stupid, infamous, scribbling woman" through a widely disseminated characterization (Mahl and Koon 224).

As an accurate imitator and parodist of her formally educated male peers, Montagu's style achieved the same tone of neutral and confident arrogance purveyed by the men in her intellectual circle. With her gender obscured, her essays also ring with a funny irony that we can appreciate, knowing they are hers. In an immodest proposal to do away with parliaments, very much in the style of Swift, we can hear the assurance of her authorial voice:

> I am very much entertained with the Variety of Censures that are passed on my harmless Paper, which I hear almost every Day with an indifferent Face, and to say Truth, without much Violence to myself, not feeling the *paternal* Affection that most Authors do for their Productions; neither my Fame nor Fortune being any way affected by their Success.—*My Acquaintance think me no more qualified for a Writer, than for a General:* and even in this Nation of Parties, I have preserved my self so unspotted by any of them, that I am not suspected of being engaged wither in *Court* or *Country* Interest [italics are mine]. (*Nonsense of Common-Sense* 29)

In this single passage Montagu has listed nearly all of the public offices for which she was *not* qualified, being a woman, yet skillfully reproduced the style of her male model. This piece becomes broad satire if one knows the author, and her peer audience probably did (see italics). But it also works as public satire in its disinterested tone and conventional humility topos. Her attitude markers show an authorial self-confidence that could result from her anonymity but probably resulted from her command of a masculine education and language and her facility in a male genre.

Montagu's only available rhetorical context was her class, providing both occasion and audience, and this class was the one privileged by hereditary right to the Western intellectual tradition. She assumed diverse roles in relationship to her audience, but coming from the same class, she generally performed as social gadfly in the same way that Pope, Addison, Swift, and Congreve did. In her periodical essays, she took on a male persona similar to theirs. Even when she promotes a feminist agenda, she appeals to contemporary aristocratic values, which were inherently masculine. For example, when advocating that women be valued for their intelligence and not constructed as brainless ignoramuses, she uses the following analogy: "I would not every Day tell my Footmen, if I kept any, that their whole Fraternity were a Pack of Scoundrels; that Lying and Stealing were such inseparable Qualities to their Cloth, that I should think myself very happy in them, if they confined themselves to innocent Lies, and would only steal Candles Ends" (*Nonsense of Common-Sense* 27). The patriarchal point of view here equates women with servants. But Montagu's class is the only institutional context from which she can speak. Though she subscribed to Whig politics, her cosmopolitan cachet and class-consciousness dominate her writing, despite her egalitarian claims.

Like her male peers' prose, Montagu's flows by virtue of subordinators, summative and resumptive modifiers, and the colon and semicolon. Her lengthy and complex periods mimic well the masculine style. This verbose style was soon to come under criticism in favor of "plain speech," by supporters of the new science. But it was very much the vogue during Montagu's prolific writing life. Witness Swift: "I do therefore humbly offer it to public consideration, that of the hundred and twenty thousand children already computed, twenty thousand may be reserved for breed, whereof only one fourth part to be males; which is more than we allow to sheep, black cattel, or swine; and my reason is that these children are seldom the fruits of marriage, a circumstance not much regarded by our savages, therefore one male will be sufficient to serve four females [mechanics regularized by modern publishers]" (Bate et al. 739) Montagu composes this Swiftian sentence in *The Nonsense of Common-Sense III,* when she facetiously proposes the use of singing statues to avoid the exorbitant fees of foreign opera stars:

> Beside this Advantage, with respect to the Action, I must take Notice, that this Project will be a great Ease to the ingenious *Superintendant of the* English *Diversions,* as his witty and facetious Countrymen are pleased to call him, and to the Directors of the *Academy of Musick,* who have often been obliged to use all their Art, and all their Politicks, to pacify the domestick Feuds of the *Opera* Stage, and to reconcile the several Actors and Actresses to one another—and to the Parts allotted them respectively; for which Purpose those worthy Patriots, to the high Emolument of their Country, and to their own immortal Renown, have often watch'd whilst others slept [italics hers]. (*Nonsense of Common-Sense* 10–11)

To achieve coherence in such a text, the author had to be a master, or mistress, of the subtleties of punctuation and subordination. Montagu's command of the conventions of language was nothing if not confident.

Like her peers, she cites classical authorities as a matter of course, not to support her position, but more imaginatively to discredit them or to flaunt her erudition, other signs of subjective confidence. She says, for instance, "I am more than ever determined to write in Defence of moral Virtue, tho I should be opposed by all the Printers, Ministers, and patriots that flourish in this Age, and think with Seneca, *Avida est Periculi Virtus*" (*Nonsense of Common-Sense* 31).

Why would Montagu's society have perpetuated a prejudice so significant against a female author of her caliber when, for more than a hundred years, women of fortunate circumstances had been writing—though fewer than a handful were paid for it? We have to examine the social dynamics that affected male, as well as female, identities and the powerful rhetorical agenda used to stabilize them.

Historic periods like Montagu's are often characterized by threats to traditional social hierarchies resulting from a rising, landless, and wealthy middle class. Besides this cultural phenomenon, the Hanoverian succession, Robert Walpole's Spanish policy and excise tax, his attempts to control the press, and the South Sea Bubble all contributed to social instability. The aristocracy saw wealthy burghers undermining upper-class hegemony. Both aristocratic and bourgeois men sought power and influence by maintaining wealth in families. Neither wanted interference or competition from women, whose social experience might not support masculine public agendas.

Historically, when male identities have been in flux, reification of women has usually resulted, in an attempt to objectify their peculiar experience and marginalize it for greater social control. Other periods in which the phenomenon can be seen were Athenian Greece—when citizenship excluded all categories of residents, including women, who were not native born, property holding men—and pre-civil war and interregnum England—when wealthy middle-class men threatened the authority of propertied aristocrats. Unattached daughters and widows had to become *femmes coverts* to prevent their inheriting titles and property they could bestow at their own discretion. Queen Anne's reign presented the same problem to monarchical power posed earlier by the reign of Elizabeth I, a female monarch "covered" or governed by no male authority. The philosophical question "What is man?" in such rhetorical moments is highly gendered. The female corollary becomes "What are women *for*?" The answer is usually the implementation of masculine social agendas. Women become merely instruments for achieving patriarchal power and stability. They are defined by their biology as the producers of legitimate heirs and are socialized into ignorance to prevent their redefining public social structures.

Articulators of constructivist epistemology Peter Berger and Thomas

Luckmann maintained that marginal social realities, such as women's, pose the most acute threat to taken-for-granted, routinized existence. Such realities have to be integrated into the paramount reality. Australian linguist Cate Poynton has since argued that language is the means by which men have exercised power over women and socially conditioned them into inferior gender roles (4). Once domesticated and denied identity-forming social discourse, women offered little threat to the comfortable efficiency of masculine social, political, or economic arrangements.

Montagu's public authorial subjectivity reveals, however, no specifically feminine "realities." Her domestic life receives written attention only in her personal letters to her husband and children. Even in them her voice is more paternal than maternal. Advice to her son and daughter turned on issues of education, social standing, money management, political positioning, and public rules of decorum—the advice that typically came from the family patriarch, and in Montagu's case, the only kind of parental advice she had to emulate. In her almost exclusive focus on public issues and social critique, Montagu's views were either taken to be a man's or discounted for being a woman's.

Montagu's forays into political rhetorical arenas were always anonymous, but her subtle critiques of gendered privilege would have jeopardized the contemporary balance of social power, particularly that between unpropertied and uneducated women and the male proprietors of every social institution from the family to the government, including the cultural. This probably explains why her periodical essays in *The Nonsense of Common-Sense* remained forgotten until Robert Halsband published the manuscripts in the twentieth century.

Literary and intellectual life under such circumstances was hardly possible for most women in Montagu's milieu. Silencing women thinkers was the most effective way to maintain the high-culture status quo and the elitist prerogatives of those possessed of classical educations. Silenced, women were denied the nomic, or meaning-bestowing, social dialogues to articulate intellectual identities and refute masculine depictions that constructed them as inferior in mind, body, and spirit. Aristotle's verdict had not been overturned.

Given the influence of neoclassic thought on eighteenth-century rhetoric, prevailing discourse perpetuated the misogynous defamations that constructed women as irrational, immoral, and evil, which had regularly surfaced in Western culture since Aristotle. When women's reality would have threatened patriarchal control of social reality, public forums had excluded women's voices. Montagu's male peers were determined to protect their exclusive right to determine not only cultural taste but all public social institutions as well. Not being privy to hegemonic discourse, women had no access to the mechanisms of their own exclusion and repression and could not stage a successful rhetorical response. Indicative of their silencing in Montagu's era is that neither she nor Eliza Haywood was mentioned in histories of the periodical essay until the late twentieth century.

Feminist epistemologists such as Elizabeth Gosz, Susan Hekman, and Lorraine Code, who have explored how women come to know, have also concluded that women's constricted intellectual life and marginalized existence have been accomplished by masculine value systems embedded in dominant discourse. Montagu's male contemporary Richard Steele was able to identify a sonnet as being written by a woman, for example, because of its poor grammar and misspellings, and grammarian Thomas Wilson said a woman lost admiration when she wrote because of the "silliness of her Words" (Coates 24, 27). Women's writing generally *did* evince ignorance, of both Western culture and its formal linguistic conventions, because of their lack of formal education.

In controlling public rhetoric, men such as Pope, Steele, Addison, and Swift had the power to define women, as both social beings and as writers. In forcing adherence to the conventionally authoritative and allusive neoclassic style they had internalized, they ensured that a woman's voice without that education was easily identifiable. What they did was to define women *out* of public discourse, and women had no rhetorical stance from which to refute that definition. Montagu was almost unique in her context because she was *not* disadvantaged in this way, but she was too well acquainted to escape detection and consequently criticized for having spoken where she might be heard at all. Private discourse was one thing, but the modes and channels of distribution made almost all writing public, and Montagu circulated at the hub of her culture's rhetoric.

Cate Poynton has elaborated a descriptive tool for analyzing the tenor relationship between speaker and audience that explains the way masculine social power controls public language. *Tenor* is a function of power, contact, and affect and is subject to the institutional context for discourse. In all these regards, men have had the discursive advantages. Their power rested on their force, authority, status, and expertise, which were socially constructed as male attributes and fostered by elitist educations. Men were stronger and held social authority because they occupied higher social positions (men of all classes were generically superior in public domains to women of any class). They thus monopolized the expertise in every public institutional context—politics, education, art, religion, medicine, commerce, science, and literature.

Since women were subordinate to men in these rhetorical situations, but could not avoid frequent and long-term contact with them, male social arrangements engendered a loss of affect on the part of both men and women. Men feared insubordination and exercised increasing control. Women feared abuse and chafed under control. In such an environment, public rhetoric had to socialize everyone to his or her position. Men's role was to govern, and women's role was to be silent and governed, a major Western premise going back to Aristotle and revived in every era in which classical learning has been valued.

Montagu, however, was an exceptional woman, both for her era and even for ours. If public life was a drama played by male actors, she stole the script, learned the lines, and played a trouser role. She did not realize an identifiably female persona, because her education was classical and her conversants were high-profile men. But she did not succeed as an author nevertheless, even though most of her work was virtually indistinguishable from that of her male peers.

For one thing, she never intended to succeed. Commensurate with her aristocratic class identification, she harbored a prejudice against writing for money. Fame, she probably would have enjoyed, but that was not allowed her. Instead, Alexander Pope gave her infamy, and he had a socially sanctioned right to do so. By speaking in a public forum, Montagu had violated the other two dictums for women as well—she was both disobedient and lewd. The advantages of a good mind, a well-stocked library, determination, and opportunities to converse with the intellectual lights of her period availed her little. Masculine interlocutors Pope, Addison, Congreve, John Gay, and even Voltaire had helped her construct her masculine subjectivity as social wit, gadfly, poet, and critic through dialogic processes explored by such linguistic theorists as Mikhail Bakhtin and Lev Vygotsky, but they also had the power to deny her a rhetorical platform to voice it.

Montagu's authorial identity can be explained by a combination of these contemporary linguistic and rhetorical theories. Bakhtin determined that identity is a linguistic, dialogic construct that takes place between speaker and audience. Vygotsky demonstrated that reflective thought is actually internalized conversation, and constructionist social psychologists, such as Edward Sampson, B. R. Slugoski, and G. P. Ginsburg, have argued that the concept of an identifiable personal identity is a phenomenon restricted to Western bourgeois males from the Renaissance forward. Prior to that time, humans were all considered to possess identical souls made in the image of God. Capitalistic individualism, however, required the individual to distinguish himself from his peers in order to compete. Individualism became a class and then a male prerogative. The public rhetoric of Montagu's capitalistic milieu bred these values in an attempt to favor the economic survival of the privileged through attenuating identity development of potential competitors.

The model of expressive discourse developed by rhetorician James Kinneavy provides another explanation for women's not developing rhetorical subjectivities as readily as men. Kinneavy defined expressive discourse as the use of language to express "the personal stake of the speaker in the discourse" (393). Using phenomenological philosophy and the existentialism of Jean-Paul Sartre, he claimed that three types of consciousness constitute the self: "Being-for-Itself," "Being-for-Others," and "Being-in-the-World." Being-for-Itself is the individual's presence to him- or herself, what that presence has made of itself and what it is attempting to make of itself.

But that identity cannot be realized unless joined with Being-for-Others and Being-in-the World. This is precisely the point at which Montagu *was* disadvantaged. These other aspects of consciousness require social interaction through language. The Being-for-Itself has to be externalized and objectified through dialogue—*and be responded to*—before it can be internalized as identity. Thus, since Montagu does reveal an identifiable subjectivity, that subjectivity is masculine, because the dialogues in which she participated were with men about male concerns, but the "Others" with whom she was able to converse did not allow her to do so "in the World"—the public sphere—where a truly public identity could be constructed.

Though Montagu had the necessary nomic conversation to define herself through language, it was a masculine language, and her masculine identification is visible in her work. Her public rhetoric in *The Nonsense of Common-Sense,* which she wrote on request in support of Walpole's social programs, showed her to be an informed political conservative who spoke knowledgeably about such issues as opera, trade, politics, and literature and revealed her as a keen social analyst. However, her detractors were able to discredit them, because they could reveal who wrote them—and they did.

Though conventionally anonymous, the works of highly visible authors like Pope and Addison never were. Montagu's works too were traced to her. For that she suffered public criticism, principally from her sometime-admirer Pope. Not having stylistic or rhetorical grounds, his criticism had to be an *argumentum ad hominem,* more accurately *ad mulierum.* Instead of addressing her arguments, he denigrated her personally as a literary slattern, giving her epithets like "Lady Airy," "Sappho," "lewd Lesbos," "Slipshod W—," and "bitch," whereas he had once said her mind was the equal of a man's (Halsband 140–41, 147). Her only crime was in being a woman whose public work could be identified.

Montagu had little difficulty imitating such neoclassical dictums as Pope laid down in his "Essay on Criticism": adhere to nature's own "methodized" rules, not slavishly, but as the means to a natural end; study Homer, Virgil, and Horace for models; and let wit show in humility and plainness of expression rather than in overwrought conceits. What is ironic is that neither she nor Pope could confine their "art" within them. Both violate them with impunity, and Pope would defend his practice with his first rule: the end justifies the means.

Like Pope, Montagu can cite Virgil and compose virtuosic and ostentatious passages full of obscure classical allusion too. But he has the rhetorical authority to accuse her of violating his second and third rules, *and to make it socially real:* "Do as I say and not as I do." She has no authority to refute defamatory accusations, even when her actual texts demonstrate she could. Pope broke stylistic rules in inventing the alexandrine line, but it is the prerogative of dominant speakers to "make the rules." Nowhere does Pope specifically criticize Montagu's diction, choice of genre, or textual strategies to support his slatternly epithets.

Because Montagu's texts are anonymous and express a masculine persona, they speak with authority in most instances. Only in conversations in which she confers superior power on her male conversant does she evince the language of subordination. She generally identified so entirely with a masculinist viewpoint that she often criticized women in the same way a man would have. For example, in *Nonsense of Common-Sense,* numbers I and II, she sounds very much like Swift when she satirizes women's propensity for buying foreign luxury goods: "I begin with the Regulation of the present Mourning, which is so highly advantageous to the Woollen Manufacture, the staple Commodity of these Kingdoms, the Growth of our own Lands, and the Support of the Poor, reduced now to a very low Ebb, by the Luxury and ill Taste of the Rich, and the fantastick Mimickry of our Ladies, who are so accustomed to shiver in Silks, that they exclaim at the Hardships of Warmth and Decency" (*Nonsense of Common-Sense* 1737–38, 2).

However, in her frustrated love letters to Count Francesco Algarotti she reveals an uncharacteristic subservience. It's difficult to imagine the Montagu of her other work uttering these words: "How timid one is when one loves! I am afraid of offending you by sending you this note though I mean to please. In short I am so foolish about everything that concerns you that

I am not sure of my own thoughts" (*Complete Letters II* 103-04, 501). Even in her courtship negotiations with Wortley Montagu, she had adopted the rational tone that suppressed affect: "You think if you marry'd me I should be passionately fond of you one month and of some body else the next. Neither would happen. I can esteem, I can be a freind, but I don't know whether I can Love" (*Complete Letters I* 30).

Rarely does Montagu externalize a feminine point of view, though she is capable of a telling feminist critique. When, for instance, she remonstrates against men's treating their wives like deceitful dullards ("The Country Squire is confirmed, on the elegant Choice he has made, in preferring the Conversation of his Hounds to that of his Wife" [*Nonsense of Common-Sense* 25–26]), she does so from a male perspective. When she criticizes Fielding's treatment of a female character, she even employs conventional misogyny: "Charlotte acts with an Ingratitude that I think too black for Human Nature, with such coarse Jokes and low expressions as are only to be heard amongst the Lowest Class of People. Women of that Rank often plead a right to beat their Husbands when they don't cuckold them, and I believe this Author was never admitted into higher Company, and should confine his Pen to the Amours of Housemaids" (*Complete Letters II* 96).

In writing anonymously from her class position, the tenor relationship between her and her readers is one of equality, and Montagu's self-assured tone, particularly in her satirical pieces, is evident. Sounding convincingly like a man, Montagu used the first person confidently and employed the same self-reflective disingenuous humility that male peers like Swift employed. Witness this Swiftian disclaimer: "'Tis no way my interest (according to the common acceptation of that word) to convince the world of their errors; that is, I shall get nothing by it but the private satisfaction of having done good to mankind, and I know no body that reckons that satisfaction any part of their interest'" (Halsband 111).

When Montagu's male audience exerted some power over her and knew who she was, her textual metadiscourse reveals her sense of powerlessness. The only evidence of this lack of verbal power is in her Algarotti letters. One letter of about 340 words, for example, contains the following strategies often considered feminine (Coates; Poynton; Vande Kopple) and probably resulting from a sense of powerlessness: ten conditional or qualifying modals, two validity markers, 34 percent intransitive verbs, one citation of authority, five evaluative or "empty" adjectives, two intensifiers, and nineteen expressions of emotion (*Complete Letters II* 106). For none of her other audiences does she use so many of these expressions. In her letters to Algarotti we see strong positive and negative affect and little of the neutralized neoclassical tone: “Yes, I would spend the morning writing to you even if you should be furious. I have begun to scorn your scorn, and in that vein I no longer wish to restrain myself” (*Complete Letters II,* 237, 513).

When her metadiscourse refers to her authority as writer in self-reflexive ways, it is typically ironic and confident: “I am very much entertained with the Variety of Censures that are passed on my harmless Paper, which I hear almost every Day with an indifferent Face, and to say Truth, without much Violence to myself, not feeling the paternal Affection that most Authors do for their Productions; neither my Fame nor Fortune being any way affected by their Success (*Nonsense of Common-Sense* 29).

Like male authorities, she often criticized other authors’ work with biting wit, telling Voltaire, for example, that the English in his *Essay on Epic Poetry* was too good to be written by him, but too poor to be authored by a distinguished person (Halsband 120).

Her authorial confidence is usually demonstrated by the way she uses her attitude and validity markers and her citation of authorities. Rather than expressing a genuine diffidence, they are almost always ironic and actually express assuredness in the accuracy of her critique: “I am willing to believe there yet remains so much Politeness in the Kingdom of *Great Britain,* that a great Number of both Sexes are still capable of being delighted with what is rational” (*Nonsense of Common-Sense* 30).

The only explanation for her failure as an author is that femaleness as it was socially constructed in her era allowed no access to public rhetorical forums. So even though she did a credible job of assuming a masculine stance and acquiring an authentic masculine voice, her gender was also public knowledge. Her work was marginalized because she was by definition not a public person. As a woman she was socially invisible. Her voice, style, and genres were those of prevailing male discourse, but her work disappeared for 250 years, when that of her masculine contemporaries and conversants became canonical.

For Bakhtin, *genre* is the particular form any concrete utterance takes in a given speech situation. The content, style, and compositional structure are all determined by the sphere of communication—or register. Register comprises all the dimensions of the rhetorical situation: field, tenor, and mode. We thus can see that if Montagu’s texts could be attached to her, the very fact that she wrote them would obviate her right to make them public, because they all had to be written in male-dominated fields and modes. Had she been able to keep them anonymous herself, Pope’s animosity toward her still would have turned her into a public object of scorn.

Even personal letters were publicly circulated, and an examination of men's letters of the period—Swift's, for example—reveals a stylistic self-consciousness that rarely belies a private persona. Montagu wrote voluminously, mostly letters. The circle of her correspondents was highly visible and comprised the most influential writers of the era. Her own views on social and political issues were widely known. Therefore, it was virtually impossible *not* to identify her hand behind her public texts—her satiric poetry and periodical essays.

So her male detractors had to invoke classical and conventional misogynous definitions of her, as a *woman,* because there were no artistic grounds on which to devalue her work. They simply did not want women jeopardizing their prerogative to construct rules for public behavior or control rhetorical reality making. In their rhetorical environment, men held all the power. They could define anything in their purview, and their definitions would prevail. Like Adam, they had the right to name all of creation. Masculine-constructed reality excluded "author" as a definition for women. I believe Pope's principal motive for discrediting her was simply to unmask her gender in order to damage her ethos. Once her identity was known, her work would automatically lose credibility.

We have evidence that Montagu was aware of her disabilities as a writer if her identity were known. Her intentionally public work is the most noticeably masculine. Even her letter defending widows, published by Addison in the *Spectator,* could just as easily have been written by a man. In fact, part of the humor relies on the audience's misogynistic prejudices. A woman's articulate advocacy of widows was something so unimaginable that it produced the same low humor as, for instance, Swift's creation of intelligent talking horses. A sympathetic depiction of widows was unthinkable. A male writer writing for men could use a stereotypical perception of women for humorous effect only if the audience would find the proposition outrageous.

In *Nonsense of Common-Sense,* number VI, Montagu argues for more egalitarian treatment of wives, but she writes anonymously and again uses male metaphors and a masculine point of view—it is to men's benefit to treat their wives as intelligent beings, because not doing so leaves them stupid, malign dissipaters of family capital. In order to appeal to her masculine audience, Montagu had to play on their economic self-interest. Women's conspicuous consumption was a common theme to Montagu's bourgeois male readers.

Most writing in Montagu's milieu was political, and she took a lively interest in the politics of her day, supporting Robert Walpole's government and her husband's campaigns for election. Merely by participating in the available conversation, she automatically constructed a public, and therefore masculine, identity. When she undertook a political theme, she was forced to evince a masculine style. It is easy to infer, therefore, that the author of *The Nonsense of Common-Sense* is a man, because the essays respond directly to the male-authored periodical, the *Common Sense*. Montagu's loyalty to Walpole would also not have allowed her to jeopardize his public image by her support had she suspected that her anonymity could not be maintained. Yet *Nonsense* received virtually no public response and was written right out of Western literary history.

In conclusion, Montagu was prevented from constructing a public rhetorical identity simply because she was a well-known *woman*. Her work evinced confidence as a writer that only her classical learning, exclusive exposure to the dominant male writers of her period, and appropriation of masculine discourse could have given her. Had she written under a male pseudonym and managed to keep her gender a secret, she probably would have been taken as seriously as her male peers. She would even have added to the public conversation because of her sociopolitical positioning, cosmopolitan voice, and international experience. Her only female rival would have been Eliza Haywood, who came from a very different socioeconomic background and wrote for money. Nevertheless, Montagu's views and style were well known among her circle of literary and political conversants. Though the period's convention among the literary elite was to publish anonymously (it would have been déclassé to seek money or fame through their work), the primary mode of distribution was through regular personal contact. So when Pope quarreled with Montagu, he vented his enmity publicly in order to capitalize on her gender identity and thereby discredit her work. As a result of this notoriety, she suffered enormously and exiled herself to Italy for the rest of her life, with her husband's support. She continued a voluminous private correspondence, both witty and serious, with acquaintances and family and kept abreast of events "at home." But she set foot there only at the end of her life.

All Pope had had to do was invoke Aristotelian misogyny that constructed women as stupid, disobedient, and lascivious. By thus savaging Montagu in print, he created identification with *his* audience that only enhanced his ethos. Swift, too, had been merely voicing communal wisdom when he referred to Eliza Haywood as a stupid, infamous scribbler because she was a woman writing in a public forum (Mahl and Koon 224). Montagu played her trouser role convincingly, but because of her particular rhetorical context, she was too well known not to be recognized. Her body of work having been suppressed and forgotten until the mid-twentieth century has added impetus and incentive to feminist scholarship on her period and fills a conspicuous gap between Mary Astell and the Bluestockings, of whom one was her niece.

Works Cited

Arthur, Marilyn B. "Early Greece: The Origins of the Western Attitude toward Women." *Arethusa* 6 (1973): 7–58.

Baecker, Diann Lynn. "Rhetoric's Role in the Development of the Bourgeois Public Sphere: A Study of Women's Responses to Rhetorical Texts in Eighteenth-Century England." *DAI* 61, no. 07A (2000): 2691.

Bate, Walter J., et al., eds. *Major British Writers.* New York: Harcourt, Brace, 1959.

Berger, Peter L., and Thomas Luckmann. *The Social Construction of Reality: A Treatise in the Sociology of Knowledge.* Garden City, NY: Anchor Books, 1967.

Bridenthal, Renate, and Claudia Koonz. *Becoming Visible: Women in European History.* Boston: Houghton Mifflin, 1977.

Cantarella, Eva. *Pandora's Daughters: The Role and Status of Women in Greek and Roman Antiquity.* Trans. Maureen B. Fant. Foreword Mary R. Lefkowitz. Baltimore: Johns Hopkins UP, 1981.

Coates, Jennifer. *Women, Men, and Language: A Sociolinguistic Account of Sex Differences in Language.* London: Longman, 1986.

Code, Lorraine. *What Can She Know? Feminist Theory and the Construction of Knowledge.* Ithaca, NY: Cornell UP, 1991.

Eger, Elizabeth, Charlotte Grant, Cliona O'Gallchoir, and Penny Warburton. *Women, Writing, and the Public Sphere, 1700–1830.* Cambridge: Cambridge UP, 2001.

Ferguson, Kathy E. *The Man Question: Visions of Subjectivity in Feminist Theory.* Berkeley: U of California P, 1993.

Fraser, Nancy. "Pragmatism, Feminism, and the Linguistic Turn." *Feminist Contentions: A Philosophical Exchange.* Eds. Seyla Benhabib, Judith Butler, Drucilla Cornell, and Nancy Fraser. New York: Routledge, 1995.

Gosz, Elizabeth. "Contemporary Theories of Power and Subjectivity." *Feminist Knowledge: Critique and Construct.* Ed. Sneja Gunew. London: Routledge, 1990. 59–120.

Graff, Harvey J. *The Legacies of Literacy: Continuities and Contradictions in Western Culture and Society.* Bloomington: Indiana UP, 1987.

Halsband, Robert. *The Life of Lady Mary Wortley Montagu.* Oxford: Clarendon, 1956.

Hekman, Susan J. *Gender and Knowledge: Elements of Postmodern Feminism.* Boston: Northeastern UP, 1990.

Jones, Vivien, ed. Introduction. *Women and Literature in Britain, 1700–1800.* Cambridge: Cambridge UP, 2000.

Justice, George L. Introduction. *Women's Writing and the Circulation of Ideas: Manuscript Publication in England, 1550–1800.* Eds. George L. Justice and Nathan Tinker. Cambridge: Cambridge UP, 2002.

Kinneavy, James L. *A Theory of Discourse: The Aims of Discourse.* Englewood Cliffs, NJ: Prentice-Hall, 1971.

Lawson, John, and Harold Silver. *A Social History of Education in England.* London: Methuen, 1973.

Looser, Devoney. *British Women Writers and the Writing of History, 1670–1820.* Baltimore: Johns Hopkins UP, 2000.

Mahl, Mary, and Helene Koon, eds. *The Female Spectator: English Women Writers before 1800.* Old Westbury, NY: Feminist Press, 1977.

McKeon, Michael. "Historicizing Patriarchy: The Emergence of Gender Difference in England, 1660–1760." *Eighteenth-Century Studies* 28.3 (Spring 1995): 295–321.

Montagu, Lady Mary Wortley. *The Complete Letters of Lady Mary Wortley Montagu.* Vol. I. Ed. Robert Halsband. Oxford: Clarendon, 1965.

———. *The Complete Letters of Lady Mary Wortley Montagu.* Vol. II. Ed. Robert Halsband. Oxford: Clarendon, 1966.

———. *The Complete Letters of Lady Mary Wortley Montagu.* Vol. III. Ed. Robert Halsband. Oxford: Clarendon, 1967.

———. *The Nonsense of Common-Sense, 1737–1738.* Ed. and notes Robert Halsband. Evanston, IL: Northwestern UP, 1947.

Okin, Susan Moller. "Patriarchy and Married Women's Property: Questions on Some Current Views." *Eighteenth Century Studies* 17 (1983/1984): 121–38.

Poynton, Cate. *Language and Gender: Making the Difference.* Oxford: Oxford UP, 1989.

Rogers, Katharine M. *Feminism in Eighteenth-Century England.* Urbana: U of Illinois P, 1982.

Skinner, Gillian. "Women's Status as Legal and Civic Subjects: 'A Worse Condition than Slavery Itself'?" Jones 91–110.

Vande Kopple, William J. "Some Exploratory Discourse on Metadiscourse." *College Composition and Communication* 36 (1985): 82–93.

3

Princess Sarah, the Civilized Indian

The Rhetoric of Cultural Literacies in Sarah Winnemucca Hopkins's *Life among the Piutes*

Malea Powell

> We travel to our place in the world by the grace of others' words. The shape of every experience known only by its nestling in among the soft folds of our history.
>
> Kimberly Blaeser, *Reinventing the Enemy's Language*

This is a story.[1]

As a graduate student in a well-known doctoral program in rhetoric and composition, I rarely read scholarly work that ventured into the long history of American Indians on the North American continent. Most of what I did eventually find was either hopelessly simplistic or romantic, or was written by the small circle of fellow Native scholars whom I gradually came to know. There was much more scholarly work by or about Indians available in the fields of literature and literary history, but I gradually came to realize that few scholars of the history of rhetoric write about Native peoples at all, and even fewer are willing to address the complex interactions that have occurred between Native peoples and the European/Euro-American colonists over the past five-hundred-plus years. While it is true that the rhetorical histories of women and so-called minority cultures in the United States have, as a group, been much unattended to, the rhetorical history of American Indians has been even more ignored. Even scholars of nineteenth-century American rhetoric have left untouched the vast amount of materials produced during the Indian reform era (1840–1920) by both Native and non-Native participants, an oddity considering our recent penchant for recovery of women's rhetoric since this large and influential social movement was powered mostly by women. As a scholar whose specialty is American Indian rhetorics, I hope that the following story about American Indian woman intellectual and activist Sarah Winnemucca Hopkins will become just the beginning contribution in a scholarly conversation about American Indians and American Indian women, particularly one that looks closely at the complicated and frequently contradictory ways in which subjectivity was made possible for such women. Winnemucca and others like her faced difficult rhetorical circumstances in which they had to weigh carefully the price of convincing Euro-American audiences of the worthiness of their "cause" against the risk of both alienating their own people and reinscribing dominant ideas about the dependency of Native peoples. The kind of understandings that can arise from such close listenings, and from the willingness to see contradictory subjectivities as always already simultaneous and necessary for those listenings to begin, will also lead us to a richer, much more complicated conceptualization of the history of rhetoric.

The 1883 publication of Sarah Winnemucca Hopkins's *Life among the Piutes: Their Wrongs and Claims* marks her as "the only Indian woman writer of personal and tribal history during most of the nineteenth century" (Ruoff 261). Winnemucca is widely hailed as the first American Indian woman autobiographer in the United States.[2] The texts of early Native writers are especially problematic, not only in terms of questions of editorship and authorship but also in terms of how they are read and received today.[3] Most often, American Indian texts, especially autobiographies, are read literally as "authentic" expressions of Indian cultures, simple point-of-view retellings of particular events. These texts are rarely seen as deliberately rhetorical, created in a manner that is consciously and selectively representative with a specific (dominant) audience's needs in mind.[4] While such assumptions concerning the rhetorical abilities of Native writers could undoubtedly be traced to the psychology of colonialism and empire that created "America," such an analysis is not the point of my tellings in this essay. Instead, I begin with the assumption that Winnemucca's text *is* a rhetorical performance, one in which she represents herself as a participant in the kinds of Indian-ness that would have appealed to her late-nineteenth-century reformist audience, that is, the "civilized Indian" and/or the "Indian Princess."

Further, her textual performance needed to persuade her audience not only that she was civilized, but also that her representation of events was accurate so that these influential reformers would be moved to lobby for specific changes in Bureau of Indian Affairs (BIA) policies that would help her people, the Northern Paiutes.[5] My tellings will examine some of the ways that Winnemucca creates and presents a public/textual "self" who could respond to the needs and desires of her audience. Specifically, I will focus on the tactics that Winnemucca uses in *Life among the Piutes* (hereafter referred to as *Life*) to represent herself textually as a fit representative for the Paiutes—both an authentic *and* civilized Indian, a literate practitioner of both Euro-American and Paiute cultural discourses.[6] Further, I will also examine some of the ways Winnemucca uses her knowledge of the conventions of Euro-American discourse to connect with and persuade her readers. It is this, her simultaneous participation in multiple cultural discourses, that not only marks Winnemucca's textual "self" but also becomes, as I have argued elsewhere, a necessary tool for many American Indian intellectuals whose participation in American scholarly discourses is already predicated on notions of "America" that erase living Indian peoples from the landscape and replace us with varying images of savagery—feathered, blood-thirsty warriors, noble disappearing savages, and desexualized Indian princesses.[7]

In "The Pocahontas Perplex," Rayna Green traces the image of the Indian woman as a "Princess." Green claims this image first appeared in 1575 in European iconographic representations of America, a "bare-breasted, Amazonian Native American Queen" who reigned as the sole iconographic representation for the Americas until 1765, when new images emerge (16). Slimmer and "less barbarous," the Princess is "more 'American'" and less Latin than her mother and is "armed, usually with a spear, but she also carries a peace pipe, a flag, or the starred and striped shield of Colonial America" (17). In fact, she also often stands as a handmaiden to American independence alongside "the Sons of Liberty, or later, with George Washington" (17). The Princess's (i.e., Pocahontas's) iconographic relationship to the European/Euro-American men who supposedly created America is, of course, perplexed in the face of real Native women who intrude not only onto the symbolic foundations of "America," but whose presence on the land is also seen as an intrusion into the literal progress of colonization of the land by these new "Americans." Thus, writes Green, this "Pocahontas perplex" becomes "a controlling metaphor in the American experience," whereby the Princess and her savage counterpoint, the "Squaw," are defined in terms of their relationships to white men (18).

The authenticating device for the Princess, the "good Indian" woman, is her kindness, her reasonableness, even her trust and love, toward white men combined with her ability to see other Indians as "savages" or as children, both often figured in her conversion to Christianity. The Princess is seen as "more Caucasian than her fellow natives" and more tragic, since in order to become the Princess she must "defy her own people, exile herself from them, become white, and perhaps suffer death" without ever a hint of her availability as a sexual object (18). The Squaw, on the other hand, is signified by "the presence of overt and realized sexuality" and by "the same vices attributed to Indian men," such as drunkenness and violence (19). Both of these figures—the Princess and the Squaw—are, of course, intimately connected with similar ways of configuring Indian men, with all the understandings of either Indian men or women wrapped up in their relationships to whites. And both fit with the discourse of Manifest Destiny—the Squaw's removal/disappearance is easily "understood as necessary to the progress of civilization," a process to which her civilized sister, the Princess, has already sacrificed herself (21). Stuck between frying pan and fire, real Native women become almost impossible to see.

The Indian reformers of the late nineteenth century most certainly believed that the salvation of the tribes meant the sacrifice of the savage to Christianity and civilization.[8] While reform groups such as the Boston Indian Citizenship Committee, the Women's National Indian Association, the Indian Rights Association, and the Lake Mohonk Friends of the Indian bore a passing similarity to previous reform groups in that "they were driven by a sense of Christian mission," their work took on a critically different stance in relation to reservation lands for Native peoples (Hoxie 12). Under the "peace policy" instituted during President Ulysses Grant's administration, an attempt was made to force all Indian nations, even those exempt from removal, onto reservations for their own "protection." Religious groups (Quakers, Catholics, Methodists, etc.) were given control of both BIA-appointed offices and the Board of Indian Commissioners. The new reformers, however, were aggressively antireservation, and their work "revolution[ized] the relations of Indians with the rest of the nation," forcing Congress into a program of rabid antitribalism and private property reform (Prucha 609). The Indian Rights Association, in their *Second Annual Report* (1885), blatantly stated that their intent was to secure "for the Indian" three things: "Law," "Education," and "a protected individual title to land, . . . the entering-wedge by which tribal organization is to be rent asunder" (43). That same year, in the *Seventeenth Annual Report of the Board of Indian Commissioners* (1885), Merrill Gates, who presided over the Lake Mohonk Conference for several years, wrote that "the aim of legislation for the Indian should be to make him as soon as possible an intelligent, useful citizen" and that "Indian reservations . . . insulate Indians from civilization, cultivate vice, and [are] a domain for lawlessness licensed by the United States" (55–56).

The culmination of these reform groups came in the passage of the General Allotment Act, or the Dawes Act, of 1887. The Dawes Act was designed to allot a quarter section of 160 acres to the head of each Indian family. Indians who refused or failed to select an allotment would have one selected for them by the Secretary of the Interior. The new land "owner" would not, however, receive a patent for the land until it had been held in trust for twenty-five years by the Office of the Secretary of the Interior; the land could not be sold or its title encumbered by its "owner." Further, when the land patent was finally issued, the landowner became subject to state and federal laws, and U.S. citizenship would be granted to those Indian landowners who had "resided separate and apart from the tribe" and had "adopted the habits of civilized life," thus eradicating treaty obligations and cultural distinctiveness in one fell swoop. All reservation lands left over after the initial allotment were to be purchased by the government, the moneys from that purchase being held in trust "for the education and civilization of the former tribe members" (Berkhofer 174). Unfortunately, an 1891 legislative act enabled allotted lands to be leased for agriculture, mining, and lumbering, while other provisions of the act—reservation courts/police and citizenship for "reformed" Indians—did not come about in any substantial manner before the 1930s. Before the Dawes Act went into effect, Native nations held 138 million acres. Sixty percent of that land was lost through the sale of "surplus" lands, 20 percent was lost through "disposal of allotments," and an unknown amount was leased in perpetuity (175).

It was during the birth of these late-nineteenth-century reform groups and their ideas about the civilizability of Indians that Winnemucca entered the picture. Sarah Winnemucca was born "somewhere near 1844" near the sink of the Humboldt River in what is now Nevada (*Life* 5). Born the granddaughter of Truckee, self-proclaimed chief of all the Paiutes, Winnemucca spent her life as a spokesperson and advocate for her Northern Paiute peoples. She experienced her first contact with whites when she was about four years old. Winnemucca was terrified of the white men she saw, because with their beards and light eyes they resembled owls, the form taken by a Paiute bogeyman known as the "Cannibal Owl," who was rumored to carry off bad children, pound their flesh into a pulp, and happily eat them (Canfield 5). Winnemucca gradually overcame many of her childhood fears about whites and spent much of her life living and working within Euro-

American culture, learning Spanish as a young girl during an extended stay with her grandfather in Santa Cruz, and teaching herself to read and write in English while working as a domestic servant in Virginia City. She also worked as an interpreter for the army and various Indian agents, and as a teacher at several "Indian" schools. Winnemucca had especially close contact with government officials, particularly Indian agents, who, in her mind, often mistreated the Paiutes for their own selfish gain. It was this mistreatment that prompted her first public lectures in San Francisco in 1879, in which she directly criticized the practices of a particular Indian agent, William V. Rinehart, who was stationed at the Malheur Reservation in eastern Oregon, where the Paiutes were reserved.

Rinehart's behavior has been cited as one of the major causes of the Bannock war of 1878, when Paiutes joined with Bannocks and, because of the deplorable conditions on the reservations, literally took to the surrounding hills to hide from the government, periodically "borrowing" supplies from nearby settlers and reservation stores. When the army was called in, General Oliver Otis Howard contacted Winnemucca and asked her to serve as his liaison with these "renegade" Paiutes. This group of Paiutes was taken to the Yakima Reservation (in present-day Washington State), quite far from the Paiutes' previous home at Malheur, and kept there as prisoners. For her service and peacekeeping efforts, the army gave her five hundred dollars, which she promptly spent to travel to San Francisco, where her public performances as "The Princess Sarah" and her lectures concerning the Bannock war and the Paiutes' problems at the Yakima Reservation were a great success.[9] Within a month, Winnemucca, her brother Natchez, and her father, Old Winnemucca, were called to Washington, D.C., for a meeting with Carl Schurz, the Secretary of the Interior in charge of the Bureau of Indian Affairs, and with President Rutherford B. Hayes. During this trip Winnemucca was introduced to Elizabeth Palmer Peabody, the famed transcendentalist, who offered to finance Winnemucca in a series of East Coast lectures. Winnemucca was even more of a success in the East than she had been in San Francisco. In full Indian Princess regalia—"fringed buckskin and beads . . . a gold crown on her head and a wampum bag of velvet, decorated with an embroidered cupid"—she delivered over three hundred lectures from April 1883 to August 1884 (Canfield 201). During the lecture tour, Winnemucca became frustrated at the relatively small amount of information she was able to convey in a single lecture, so she decided to write a book; *Life among the Piutes* was published, with Peabody's financial support and Mary Mann's unobtrusive editing, in 1883. Following its publication, the BIA launched an extensive campaign to discredit Winnemucca, based mostly on

Rinehart's accusations concerning her character.[10] Ultimately, she returned to Lovelocks, Nevada, and began, again with Peabody's financial support, a bilingual school for Paiute children. Winnemucca died in 1891.[11]

With these briefest bits of context and history in mind, I want to now focus on the tactics Winnemucca uses to authenticate and authorize herself as that most contradictory of subjects—a *civilized Indian*—which she does partly by embracing the Indian princess image in her public performances and partly through a textual presentation of herself in *Life* as a literate practitioner of Euro-American cultural discourse at the same time she clearly represents herself as Paiute. Winnemucca's significant contact with Eastern reform groups is well documented. Newspaper accounts of her speaking engagements are numerous, as are her associations with the literary and cultural elite: she spoke in the homes of Emerson, Whittier, and Senator Dawes; had frequent conversations with Dawes concerning the wisdom of allotment versus the corruption of the reservation system; and was the subject of two publications by Peabody (*Sarah Winnemucca's Practical Solution of the Indian Problem* [1886] and *The Piutes* [1887]). Winnemucca's oral performances during her East Coast tour are echoed in the "lectures" she includes in *Life*. For example, the second chapter in *Life*, "Domestic and Social Moralities," is undoubtedly similar to the early lecture she delivered in Boston for an audience of women only, in which she "spoke of the domestic education" given to Paiutes "of both sexes," a lecture "which never failed to excite the moral enthusiasm of every woman that heard it" (Canfield 203, Peabody, *Paiutes* 5). Because instances of Winnemucca's careful construction of her "self" for her audience abound in *Life*, I want to begin with a significant episode in which Winnemucca presents the relationship of the Paiutes to English-language writing and letters. Her characterizations here set the tone for much of what follows in her text.

Early in *Life*, Winnemucca writes about the Paiutes' reaction to a letter Chief Truckee received from his "white brothers" during the time he worked as a guide for settlers traveling through the Sierras.

> He then showed us a more wonderful thing than all the others that he had brought. It was a paper, which he said could talk to him. . . . He said, "This can talk to all our white brothers, and our white sisters, and their children. Our white brothers are beautiful, and our white sisters are beautiful, and their children are beautiful. He also said the paper can travel like the wind, and it can go and talk with their [white] fathers and brothers and sisters, and come back to tell what they are doing, and whether they are well or sick." . . . our doctors and

> doctresses said—"If they can do this wonderful thing, they are not truly human, but pure spirits. None but heavenly spirits can do such wonderful things." (18–19)

The Paiutes' expressed wonder at the "magic" of print text is immediately followed by a caution that a people who can perform such "magic" can also make their "hearts bleed" through "mischief" (19). Notice, though, how Winnemucca's telling of this story reinforces the goodness of white people, a goodness she attributes throughout the texts as her grandfather's trust of his white brothers. The spirits here are "heavenly," the white family is "beautiful" (19). Though his people protest Truckee's version of whites by pointing out that "their blood is all around us, and the dead are lying all about us, and we cannot escape it," their protestations "did not go far with [Winnemucca's] grandfather" (19).

Truckee becomes a pivotal character in *Life* because of his trust and faith in the goodness of whites, and because of his knowledge of the power of the written word. The letter, which Truckee calls his "rag friend," is a symbol of the goodness and powerfulness of white people, and of their high regard for him as a true and loyal friend. "'Just as long as I live and have that paper which my white brothers' great chieftain has given me, I shall stand by them, come what will.' He held the paper up towards heaven and kissed it, as if it was really a person. 'Oh, if I should lose this,' he said, 'we shall all be lost'" (22). Truckee's letter signifies a social contract between Paiutes and whites, and it is this social contract that gets reiterated each time any letter appears in the text. Letters and English-language writing play a significant role in Winnemucca's representation of herself not just as "civilized," but as a translator of words that demands she also be a translator of cultures, that is, a civilized Indian. Letters become the prime conduit through which Winnemucca articulates and describes her "self" to her audience. Throughout *Life,* Winnemucca consistently constructs herself in relation to letters—from the army, the BIA, Secretary Schurz, and others—especially in relation to her ability to decode and mediate Euro-American knowledge through her English-language skills. Winnemucca's position as an interpreter, as a speaker and reader of the language of the "white father," is how she defines both her value to the Paiutes as a member of the Indian community and her value to Euro-Americans as a civilized Indian. However, that construction is vexed on both sides, since the very quality that makes her "authentic" in one cultural discourse is what makes her an object of suspicion in the other discourse.

Remember, though, that *Life* is a text written for a Euro-American audience with particular beliefs about Indians and with specific political goals in mind; it was not written to record events for the Paiutes. Winnemucca's relationship to letters from (mostly) white men stands in for Green's Princess's direct relationship to white men, out of which her designation as a good Indian arises. Winnemucca's vexed position as translator moves her into an area of ambivalent subjectivity, a simultaneous participation that deftly highlights the problematics of being a translator without reducing herself to victimization. Further, by echoing the moral imperatives inherent in such a position, Winnemucca's text echoes a position that had been raised by reformers themselves—for example, Helen Hunt Jackson's *A Century of Dishonor* (1881), a text that Jackson intended as "a Record of our Broken Treaties" (qtd. in Mathes 33).[12] *A Century of Dishonor* is a collection of narratives about past injustices, what Jackson calls "a sketch" that will "show our causes for national shame in the matter of our treatment of the Indians," in which Native peoples are portrayed throughout as the "weak and helpless" victims of the "dishonorable conduct" of the U.S. government (7, 27, 18).

The kind of moral outrage and fervor that Jackson hopes to stir up is part of the discursive norm that Winnemucca takes for granted and uses throughout her text, but it is especially at work in the last chapter of *Life*, "The Yakima Affair." The text describes how Winnemucca, her father, and her brother went to Washington, D.C., in 1880 to meet with Secretary Schurz and President Hayes about the various problems being experienced by the Paiutes. Secretary Schurz gives them a letter that seems to respond to their concerns. Winnemucca cites the letter in full within her text. In it Schurz writes that "the Pi-Utes . . . are to have lands allotted to them in severalty . . . under the instructions of their agent," that the Paiutes who "went to the Yakima Reservation" may "rejoin their relatives . . . without expense to the government for transportation" (223–24). Shortly before her citation of the letter, Winnemucca describes one encounter with Schurz in which he promises to "send enough [canvas] to make your people one hundred tents" and asks Winnemucca to issue the canvas when she returns to Lovelocks, Nevada (221). The next few pages of text are filled with Winnemucca's representation of her negotiations with Schurz—much of which consists of him agreeing to some of her demands if she will agree not to lecture while she is in Washington, D.C.—and her encounter with the president. Following this she cites the letter, and then Winnemucca describes what happens once she, her father, and brother arrive home:

> When we got home we told our people to go to Lovelocks, and be ready to receive some tents that were to be sent for them. . . . While we were waiting we almost starved. I wrote the Secretary of the Interior for God's sake to send us something to eat. He answered my letter telling me to take my people to the Malheur Agency. Just think of taking my people, who were already starving, to go three hundred miles through snow waist-deep. I told my people what the letter said. They all laughed and said,—"We are not disappointed. We always said that the Big Father was just like all the white people." What could we say? We were only ashamed because we came and told them lies which the white people had told us. (224–25)

Winnemucca makes clear here, and throughout this final chapter, that the words she uses to convey the government's promises "are not my own words, but the words of the agents and the soldiers" (236). The problem of being only a translator of words is clear—those words may be false. Even the admission above that the Winnemuccas have conveyed the "lies which the white people had told us" is one that highlights the importance of cultural translations as well as simply language translations. After Winnemucca reads Schurz's letter to the Paiutes at Lovelocks, she puts the cultural translation in the mouth of another Paiute, Captain John: "I have lived many years with white people. . . . I have never known one of them to do what they promised. I think they mean it just at the time, but I tell you they are very forgetful. . . . These are your white brothers' ways, and they are a weak people" (225). Even so, Winnemucca continues the narration here with her preparations to go to Yakima, believing that because she is "armed with a paper signed by Secretary Schurz," she will "not have anything to do but to go there and get them [the Paiutes]" (226). While she allows her belief that whites may lie when it is just their spoken word that binds them to be spoken by another character in the text, she still maintains her faith in the power of the written word, "the beautiful paper that the Great Father gave me, and what beautiful things they were going to do for us" (227).

It is important here to note that Winnemucca is representing these events with a persuasive end in mind. Her book was published three years after the events that she describes, and each copy contains a petition asking the "Honorable Congress of the United States" to return the Paiutes to the Malheur Reservation, "especially that portion of the tribe arbitrarily removed . . . to the Yakima Reservation" (247). This petition is followed by a note from Mary Mann requesting that "whoever shall be interested by this little book or by Mrs. Hopkins's living word" should copy the petition, obtain signatures to it, and send it on to Mann in Boston (247). Winnemucca needs her audience of Eastern readers to see her portrayals as believable, but in order to be so, she must play to the stereotypes of Native peoples, like the Indian princess or the childlike and trusting ward, that reformers were likely to believe. Her faith in the written word demonstrates that she not only learned the lesson of trusting whites from her grandfather but also that she believes this "civilized" tool—the written word—would be powerful enough to make changes in the material conditions of daily life for the Paiutes at Yakima. Even though she is trying to set herself apart from the Paiutes here, and to seem more like a reformer, she still represents herself as an Indian insofar as she is still willing to trust the federal promises symbolized by the letter—a trust that Jackson, Peabody, and other reformers knew to be misdirected. Her representation here, I believe, is deliberate and effective.

When Winnemucca at last reaches Yakima, she does "not say anything for four days," but her brother Lee "told everything to our people" (234).[13] When Winnemucca finally does meet with Father Wilbur, the Indian agent there, he is angry about the letter and entreats her to be silent about its contents: "I don't want you to tell them of this paper or to read it to them" (234). Wilbur offers to pay her fifty dollars plus the money he owes her for interpreting, and he offers to request her as an interpreter at Yakima if she "will not tell them [the Paiutes]" what the letter "says" (234). Winnemucca writes: "I did not promise, and went away. I did not say anything for five or six days" (235). To the Paiutes, her silence is seen as a sign of her betrayal; they believe that she has "sold [them] to Father Wilbur" (235). Her refusal to read them the letter, to translate for them, is seen as having the power to undo whatever promise was made in Washington: "We are told that she has a paper, which has been given to her by the mighty Big Father in Washington, and she has burnt it or hid it, so we don't know. . . . Our paper is all gone, there is nobody to talk for us" (235). That the printed/written text has power only insofar as Winnemucca is willing to read it leaves Winnemucca's "self" empowered only through her role as a translator; she maintains a favorable position within the tribe through her ability to interpret the dictates of the "spirit" within the "rag friend," to speak in the magical voice of the white father.

Throughout the text there is little mention of Winnemucca's "personal" struggles except as they relate to her people. While much of the text is taken up with Winnemucca's representation of encounters with various Indian agents, she rarely writes of her own marital problems (she was married several times and her last husband, Lewis Hopkins, gambled heavily) or of her employments outside translating (she worked as a domestic servant for several years). Furthermore, anyone reading the text would believe that Winnemucca lived with the Paiutes on the reservation, when in fact she spent most of her adult life living in towns like Lovelocks, Carson City, and Virginia City. When Winnemucca does mention her "personal" life, it is to make a specific point to her readers, such as the early anecdote about being buried alive:

> There was a fearful story they told us children. Our mothers told us that the whites were killing everybody and eating them. . . . Oh, what a fright we all got one morning to hear some white people were coming. . . . So they went to work and buried us, and told us if we heard any noise not to cry out, for if we did they would surely kill us and eat us. . . . Oh, can any one imagine my feelings buried alive, thinking every minute that I was to be unburied and eaten up by the people that my grandfather loved so much? (11–12)

Surprisingly, the point of this story is not only to demonstrate the superstitious beliefs that Paiutes held about whites during early contact but also to assert Winnemucca's position, her tireless work on behalf of her people and her Christianity. She ends the anecdote with: "I was once buried alive; but my second burial shall be for ever, . . . I shall be in the sweet rest of peace,—I, the chieftain's weary daughter" (12).

Winnemucca's "personal" life is not as important here as how the events of her life connect and separate her from her community. When Winnemucca tells the Yakima Paiutes that she will "telegraph to the Big Father in Washington" and that she will "work for them while there was life in my body" (241), she is clearly marking out a "self" that will always be defined in relation to her community and to her function within that community. However, through this final encounter with the Paiutes at Yakima, Winnemucca represents herself and her relationship to the letter as one that is highly vexed. In response to their accusations of her betrayal, Winnemucca writes: "I have suffered everything but death to come here with this paper. I don't know whether it speaks truth or not. . . . I have told you many things which are not my own words, . . . I know I have told you more lies than I have hair on my head. I tell you, my dear children, I have never told you my own words; they were the words of the white people, not mine" (236). And it is this, being put in the position of conveying lies to her people, "finding it impossible to do anything for my people," that prompts Winnemucca to "come to the East and talk for them" (246). It is this, also, that prompts her to entreat her readers to action: "I pray of you, I implore you, I beseech of you, hear our pitiful cry to you, sweep away the agency system; give us homes to live in, for God's sake and for humanity's sake" (242–43).

Letters, then, act as a signifier whereby Winnemucca is authorized and authenticated as "real"—her willingness to translate them marks her as a "real Indian" (or not) for the Paiutes, and her ability to translate marks her as "really civilized" for her white audience. Once believable to her audience as conversant in their cultural discourse, she uses the conventions of that discourse to persuasive ends. For example, to create a sense of similarity between herself and her audience, Winnemucca frequently employs the direct-address techniques cited above that were a staple of many other sentimental texts from this time period. As she does so, she carefully negotiates the representation of her "self" as both apart from and a part of Paiute culture. For example, when Winnemucca introduces the story of her grandfather's death—"But how can I describe the scene that followed [Truckee's death]? Some of you, dear reader[s], can imagine"—she links a personal and tribal tragedy and reaches out to her readers as capable of empathizing with such an event (69). Much of the text of this scene is delivered in this kind of simultaneous translation. "Every one threw themselves upon his body, and their cries could be heard for many a mile. I crept up to him. I could hardly believe he would never speak to me again. I knelt beside him, and took his dear old face in my hands, and looked at him quite a while. I could not speak. I felt the world growing cold; everything seemed dark . . . I think if he had put out his hands and asked me to go with him, I would gladly have folded myself in his arms" (69). Winnemucca almost immediately casts the Paiute people gathered at her grandfather's deathbed as participants in her grief: "Such a scene I never had seen before. Everybody would take his dead body in their arms and weep" (70). She carefully draws her audience into her construction of herself as a member of the tribe; at the same time, she maintains a distance from the tribe by establishing a direct relationship with her readers. Immediately following this is a detached description of Paiute burial procedures, which include burying the deceased's possessions with him, and more direct audience address. "Now, my dear readers, I do not want you to think we do this thing because we think the dead use what we put in. . . . No, no; but it is the last respect we pay for our dead" (70). This mediation is adept.

Winnemucca's writing shows a clear sense of the values of her Euro-American audience. Winnemucca was first exposed to Euro-American religious practices while staying on various ranches and with various white families during her own family's trip to California when she was just a child. As an adult, Winnemucca claimed to be Methodist, though her strongest critiques of missionary work among the Paiutes were also aimed at Methodists. That she learned the language of Protestant Christian reform is clear. An 1879 *Daily Alta California* report on her San Francisco lectures characterized her "sententious sentences" as "bear[ing] a striking similarity to the poetry of Holy Writ," attributing the similarity to her claims of Methodism and to "her reading of the Old Testament" (qtd. in Canfield 166–67). In this often-quoted passage from *Life,* her adeptness at producing and revising Protestant Christian discourse is clear:

> Oh, for shame! You who are educated by a Christian government in the art of war; the practice of whose profession makes you natural enemies of the savages, so called by you. Yes, you, who call yourselves the great civilization; you who have knelt upon Plymouth Rock, covenanting with God to make this land the home of the free and the brave. Ah, then you rise from your bended knees and seizing the welcoming hands of those who are the owners of this land, which you are not, your carbines rise upon the bleak shore, and your so-called civilization sweeps inland from the ocean wave; but, oh, my God! leaving its pathway marked by crimson lines of blood and strewed by the bones of two races, the inheritor and the invader; and I am crying out to you for justice. (207)

In this passage, Winnemucca uses Christian revival language techniques and further uses the "Christian" roots of European immigration both to remind her audience of the "greatness" of their "forefathers" and to let them know that she is knowledgeable about white people in a way that they are not knowledgeable about Indian peoples. The positioning here is delicate. She does not flatter her audience when she points out the destruction their "civilizing" has initiated. What I find most significant about this passage is that she cites the damage done to "two races," insinuating that the violence done to Indian peoples by Euro-American settlers is as much a problem for the whites who will read her book as it is for the Indians she claims to represent. Her plea for justice emphasizes this "double jeopardy" situation—if those to whom she is speaking/writing do not help her (and, by association, all Indian peoples) to attain some sort of "justice," then they will be on the side of violence and bloodshed, not on the side of peace and humanity. White audiences could gain "salvation" through supporting Winnemucca's cause. And the way to justice was made easy—at each of her lectures, and in the back of her autobiography, there was a copy of her petition to Congress on behalf of the Paiutes.

This mediation between representations of her own Indian-ness and her reader's beliefs about Indian-ness permeates her story. She very carefully plays on the Eastern ladies' Christian sympathy through her attack on the "bad" Christian agents who dealt blow after blow to the Paiutes with their swindling and dishonesty, and she balances this with the hard work and honesty of the Paiute people, stereotypical simple and childlike wards, who need their honest agent, Mr. Samuel Parrish: "You are my children," Parrish says to the Paiutes, "I have come to show you how to work" (106). Old Winnemucca answers with, "We will all work at whatever our white father says we must work at" (108). The Paiutes are grateful and happy to be taught how to work by Parrish and declare that he is "the best father we ever had in all our lives" (109). This configuration of the Euro-American as father is, of course, extended even to the "Great White Father" in Washington, D.C. While Winnemucca connects this attribution of the name "father" to figures of authority as a traditional Paiute term of respect for the power of the father figure, in fact the trope was in common usage throughout the nineteenth century and was especially useful to the paternalistic policies/attitude of the federal government in regard to tribal nations during the last half of the century.[14] Even so, the trope still held rhetorical power, especially among reform groups in the East; if Winnemucca wanted her readers to feel shame, anger, and responsibility at the way the Paiutes were being treated, then the image of an abusive and neglectful father, who provided a poor example for the simple and childlike Indians, was one that was certain to pinch a sympathetic nerve.

For those who need more direct proof of Winnemucca's rhetorical awareness, there is a passage, about halfway through *Life,* when, embroiled in a discussion with her cousin Oytes, Winnemucca reveals the crux of her rhetorical tactics: "I have lived a long time with white people, and I know what they do. They are people who are very kind to any one who is ready to do whatever they wish" (113). Winnemucca was an influential American Indian woman and an important figure both in the rhetorical history of women and the rhetorical history of the United States. And Winnemucca's ability to participate in both Euro-American and Paiute cultural practices, her literacy in both of those cultural discourses, marks an important moment for those of us who "study Indians" as well. Winnemucca's ultimate solution was not the "torn between two worlds" victimization still too often attributed Native peoples and Native scholars, which leaves American Indians who didn't "disappear" in the position of being victims of our own subjectivity. Instead, her solution was rhetorical—to pick and choose from both cultural systems, to participate in both in such a way that she gestures toward a new possibility for those of us "civilized Indians" who continue her project of resistance and negotiation in the face of the ongoing project of the rhetoric of empire at work in these United States even today.

Notes, or Other Stories

Portions of this essay appear in a different framework in "Rhetorics of Survivors: how American Indians use writing," *CCC* 53.3 (February 2002).

1. My use of the word "story" throughout my work is based on my understanding of the power of stories to create the world and our ability to live in the world. Stories are never "just stories"—they have ideological and material effects; they are alive; and they are all we have.

2. I refer to Sarah Winnemucca Hopkins throughout this essay as "Winnemucca" since that is the name with which she most often allied herself and is the identity through which she claimed her cultural capital as a Paiute. Also, the tribal name "Paiute" was unregularized in the nineteenth century. I use "Paiute" unless I am quoting a source that uses a different spelling (Piute, Pah-utes, etc.).

3. For a critical analysis of the forms of American Indian autobiography, particularly the "as told to" stories of nineteenth-century figures, see Hertha Dawn Wong's *Sending My Heart Back across the Years* (New York: Oxford UP, 1992).

4. For an example of this in relation to Winnemucca's text, see H. David Brumble's study of Winnemucca in his *American Indian Autobiography* (Berkeley: U of California P, 1988), in which Brumble characterizes Winnemucca's text, along with the as-told-to narratives of Chief Joseph White Bull and Two Leggings, as "preliterate."

5. In addition to being an advocate for allotment of reservation lands, mostly due to the abuses she had witnessed BIA agents indulge in at the expense of her people's welfare, Winnemucca and her father wanted a reservation set aside for the Paiutes on their traditional lands near Fort McDermit. Legislation establishing such a reservation passed Congress in July of 1889.

6. I'm using the concept of "literacy" in a broad way to indicate the familiarity of a subject with the rules and tools of particular cultural discourses. While print literacy is often a component of such knowledge, it is only one kind of participation in the discourses of a culture and, thus, is more limiting a definition than I have in mind.

7. For elaborations of these arguments, see Malea Powell, "Blood and Scholarship" (in *Race, Rhetoric, and Composition,* ed. Keith Gilyard [Portsmith, NH:

Heinemann Boynton/Cook, 1999], 1–16) and "The X-Blood Files" (in *Native American Literary Strategies for the Next Millennium,* eds. P. Jane Hafen and Gwen Griffin [Reno: U of Nevada P, forthcoming]). For further study regarding the function of Indians in the formation of "American" identity, see Roy Harvey Pearce's *Savagism and Civilization* (Berkeley: U of California P, 1988), Richard Drinnon's *Facing West* (New York: Schocken, 1990), and Richard Slotkin's *Regeneration through Violence* (Middletown, CT: Wesleyan UP, 1973).

8. For more information on Indian reform, see Christine Bolt's *American Indian Policy and American Reform* (Boston: Allen and Unwin, 1987); Henry Fritz's *The Movement for Indian Assimilation, 1860–1890* (Philadelphia: U of Penn P, 1963); Frederick Hoxie's *A Final Promise* (see works cited); Robert Keller Jr.'s *American Protestantism and United States Indian Policy, 1869–1892* (Lincoln: U of Nebraska P, 1983); Robert Mardock's *The Reformers and the American Indian* (Columbia: U of Missouri P, 1971); Valerie Mathes's *Helen Hunt Jackson and Her Indian Reform Legacy* (see works cited); and Francis Paul Prucha's *The Great Father* (see works cited).

9. These performances in San Francisco were not the first time that Winnemucca had appeared on stage. In 1864 Winnemucca, her father, her sister Elma, and several young Paiute men had appeared in a series of "Tableaux Vivants Illustrative of Indian Life," first in Virginia City then in San Francisco, in order to raise money to feed the Paiute bands led by her father.

10. This incident is covered more fully in Malea Powell, "Sarah Winnemucca Hopkins: Her Wrongs and Claims," forthcoming in *Native American Rhetorics,* ed. Ernest Stromberg, press to be determined.

11. The brief biography here was compiled from Winnemucca's own account of her life in *Life* and from Canfield's *Sarah Winnemucca of the Northern Paiutes* (see works cited).

12. Appearing in the appendix of Jackson's book is an 1870 "Letter from Sarah Winnemucca, an educated Pah-ute Woman."

13. The few pages between Lovelocks and Yakima are especially interesting in Winnemucca's narrative. It is one of the few places where she talks frankly about the dangers she faces being an Indian woman in "frontier" territory. There are several accounts of being chased by men and barely escaping assaults.

14. For a more detailed historical analysis of this phenomenon, see Francis Paul Prucha's *The Great Father* (see works cited).

Works Cited

Berkhofer, Robert F. *The White Man's Indian: Images of the American Indian, From Columbus to the Present.* New York: Vintage, 1979.

Blaeser, Kimberly. Introduction to "Rituals, Yours—and Mine." *Reinventing the Enemy's Language: Contemporary Native Women's Writings of North America.* Eds. Joy Harjo and Gloria Bird. New York: W. W. Norton, 1997. 113.

Canfield, Gae Whitney. *Sarah Winnemucca of the Northern Paiutes.* Norman: U of Oklahoma P, 1983.

Gates, Merrill E. "Land and Laws as Agents in Educating Indians." *Seventeenth Annual Report of the Board of Indian Commissioners* (1885). Reprinted in *Americanizing the American Indians: Writings by the "Friends of the Indian," 1880–1900.* Ed. Francis Paul Prucha. Cambridge: Harvard UP, 1973. 45–56.

Green, Rayna. "The Pocahontas Perplex: The Image of Indian Women in American Culture." *Works Massachusetts Review 16,* Autumn 1975.

Hopkins, Sarah Winnemucca. *Life among the Piutes: Their Wrongs and Claims.* Boston: privately printed, 1883. Reprint. Bishop, CA: Chalfant Press, 1969.

Hoxie, Frederick E. *A Final Promise: The Campaign to Assimilate the Indians, 1880–1920.* Lincoln: U of Nebraska P, 1984.

Indian Rights Association. "Statement of Objectives" from *Second Annual Report of the Executive Committee of the Indian Rights Association* (1885). Reprinted in Prucha, *Americanizing the American Indians* 42–44.

Jackson, Helen Hunt. *A Century of Dishonor: A Sketch of the United States Government's Dealings with Some of the Indian Tribes.* Boston: Roberts Bros., 1881. Reprint. New York: Indian Head Books, 1993.

Mathes, Valerie Sherer. *Helen Hunt Jackson and Her Indian Reform Legacy.* Austin: U of Texas P, 1990.

Peabody, Elizabeth Palmer. *The Piutes: Second Report of the Model School of Sarah Winnemucca, 1886–87.* Cambridge: John Wilson & Son, 1887.

———. *Sarah Winnemucca's Practical Solution of the Indian Problem: A Letter to Dr. Lyman Abbot of the "Christian Union."* Cambridge: John Wilson & Son, 1886.

Prucha, Francis Paul. *The Great Father: The United States Government and the American Indians,* vols. 1 and 2. Lincoln: U of Nebraska P, 1984.

Ruoff, A. LaVonne Brown. "Three Nineteenth-Century American Indian Autobiographers." *Redefining American Literary History.* Eds. A. LaVonne Brown Ruoff and Jerry W. Ward Jr. New York: Modern Language Association, 1990. 251–69.

4

Cooper and Crummell

Dialogics of Race and Womanhood

Elizabeth West

It is somewhat ironic that in her 1892 signature publication, *A Voice from the South,* Anna Julia Cooper would offer such unequivocal praise for Alexander Crummell, a man who had a longstanding reputation for teetering at the extremes of Puritanical rigidity. In spite of his stoicism and inflexibility, Crummell's widely circulated essay "The Black Woman of the South: Her Neglects and Her Needs" (1883) inspired sympathy and aid for black women in the postbellum South. In this work Crummell articulates an ideology of black womanhood that he has shaped for decades before the Civil War and that remained for the most part unchanged. This constancy is found in the clearest and most steadfast convictions as well as the ambiguities in his work.

Simply due to the length of his career, Crummell is an important figure, for he sheds light on the transition of African Americans from the nineteenth-century antebellum period to the closing years of the century. Born in 1819 to free black parents in New York, Crummell grew up in a community of black antebellum activists. His father, Boston Crummell, was among those blacks who founded the first African American newspaper, *Freedom's Journal,* and both Crummells regularly participated in black conventions held throughout the antebellum North (Moses 13). Although Crummell spent more than twenty years away from America—nearly five (1847–1853) in England pursuing a degree at Queen's College and nearly twenty (1853–1872) in Liberia as a missionary—he was nevertheless a significant voice for the abolitionist cause. Crummell's writings provide meaningful insight into the philosophy of one of the most prolific and published black writers in the nineteenth century. His postwar works—in particular, his most passionate plea for black women—can be studied in concert with Cooper's writings. The dialogic resonations between Cooper's and Crummell's writings tell us much about how class and gender informed rhetorics of black womanhood in the closing decades of the nineteenth century.

Alexander Crummell and Anna Julia Cooper were unlikely contemporaries. Cooper, born a slave in North Carolina in 1858 to her slave mother and her mother's master (Hutchinson 4), was decades younger than the august and revered Crummell, but was closer to the degradation and poverty of which they both spoke. Though generations apart, the two would find common ground in their commitments to education and racial uplift. Upon his return to the United States in 1872, Crummell was assigned the pastorship of a leading group of black Episcopalians in Washington, D.C. He would grow this group into St. Luke's Episcopal Church, one of the most prestigious black churches in late-nineteenth-century Washington. As a member of St. Luke's and the community of black scholars and activists in Washington, Cooper would come to know Crummell well, so well that she would deliver an 1894 address honoring him for fifty years of service to the church.

Together, the writings of Crummell and Cooper provide a more complete picture of Crummell, revealing his important place among the black elite, and particularly his influence on the rhetoric of black womanhood that grew out of this influential group. While Crummell has been less recognized for his interest in women's issues, Cooper's references to Crummell, as well as her reverberations of his most resolute philosophical ideals, highlight his influence not only among African American male leaders but among women as well. Crummell and other "prominent post-Reconstruction black male leaders . . . were the targeted audiences for much of her persuasive discourse" (Logan 115). A telling revelation of how Crummell and Cooper represent the sometimes strained gender relations between the male and female black elite at the close of the nineteenth century is evidenced by the tension between Crummell's 1883 essay "The Black Woman of the South" and Cooper's 1886 essay "Womanhood: A Vital Element in the Regeneration of a Race." Cooper's essay, the first in her collection *A Voice from the South: By a Black Woman of the South,* whose title itself is a response to and perhaps a signifying on Crummell's widely circulated pamphlet "Black Woman of the South,"[1] immediately engages Crummell in a dialogue. There lies a level of irony in Crummell's being the author of "The Black Woman of the South": he is alien to the experience for which he claims authoritative voice. He is a freeborn black Northern male, taking up pen and paper to articulate the trials of the newly freed black female population of the South. But Cooper, who was often candid in her criticisms of black men, is less so in her answer to her pastor's work. The title of her collection, *A Voice from the South,* clearly signifies on one who supposes himself an authority on the South, but who is himself not of the South. Identifying herself as a voice *from* the South, Cooper unseats her predecessor with her subtitle—*By a Black Woman of the South.* Crummell speaks as an outsider, while Cooper is herself the embodiment of the subject—the black woman of the South.

Cooper's clever title gives voice and subjectivity to the black woman, but her rhetoric of female empowerment is not always explicit or primary in her work. This is exemplified early in the essay "Womanhood," which at the onset seems to merely affirm the rhetoric of female domesticity. Like Crummell, Cooper grounds her discourse on civilization and human progress in a number of Western and biblical paradigms. She echoes Crummell's early works that appropriate the social and ideological discourse of leading nineteenth-century European scholars, particularly with her references to François Guizot's and Thomas Maucaulay's works that affirm woman's central contribution to the making of civilization. Cooper argues that the destined progress and prominence of America lies in the hands of its womanhood, and she cites Maucaulay, who has said, "'You may judge a nation's rank in the scale of civilization from the way they treat their women'" (12). She follows with a quote from Ralph Waldo Emerson, who makes a similar claim: "'I have thought that a sufficient measure of civilization is the influence of good women'" (12–13). From Guizot's account of women in the feudal system, Cooper again emphasizes the significance of woman in the shaping of the civilized world. Drawing from such respected scholars, Cooper also demonstrates her own learnedness. More importantly, however, she lulls her conservative audience into momentary ease with authoritative sources that ostensibly confirm a patriarchal discourse. Her male audience is not disturbed by her affirmation of woman's central role in nation building, because while woman may be hoisted onto an ideological pedestal, she is there unempowered. Maucaulay's words have not raised woman by virtue of her own power but, as he says, by virtue of how "they" (men) treat her. The well-treated woman of Maucaulay's vision is no less objectified than the ill-treated woman among barbarians. While the passage from Emerson is less an objectification of woman, he too fails to paint woman as an empowered figure. Emerson's "good women" do not challenge nineteenth-century notions of the domestic and dependent woman. In fact, Lydia Maria Child, a leading abolitionist and women's rights advocate, criticized Emerson for his denigrating vision of woman. In her 1843 essay "Women's Rights," Child recalls a lecture by Emerson that she thought inspired the male spirit while doing little more than subjugating woman once again to the realm of man's object. Cooper offers no such critique of Emerson, but rather calls on Emerson as an intellectual ally.

Cooper's intellectual alliance with Western patriarchal figures suggests her compliance with their gendered ideals, but there are critical moments in her writing that compromise this generalization. The ambiguity of Cooper's message becomes apparent with her critique of Western chivalry as a system of privilege that has left many women alienated: "Respect for woman, the much lauded chivalry of the Middle Ages, meant what I fear it still means to some men in our own today—respect for the elect few among whom they expect to consort" (14). Here, Cooper opens up her discussion for a critique of gender and class as she condemns the class-dominated gender rhetoric of Western society. But as Mary Helen Washington has pointed out, in the introduction to the 1988 Schomburg republication of Cooper's text, Cooper fails to offer a sustained discussion on gender and class. According to Washington, Cooper "is never able to discard totally the ethics of true womanhood, and except for the one passage about black laundry women, she does not imagine ordinary black working women as the basis of her feminist politics" (xlvi).

Cooper's assessment of chivalry falls short of serious interrogation as her critique is buried in her return to the image of woman as ultimately dependent on man's protection. This ideological wavering is especially evident in a compelling passage that asserts woman's equality. Arguing that Christ confirmed the redemption of woman from the fall of Eve, Cooper maintains that woman's equal place was made clear by Christ: "throughout his life and in his death he has given to men a rule and guide for the estimation of woman as an equal" (18). Her suggestion of the equality of men and women is, however, inherently compromised by the suggestion that the system of male and female equality is to be administered by man. In this same passage, the assertion of sexual equality is undermined further as Cooper describes Christ's valuation of woman as a "sacred charge to be sheltered and cared for with a brother's love and sympathy." Once again, Cooper's rhetoric of sexual equality collapses into a gender hierarchy that renders woman a ward of man.

While Cooper's assertions of sexual equality signify her resistance to the male-dominated rhetoric of late-nineteenth-century America, her repeated acquiescence to a discourse that ties womanhood to domesticity ironically ties her more firmly to the patriarchal ideals that she attempts to overturn. Her numerous affirmations of the primacy of the black woman's role as homemaker and nurturer echo the sentiments of black male elites who, like Crummell, identified the black woman's role in racial uplift as primarily that of homemaker. Just as Crummell had from his earliest works maintained that woman's place in the home signified the civility of a people, Cooper reiterated this reading of woman's place. She argued that "the position of woman in society determines the vital elements of its regeneration and progress" (21). And again, like Crummell, who maintains a rhetoric of gender essentialism, Cooper links woman's central role to her nature. The primacy of woman's role in civilization building is not the result of being "better or stronger or wiser than man, but from the nature of the case, because it is she who must first form the man by directing the earliest impulses of his character" (21). Woman, then, through natural design, is especially fit for her role. She is the physical source from which human life springs, and thus is also the earliest source for shaping human character and caring for the dependent offspring.

The arguments offered here by Cooper have been voiced by philosophers and activists before her. She acknowledges this fact and that she has been preceded by one who has already posited this argument in defense of the black woman of the South. She concurs with Crummell's general plea for the black woman of the South and his summary of her needs, but she also challenges him. Cooper is shrewd, however, softening her criticism with an initial offer of respect and reverence. She acknowledges Crummell as the authority who has preceded her in calling public attention to the needs of Southern black women, and she acknowledges the enormous challenge to follow his work: "'Cursed is he that cometh after the king[,]' and has not the king already preceded me in 'The Black Woman of the South'? They have had both Moses and the prophets in Dr. Crummell and if they hear not him, neither would they be persuaded though one came up from the South" (24). Cooper's adroitness here lies in her deference to Crummell's authority, which, ironically, highlights her as the more fitting authority. While she identifies Crummell as the "king," she points out that she is the very subject of which he speaks—she is a black woman from the South, not a distant observer. Drawing a parallel between herself and Crummell, whom she identifies as the embodiment of Moses and the prophets, Cooper indirectly suggests the prophetic and important nature of her message.

Cooper's acknowledgment of Crummell as her predecessor demonstrates her sensitivity to her audience. However, she privileges her status as insider and suggests that as an insider she might more ably tell of the sufferings of Southern black women. Though she unseats him as authoritative voice, Cooper maintains her alliance with Crummell by underscoring her similar alarm at a matter that had long troubled Crummell. Dating back to his missionary years in Liberia, Crummell resented the leadership and authoritative roles that white clergy assumed in the church and politics of black Liberia.[2] Cooper criticizes the white clergy of the Episcopal Church for their refusal to accept that blacks themselves are capable of addressing the circumstances of black women. She warns of the misdiagnosis that results when outsiders assume themselves authorities: "But the doctors[,] while discussing their scientifically conclusive diagnosis of the disease, will perhaps not think it presumptuous in the patient if he dares to suggest where at least the pain is. If this be allowed, a *Black woman of the South* would beg to point out two possible oversights in this southern work which may indicate in part both a cause and a remedy for some failure" (36).

By italicizing the words "Black woman of the South," Cooper calls attention to the connection between her work and Crummell's widely circulated tract, "The Black Woman of the South." Her presumption of authority is further revealed in the above passage with her metaphor of the black woman as the suffering patient: Cooper is the black woman, the patient, who, from personal experience speaks of the sufferings endured by neglected black women in the South. In addition to identifying the limitations of the white clergy to understand the black woman's struggle, Cooper identifies two problems in the missionary work of the Episcopal Church—its exclusion of black men in discussions on this issue and its dismissal of black women's central role in racial uplift (37). On the latter point she credits Crummell for having already argued for the needs of the black woman of the South, his having already laid out a proposal to meet these needs, and she notes the failure of the church to respond: "The ground has been ably discussed and an admirable and practical plan proposed by the oldest Negro priest in America, advising and urging that special organizations such as Church sisterhoods and industrial schools be devised to meet her pressing needs in the Southland . . . Yet the pamphlet fell still-born from the press so far as I am informed the Church has made no motion towards carrying out Dr. Crummell's suggestion" (42–43). Cooper criticizes the church for its failure to address the needs of black women in the South; however, she is careful not to alienate herself from the church.

Repeatedly situating her work as derivative of a legacy begun by Crummell, Cooper implies that her dialogue with Crummell is a rhetorical nexus.

Crummell has preceded her with his account of the black woman's unique circumstances, but she offers a view from another space, widening the lens through which these concerns can be viewed. Ultimately, however, Cooper reminds her male audience that her vision of the black woman's role is consistent with theirs. She endears herself to this group of clergymen with her affirmation that the uplift of the black woman will be signaled by her place as "the intelligent wife, the Christian mother, the earnest, virtuous, helpful woman, at once both the lever and the fulcrum for uplifting the race" (45). A shrewd rhetorician and thinker, Cooper is certainly aware that with these words, she confirms the ideology of female domesticity that this audience embraces, thereby rendering her presence and her message less threatening to their patriarchal sensibilities.

Cooper occasionally shifts from her conciliatory rhetoric, challenging dominant conventions of gender and even specific assertions of those she holds in high regard. This is especially evident in "Womanhood," with her judicious challenge to Crummell's dismissal of a particular group of black females. Referring to Crummell first with reverence and praise, applauding his advocacy of black women in the aftermath of slavery, Cooper shifts to a critique of his argument that it is the postbellum black woman of the South, excluding the colored, who needs to be protected and educated. In "The Black Woman of the South," Crummell maintained that black and colored women were distinct groups with different needs and opportunities: "In speaking to-day of the 'black woman,' I must needs make a very clear distinction. The African race in this country is divided into two classes, that is—the colored people and the negro population" (*Africa and America* 62). According to Crummell, with their history of privilege, colored women are in less need of aid than women of "pure negro blood," who were maintained on plantations without the benefits of civilization granted to colored women. Cooper, a "colored" woman of the South herself, responds to Crummell's construct of intraracial identities with the suggestion that he has overlooked the hardships suffered by fair-skinned black women: "I would beg, however, with the Doctor's permission, to add my plea for the colored girls of the South:—that large, bright, promising, fatally beautiful class that stand shivering like a delicate plantlet before the fury of tempestuous elements, so full of promise and possibilities, yet so sure of destruction; often without a stronger brother to espouse their cause and defend their honor with his life's blood . . . Oh, save them, help them, shield, train, develop, teach, inspire them! Snatch them, in God's name, as brands from the burning" (24–25). The melodramatic language employed here by Cooper, who is generally calculating and critical, exposes the signifying nature of this passage.

Her image of the "fatally beautiful" colored girl draws on the common nineteenth-century literary representation of the tragic mulatto. She clearly undermines Crummell's assertion that colored women have had a history of privilege, and she transposes Crummell's plea for the poor, defenseless black women of the South to her plea for the unprotected, violated colored girls of the South.

Cooper's picture of the colored girl of the South is more despairing than Crummell's black woman, who at least has been offered the protective discourse of a prominent black male voice. Her choice of the word *girls,* in contrast to Crummell's use of *woman,* suggests further that Cooper's young, abandoned females face a threat more immediate than that of Crummell's more mature black woman. The picture of young, helpless girls invoked by Cooper is more personal and troublesome than Crummell's picture of a symbolic, universal black woman. Cooper's colored girls represent the more compelling picture of youth and innocence lost, and it is the loss experienced by many, as suggested by Cooper's contrasting use of the plural *girls,* with Crummell's use of the single, iconic, and more distant *black woman.* Crummell has made a case for the needs of the black woman of the South, but his dismissal of the colored girls, particularly as highlighted by Cooper, leaves them without an advocate, and leaves him appearing at least slightly unfeeling. Crummell proclaims his right to protect the needful and worthy black woman: "for the mothers, sisters, and daughters of my race I have a right to speak. . . . And when I think of their sad condition down South, think, too, that since the day of emancipation hardly any one has lifted up a voice in their behalf, I feel it a duty and a privilege to set forth their praises and extol their excellences" (*Africa and America* 71). That he would deny his colored mothers, sisters, and daughters similar praise and protection seems callous in light of Cooper's description of their despairing place in Southern society.

Cooper's delivery of this message before the black clergy of the Protestant Episcopal Church must have left Crummell ill at ease by the implications of his earlier exclusion of colored girls. The severity of Cooper's criticism is eased, however, by her return to those ideals that strike a chord of agreement with her mentor. She returns to their mutual emphasis on the black woman's central role in racial uplift and the significance of collective race progress. She elucidates this point by recalling the then-deceased Martin R. Delany's assertion that "when he entered the council of kings the black race entered with him" (30). Cooper disagrees with Delany, arguing that on the contrary, "no man can represent the race. Whatever the attainments of the individual may be, unless his home has moved on pari passu, he can never be regarded as identical with or representative of the whole. . . . We must point to homes, average homes, homes of the rank and file of horny handed toiling men and women of the South" (30–31). She continues this argument with a rhetorical sleight of hand: she rejects Delany's tone of individualism but appropriates his metaphor. In her own words, Cooper explains, "Only the Black Woman can say 'when and where I enter, in the quiet, undisputed dignity of my womanhood, without violence and without suing or special patronage, then and there the whole Negro race enters with me'" (31). The black elite discourse of female domesticity is left unchallenged by Cooper as she makes a more compelling assertion—that the door to achievement and progress for the race will be opened not by the black man, but by the black woman. Cooper maintains that the domestic space is woman's realm, but she identifies woman as the agent of race progress, thereby suggesting that home is a political space and that leadership lies there.

Cooper argues that black women can best be prepared for their special calling through the assistance of missionary groups, and through the long-term improvement that comes with education. Like Crummell, she argues for the necessity of educating women, and her position is anchored in the prevailing rhetoric of woman's special place as nurturer and homemaker. "The position of woman in society determines the vital elements of its regeneration progress," and that role is prescribed by nature (*Voice from the South* 21). As the medium through which children are shaped into moral and useful adults, woman must be educated to fully carry out her role. Woman's duty, according to Cooper, "is one that might make angels tremble and fear to take hold!" (22). This elevation of woman's role to one exceeding angelic heights is reminiscent of Crummell's words in his earlier (1882) sermon "Marriage." Here, Crummell identifies man's advantage over the angels—his procreative powers: "The angels above have no productive powers: but man is made a fertile creature, and is possessed with the gift of fecundity. And in this one feature of his constitution, he is superior to the angels" (*Greatness of Christ* 45). In contrast to Crummell's analogy that draws on the nongendered use of the term *man* to represent humankind, Cooper draws a comparison between woman and angels. It is not woman's procreative powers that merit her comparison to angels, but rather her responsibility to train children. For Cooper it is the act of raising children that warrants special acknowledgment. That this act is assumed a responsibility especially fit for women further supports Cooper's assertion that black women will lead the way to the improvement of the race.

Crummell and Cooper emphasize the unreadiness of Southern black women for their special calling. Though both call for missionary groups to go South and actively work among the greater population of ill-prepared black women, Crummell seeks women to act as primary agents in this work. In "The Black Woman of the South," he charges Christian women with the job of uplifting their disadvantaged counterparts. It is through a "mission of 'sisterhoods'" peopled by "large numbers of practical Christian women, women of intelligence and piety, women well trained in domestic economy" that the black woman of the South will be uplifted" (*Africa and America* 75–76).

Crummell's call for a "mission of sisterhoods" was at least a quarter of a century old by this time, for he had made similar pleas for black women in Liberia during his missionary years there. In his 1860 address "The English Language in Liberia," Crummell argued that the intellectual needs of women had been ignored throughout history: "The world has been six thousand years in existence, and it has hardly yet begun to do justice to the intellect of woman" (*Future of Africa* 43). He warned that Liberia's future could not be secured if it failed to "raise [its] daughters and . . . sisters to become the true and equal companions of men, and not their victims" (44). Just as he would propose more than twenty years later in "The Black Woman of the South," Crummell recommended to this audience of fellow Liberians that female societies be formed to begin the long process of educating and preparing Liberian women to fulfill their roles in the process of civilizing Liberia (44–45). Though Crummell recommended that this education start "elementary, even in its nature; and by gradual signs, rise to something more ambitious" (44–45), he envisioned something grander in the long term. He argued that "the master need in Liberia is that of a female seminary, of a high order, for the education of girls" (45).

As revealed in a number of his late-nineteenth-century writings, the compassion for the cause of black women's education that Crummell expressed early would carry over to his leadership in the post-Reconstruction era. His support for the founding of St. Mary's Girl Academy during his pastorship, his support for the kindergarten program, and his continued public support for women's education clearly highlight his commitment to improving the circumstances of black women. But as was often the case with Crummell, there was contradiction in his rhetoric. This contradiction is especially evident in his plea for industrial education in "Black Woman of the South," and the contrasting message in "Excellence," which calls for these young black women to prepare to enter "the doors of a higher Academy" (*Africa and America* 345). He acknowledges the importance of utility and practicality to the rudiments of human existence, but to these young women

Crummell recommends higher aspirations: "you can do better, everywhere in life, by the attainment of excellence" (352). This celebration of higher learning is absent two years later when Crummell warns against overly ambitious blacks who seek impractical education. In his 1886 sermon "Common Sense in Common Schooling," Crummell tells his congregation:

> I fear we are overdoing this matter of higher learning. Everywhere I go throughout the country I discover two or three very disagreeable and unhealthy facts. I see, first of all, (a) the vain ambition of very many mothers to over-educate their daughters, and to give them training and culture unfitted for their position in society and unadapted to their prospects in life. I see, likewise, too many men, forgetful of the occupations they held in society, anxious to shoot their sons suddenly, regardless of fitness, into literary characters and into professional life. This is the first evil. (b) Next to this I have observed an ambition among the youth of both sexes for aesthetical culture; an inordinate desire for the ornamental and elegant in education to the neglect of the solid and practical. And (c), thirdly, to a very large extent school children are educated in letters to a neglect of household industry. (*Africa and America* 330)

Crummell's position here reveals both a picture of his philosophy on education and his elitism. While we might applaud his foresight on the necessity of educating women, we must also recognize that his philosophy is grounded in an ideology of classism—in some respects Crummell echoes the very aristocratic sensibilities of the privileged nineteenth-century American society that he often criticizes. His notion that the education of the masses be limited to practical learning conveys a message of intraracial class hierarchy, a message that will be transformed into the twentieth-century black elitist rhetoric of the talented tenth.

In her writings as well as in her activism, Cooper, like Crummell, expressed a belief in the necessity of an educated African American leadership. In an essay titled "What Are We Worth?" Cooper argues that education will be the critical marker that determines the future place and worth of blacks among humankind. According to Cooper, blacks, like other races, will be led by an educated leadership and will be judged by their ability to be educated and to then apply that education to the pursuit of progress. Education is a raw material that must be refined and fit "into the world's work to supply the world's need—the manufacture of men and women for the markets of the world" (*Voice from the South* 244). Education must be had by all people who hope to be of worth to humanity: it is an investment that "pays the largest dividends and gives the grandest possible product to the world—a man" (244–45).

Cooper's metaphors ring with capitalist symbolism, but she is not suggesting that the importance of education is its promise of material gain. She echoes Crummell's argument on the primacy of industry as the foundation of group survival and the elevated cultural status that is the result of more classical learning. She explains that there is a dynamic relationship between intellect and industry: "Wealth must pave the way for learning. Intellect, whether of races or individuals, cannot soar to the consummation of those sublime products which immortalize genius, while the general mind is assaulted and burdened with 'what shall we eat, what shall we drink, and wherewithal shall we be clothed.' Work must first create wealth, and wealth leisure, before the untrammeled intellect of the Negro, or any other race, can vindicate its capabilities" (261). The struggle for wealth or economic security is the most basic human quest, but wealth does not equate to what Cooper considers the higher level of human achievement—one not evidenced in the greater population. While work and wealth are fundamental human concerns, higher learning is the call for only a select few: "One mind in a family or in a town may show a penchant for art, for literature, for the learned professions, or more bookish lore. You will know it when it is there. No need to probe for it. It is a light that cannot be hid under a bushel—and I would try to enable that mind to go to the full length of its desires" (262–63).

Scholars frequently credit W. E. B. DuBois as the originator of this philosophy; however, the theory of an elite talented tenth leadership is clearly espoused by Cooper a decade before the publication of DuBois's 1903 essay "The Talented Tenth." Cooper's vision of an insightful and exceptional few who will lead the masses demonstrates the dubiousness of Houston Baker's assertion that "Cooper is not a DuBoisian but a Washingtonian" (34). She is neither. While Cooper did not contemplate philosophical and social issues in isolation, she was no less a creative and independent thinker than her male counterparts.

However, if one feels compelled to connect her class philosophy of racial uplift to a leading late-nineteenth-century race leader, Crummell is a more fitting candidate. Crummell predates both Cooper and DuBois with his early nationalist writings that imagined an educated black leadership paving the way for a prosperous Liberian nation. Crummell would carry over these nationalist ideals to his post-Reconstruction rhetoric of the 1880s. To the 1885 graduating class of Storer College in West Virginia, Crummell made clear this ideology. He explained that the educated men of the race possessed the superior minds needed to tackle the great problems of the race and to influence the elevation of the race as a whole: "Who are to be the agents to raise and elevate this people to a higher plane of being? It is to be affected by the scholars and philanthropists which come forth in these days from the schools. . . . [I]t is a work . . . which will require the most skillful resources and the wise practicality of superior men" (*Africa and America* 36).

Like Crummell, Cooper envisioned an educated elite that would lead the masses, and she too would also maintain the central role of the educated black woman in this mission: "In *A Voice From the South,* Cooper calls for a mass, female standard for evaluating the effectiveness of African-American praxis, a decade before Du Bois penned his concept of 'The Talented Tenth'" (James 44). Just as Crummell called for societies of women to aid the black woman of the South, Cooper too maintained the importance of such an effort. In contrast to Crummell, however, Cooper called for both men and women missionaries: "'I am my Sister's keeper!' should be the hearty response of every man and woman of the race," she instructs (*Voice from the South* 32). It is the united effort of black men and women that will change the lives of black women in the South. And Cooper notes that it is an effort that requires more privileged blacks to transcend class barriers. Her recommendation is far reaching as she suggests that barriers of class and sex be overridden in the greater interest of racial solidarity: "We need men who can let their interest and gallantry extend outside the circle of their aesthetic appreciation; men who can be a father, a brother, a friend to every weak, struggling[,] unshielded girl. We need women who are [so] sure of their own social footing that they need not fear leaning to lend a hand to a fallen or falling sister. We need men and women who do not exhaust their genius splitting hairs on aristocratic distinctions and thanking God that they are not as others" (32–33).

Though Cooper has called on privileged blacks to set aside their preoccupation with class, her own rhetoric of racial uplift reveals an elitist ideology that draws on education to mark class boundaries. An educated elite will lead the masses, and in Cooper's analogy that elite will consist of women as well as men.[3] Hence, outstanding women of the race must be educated. Cooper repeats this position in her writings, but her views are often carefully couched in a rhetoric of female domesticity and feminine moderation. She argues that an education for young women teaches them that more is expected of them than to "merely look pretty and appear well in society" (*Voice from the South,* "The Higher Education of Women" 78). Here Cooper alludes to a prevailing nineteenth-century middle-class ideal of womanhood. Dating back to early American Puritanism, women who dressed elaborately and drew excessive attention to themselves were marked as unwomanly and even violators of Christian ideals of womanhood. The mark of true womanhood was the modest, unassuming woman, and this is the image of womanhood that Cooper aligns with the image of educated black women. Cooper is aware of the narrow plank that she walks as she attempts to reconcile two distinct worlds. She posits the seemingly contradictory argument that education—which is associated with worldliness—will influence women to better perform their domestic responsibilities: "The earnest well trained Christian young woman, as a teacher, as a homemaker, as wife, mother, or silent influence even, is as potent a missionary agency among our people as is the theologian" (*Voice from the South* 79).

Cooper negotiates a delicate argument; she is not simply asking for a practical education for women, but is instead suggesting that the classical curriculum—deemed the educational realm of men—be opened to women. She acknowledges the often-made argument that a classical education for women may interfere with marriage. At the heart of Cooper's argument is the premise that a classical education does not put woman's femininity at risk, but rather renders her a more intellectual mate for man; and calling on the ancient poetess Sappho, Cooper further suggests that a classical education leads woman to spiritual fulfillment. While Cooper offers serious refutation to claims that too much education can be harmful to women, she later offers a witty yet piercing answer: "I have been told that strong-minded women could be, when they thought it worth their while, quite endurable" (72). Though Cooper very likely drew a humorous response from her audience, her remark hints at the spirit of female independence and empowerment that she often couched in a rhetoric that played to middle-class images of female domesticity.

Like Crummell, Anna Julia Cooper held a firm conviction in the role of woman's place in race progress, and both would emphasize the necessity of educating black women to meet this end. For Crummell and Cooper, however, the priority of higher education spilled over into a rhetoric that privileged Anglocentric conventions and ideals. Their classical learning left them accepting the dominant rhetoric of European cultural superiority. It would be too simplistic an analysis, however, to conclude that their reverence for Western culture was mere capitulation. Like other black leaders in the post-Reconstruction climate, Cooper and Crummell were aware that they faced a white public that was indifferent at best and often hostile to blacks and their unresolved place in American society. "The Race Problem in America" and "A Defense of the Negro Race" are two speech titles that exemplify the social mood that Crummell was responding to in the closing decades of the nineteenth century. As these titles indicate, race is a problem, and the presence of blacks in American society is seen as the source of that problem. In "A Defense of the Negro Race," Crummell responds to a criticism of blacks delivered in an 1882 address, "On the Relations of the Church to the Colored Race," by a white Episcopal clergyman, Dr. J. L. Tucker. Crummell answers Dr. Tucker's charges that blacks inherently lack qualities such as morality, honesty, and industry (*Africa and America* 86). In addition, Crummell cites Dr. Tucker's charge to the Northerners that they freed blacks only to leave them a burden on the white South (114). Tucker's charge was an often-articulated claim by white Southerners in their justification for the reign of terror that they would initiate in the post-Reconstruction South. This rhetoric followed the increasing public representation of the freed blacks as a blemish upon the American landscape. It is this rising antiblack sentiment that Cooper, too, is clearly aware of and responding to.

Cooper and Crummell were among those black elites who responded to inflammatory and denigrating representations of blacks by affirming the ability of blacks to adopt the ways of Western culture. Countering a rhetoric that proclaimed blacks inferior because they did not have the education and culture of Westerners, black leaders like Crummell and Cooper argued for the humanity of blacks. Cooper argued for the worth and place of blacks among all other races not by asserting the merits of black culture, but like Crummell, by affirming their ability to appropriate Western learning and culture. But it is not Western culture in general that Cooper deems the exemplum of higher civilization. What she extols are the high arts and learning of the Western world, not its common culture. She echoes Crummell's affirmation that the great achievements of Western society render it the model for rising nations.

While Cooper clearly holds European civilization as the exemplum of human progress, she, like Crummell, is quick to recall Europe's barbaric past. In her essay "Has America a Race Problem; If So, How Can It Best Be Solved," Cooper cites numerous moments in European history that exemplify Europe's early barbarism. Echoing an analogy often drawn by Crummell, Cooper cites Europe's barbaric history to argue that just as Europeans rose out of heathenism and incivility, blacks too would rise to greatness. She determines that the greatness of European civilization is not the result of an inherently superior people, but rather the result of an ever-improving humankind.

The deductive framework of Cooper's historical philosophy gives her argument authority, and her view of humankind is consistent with a dominant Western worldview that took shape during the European Enlightenment. The Enlightenment philosophy of mankind as ever learning and moving toward human perfection has remained an influential view in Western culture even today. Though Enlightenment philosophers constructed this progressive view of humankind under the presumption that humankind meant white civilization, many black leaders and scholars would appropriate this view and transform it into a rhetoric of black uplift. In like fashion, Cooper asserted a progressive theory of humankind. She shaped her argument in a rhetoric that underscored a dominant American ideology of identity: "As the European was higher and grander than the Asiatic, so will American civilization be broader and deeper and closer to the purposes of the Eternal than any the world has yet seen" (166).

Few nineteenth-century Americans would dispute Cooper's assertion that America is the betterment of her European ascendants—it was a vision dating back to Colonial American society. Cooper's ontological view of humankind as ever improving flowed logically into her race theory; hence, while Europe represented a great civilization, its greatness would be supplanted by its offspring—America. America's greatness would be expressed differently from her predecessor. America would not rise to greatness through legendary military conquests or industrial achievements but through higher principles of humanity: "the last page . . . to mark the climax of history, the bright consummate flower unfolding charity toward all and malice toward none,—the final triumph of universal reciprocity born of universal conflict with forces that cannot be exterminated" (166).

Cooper maintained that throughout history the conflicts between different races of people has served to improve mankind, and she turns to French historian François Guizot to elucidate this point: "'Take ever so rapid a glance,' says he, 'at modern Europe and it strikes you at once as diversified, confused, and stormy. All the principles of social organization are found existing together within it . . . all classes of society" (159). She adds: "While in other civilizations the exclusive domination of a principle (or race) led to tyranny,[4] in Europe the diversity of social elements (growing out of the contact of different races) the incapability of any one to exclude the rest, gave birth to the LIBERTY which now prevails. This inability of the various principles to exterminate one another compelled each to endure the others and made it necessary for them in order to live in common to enter into a sort of mutual understanding" (159–60).

From this Cooper deduces that "equilibrium, not repression among conflicting forces[,] is the condition of natural harmony, of permanent progress, and universal freedom" (160). Therefore, America, with its diversity of races, is destined to "learn that a race, as a family, may be true to itself without seeking to exterminate all others" (168). Like the European land of many races of people that eventually found a way to coexist and flourish, America and its many races of people would do likewise, Cooper argued. This mutual coexistence would then lead to America's greatness—the result of contributions of many race families. As one among many of America's race families, blacks too would contribute to the building of a great American civilization. Though blacks in late-nineteenth-century America were still clearly suffering from the aftermath of slavery, Cooper expressed confidence that their presence was a meaningful one: "I believe with our own Dr. Crummell that 'the Almighty does not preserve, rescue, and build up a lowly people merely for ignoble ends'" (173–74).

While Cooper and Crummell accepted the dominant discourse that touted the superiority of Western culture, they challenged claims of white superiority. This position seemed unambiguous to them and to many among the black elite in late-nineteenth-century America. Their views seemed unaffected by the possible contradiction between a belief in the progress of the black race and a concomitant belief in the cultural views of those who had maintained blacks in cultural and economic destitution: they seemed to believe that a clear distinction could be drawn between Westerners and Western civilization. While these arbiters of racial uplift articulated a rhetoric of race unity, their efforts have sometimes been interpreted in a contrasting light.

Scholar Kevin Gaines argues that the rhetoric and reality of this black elite leadership was often contradictory: "Amidst legal and extralegal repression, many black elites sought status, moral authority, and recognition of their humanity by distinguishing themselves, as bourgeois agents of civilization, from the presumably undeveloped black majority; hence the phrase, so purposeful and earnest, yet so often of ambiguous significance; uplifting the race" (2). Gaines further identifies this elite ideology as oftentimes grounded in patriarchal leanings that were promoted by black male leaders such as Crummell and Martin Delany (4), and he argues that "Cooper's thought, particularly her gender consciousness, both contested and reflected the assumptions of the black intelligence and black middle-class ideology" (129). Gaines underscores the integral place of Western bourgeois ideology in much of uplift philosophy, and his charge that "Cooper's writings cannot easily be disentangled from her Western ethnocentrism" (129) is a tenable reading.

However, even if we read elite ideology as simply a reification of white bourgeois values, we must still remember that uplift ideology was not a monolithic discourse. Clearly, some among the elite were committed to bourgeois values for their own self-interest, but others were committed because either they believed this represented a higher form of civilization or they simply surmised that it was a means to an end—namely, black assimilation into the larger society. Cooper and Crummell expressed a vision of hope that saw blacks emerging out of a cultural darkness. Though slavery had left them lagging behind the civilized world, blacks would rise out of this abyss to find a meaningful place in the greater society. Like other black activists of this era, Cooper and Crummell believed that black progress would be marked by the successful acculturation of blacks. They sanctioned a Western discourse of high culture that centered woman as the icon of domesticity, man as the worldly-wise provider, and European cultural mores as the universal mark of civility.

Again, Crummell and Cooper were able to embrace Western civilization as the benchmark of African American acculturation because they maintained a progressive view of the history of mankind, suggesting that later civilizations were successively more advanced than their predecessors. Whites had emerged out of their barbarism, having learned from and improved upon the cultures of earlier people. Blacks would then learn and improve upon that which they inherited from whites and would represent the nexus in the ever-improving state of humankind. With this worldview, Cooper and Crummell could accept Western culture as the model of civilization. For Cooper and Crummell this position carried no contradictions; they acknowledged no inconsistency in claiming the superiority of Western culture while concurrently challenging claims of white superiority.

The writings of Cooper and Crummell illustrate the difficulty encountered when one attempts to read the ideologies of the talented tenth into clear ideological camps. While Cooper and Crummell clearly show an Anglocentric grounding in their cultural views, they are nevertheless believers in the inevitable greatness of blacks. They measure that greatness by Anglocentric cultural markers, but their writings also reveal that theirs was not a philosophy rooted in simple acquiescence to a white worldview. Cooper and Crummell represent a tradition in African American literature of appropriating the dominant discourse and shaping it into a rhetoric of African American humanity and import. In an era marked by overwhelming antiblack sentiment, leading African American activists and scholars searched for a language to legitimize and validate a black presence in a world of whiteness. Cooper and Crummell undertook this task, not by overturning the dominant cultural rhetoric but rather by manipulating that rhetoric into a discourse of equality and inclusion. Their writings represent a black elite who, though aware of the destitution and drudgery common to black female experience, chose a rhetoric of female domesticity and gentility to construct black female identity. This seeming dismissal of black female experience is sometimes interpreted as the acquiescence of the black elite to white authority.

Often overlooked, however, is the weighty mission of answering public scorn that many of these activists undertook in their writings. While leading white female writers and activists were calling for equality of the sexes and woman's suffrage, Cooper and her black female contemporaries had to negotiate desires for sexual equality with their mission to counter a public rhetoric that marked black women as sexually loose and socially unrefined. In *A Voice from the South,* Cooper's dialogue with Crummell clearly illustrates the tenuous place of black women scholars who felt compelled to answer the public scorn of white America as well as the rising rhetoric of black male patriarchy that was constructing an icon of black womanhood from the blueprint of middle-class white womanhood. Cooper critiques black male patriarchy, but she ultimately submits to a male-dominant rhetoric that binds woman to a subordinate relationship with man. Notwithstanding her indictment of man's historical degradation of woman and her call for the education and improvement of women, in the end Cooper lays it all at the altar of female domesticity. In her essays that clearly undertake a dialogue with Crummell, Cooper exposes the shortcomings of his rhetoric, but she also restores him to the patriarchal helm. This is again particularly evident in the essay "Womanhood," where she challenges Crummell's self-appointed guardianship of black women, but she ultimately both confirms him as guardian and validates his view. It is no light matter that a black woman leader and activist with Cooper's professional and personal accomplishments yielded to a rhetoric that she so clearly questioned. Cooper's rhetorical acquiescence hints at the influence of a dominating male presence among the talented tenth.

While Crummell and his black male contemporaries may have been motivated by the highest of intentions, the Cooper-Crummell dialogue reveals how black women's voices were stifled and reshaped until they were oftentimes undistinguishable from the exclusionary dominant rhetoric of womanhood as well as the imposing rhetoric of a black patriarchal elite. The Cooper-Crummell dialogue represents a struggle for black female subjectivity; this is evident in Cooper's contrasting and conflicting images of womanhood as well as the tightrope she negotiates as she both praises and admonishes the gender rhetoric of one of the leading black voices of late-nineteenth-century America.

Crummell's patriarchal rhetoric looms like an overhanging storm cloud in the midst of Cooper's would-be feminist declarations. With Crummell as the guiding light for her emerging race rhetoric, Cooper becomes bound by the limitations of her mentor's vision. Crummell's longstanding deference to a Western worldview leaves little room for African American experience and cultural ideals. As a senior and esteemed figure among black leaders at the close of the nineteenth century, Crummell left a legacy of conflict and contradiction. Cooper and DuBois would be among the black elite leadership that would inherit the vision of black nationalism shaped by Crummell, but it would prove a vision of race unity and progress clouded by their subjugation of black experience and ideology to a dominant white bourgeois rhetoric. The inextricable connection they drew between womanhood and nation would reverberate well into the next century.

As highlighted in the Cooper-Crummell dialogue, the central place of the black woman in race work was not a contested point between black male and female leaders. The tensions in the rhetoric originate in conflicting visions of woman's specific place and in the attempt to conflate the reality of black female experience with a racialized rhetoric of universal womanhood. Crummell's writings reveal the instability of black elite ideals of womanhood. Even a staunch conservative like Crummell could not remain constant in his gender rhetoric. While he emphatically believed in the primacy of woman's domestic role, he could not ignore the reality that many black women did not have the opportunity to choose a life of domesticity and dependence. He would nevertheless stand firm in his vision of a black domestic female icon, and he found concurrence from a black elite that also embraced this gender construct. Crummell's rhetoric of womanhood and nationhood echoed throughout the closing decades of the nineteenth century and would not be seriously challenged until the dawn of the Harlem Renaissance, which ushered in a philosophy of race identity that validated an African American worldview. The black-centered worldview that blossomed during this period would effectively displace Crummell and his conservative ideologies, relegating him to near obscurity for more than half a century.

Notes

1. See Henry Louis Gates's *The Signifying Monkey* (New York: Oxford UP, 1988) for a more thorough discussion of this African American language play.

2. See Wilson Moses's 1989 biography, *Alexander Crummell,* for a detailed account of Crummell's troubles with his white superiors in Liberia.

3. See Floris Barnett Cash's discussion on the female talented tenth in her work

African American Women and Social Action: The Clubwomen and Volunteerism from Jim Crow to the New Deal, 1896–1936 (Westport, CT: Greenwood, 2001).

4. Cooper's use of "race" here represents the nineteenth-century discourse that had not firmly established white as a race. Works such as Roediger's *Wages of Whiteness* and Toni Morrison's *Playing in the Dark* are among a number of scholarly works that trace the construction of whiteness as a race in American society.

Works Cited

Baker, Houston A. Jr. *Workings of the Spirit: The Poetics of Afro-American Women's Writing.* Chicago: U of Chicago P, 1991.

Cooper, Anna Julia. *A Voice from the South.* 1892. New York: Oxford UP, 1988.

Crummell, Alexander. *Africa and America.* 1891. Miami: Mnemosyne Publishing, 1969.

——. *The Future of Africa.* 1862. New York: Negro UP, 1969.

——. *The Greatness of Christ, and Other Sermons.* New York: Thomas Whittaker, 1882.

Gaines, Kevin K. *Uplifting the Race: Black Leadership, Politics, and Culture in the Twentieth Century.* Chapel Hill: U of North Carolina P, 1996.

Hutchinson, Louise D. *Anna J. Cooper: A Voice from the South.* Washington, DC: Smithsonian Institution Press, 1982.

James, Joy. *Transcending the Talented Tenth: Black Leaders and American Intellectuals.* New York: Routledge, 1997.

Lemert, Charles, and Esme Bhan, eds. *The Voice of Anna Julia Cooper: Including* A Voice from the South *and Other Important Essays, Papers, and Letters.* New York: Rowman and Littlefield, 1998.

Logan, Shirley Wilson. "*We Are Coming*"*: The Persuasive Discourse of Nineteenth-Century Black Women.* Carbondale: Southern Illinois UP, 1999.

Moses, Wilson Jeremiah. *Alexander Crummell: A Study of Civilization and Discontent.* New York: Oxford UP, 1989.

Washington, Mary Helen. "Introduction." *A Voice from the South.* 1892. Anna Julia Cooper. New York: Oxford UP, 1988.

Works Consulted

Alexander, Elizabeth. "We Must Be About Our Father's Business: Anna Julia Cooper and the In-Corporation of the Nineteenth-Century African-American Woman Intellectual." *Signs* 20.2 (Winter 1995): 336–56.

Baker-Fletcher, Karen. *A Singing Something: Womanist Reflections on Anna Julia Cooper.* New York: Crossroad, 1994.

Carby, Hazel. *Race Men*. Cambridge, MA: Harvard UP, 1998.

Cooper, Anna Julia. Closing Remarks. Crummell, *Shades and Lights*.

Crummell, Alexander. *The Shades and Lights of a Fifty Years' Ministry: Jubilate: 1844–1894*. Washington, DC: St. Luke's Church, 1894.

Foster, Frances Smith. *Written by Herself: Literary Production by African American Women, 1746–1892*. Bloomington: Indiana UP, 1993.

Fredrickson, George. *The Black Image in the White Mind: The Debate on Afro-American Character and Destiny, 1817–1914*. Middletown, CT: Wesleyan UP, 1971.

Gatewood, Willard B. *Aristocrats of Color: The Black Elite, 1880–1920*. Bloomington: Indiana UP, 1990.

Giddings, Paula. *When and Where I Enter: The Impact of Black Women on Race and Sex in America*. New York: Bantam Books, 1985.

Harley, Sharon. "Anna Julia Cooper: A Voice for Black Women." *The Afro-American Woman: Struggles and Images*. Ed. Sharon Harley and Rosalyn Terborg-Penn. Port Washington, NY: Kennikat, 1978. 87–96.

James, Joy. "The Profeminist Politics Of W. E. B. Du Bois with Respect to Anna Julia Cooper and Ida B. Wells-Barnett." *W. E. B. DuBois on Race and Culture: Philosophy, Politics, and Poetics*. Ed. Bernard W. Bell, Emily Grosholz, and James B. Stewart. New York: Routledge, 1996. 141–160.

Lerner, Gerda, ed. *Black Women in White America: A Documentary History*. New York: Vintage Books, 1973.

Lewis, David Levering. *W. E. B. DuBois: Biography of a Race, 1868–1919*. New York: Henry Holt, 1993.

Royster, Jacqueline Jones. *Traces of a Stream: Literacy and Social Change among African American Women*. Pittsburgh: U of Pittsburgh P, 2000.

Shockley, Ann Allen, ed. *Afro-American Women Writers, 1746–1933: An Anthology and Critical Guide*. New York: Meridian, 1989.

Sterling, Dorothy, ed. *We Are Your Sisters: Black Women in the Nineteenth Century*. New York: W. W. Norton, 1984.

Tate, Claudia. *Domestic Allegories of Political Desire: The Black Heroine's Text at the Turn of the Century*. New York: Oxford UP, 1992.

Wells, Ida B. *The Memphis Diary of Ida B. Wells*. Ed. Miriam DeCosta-Willis. Boston: Beacon Press, 1995.

White, Deborah Gray. *Too Heavy a Load: Black Women in Defense of Themselves, 1894–1994*. New York: W. W. Norton, 1999.

Part 2

Representing Women's Rhetorics: Genres, Strategies, Techniques

In this section our contributors focus on the textual and rhetorical tactics that women have used to represent themselves in various roles. Women and other marginalized groups have long struggled to "come to voice." Certain genres, strategies, and techniques have come to be associated with this struggle to be part of, to interact with, and even to transform the cultural contexts in which women find themselves. Among these tactics are using the genres of collaboration and conversation, representing the relation between rhetor and audience as egalitarian or as "sisterly" and noncompetitive, and privileging the professional sphere for women over the private one. Our contributors take up these familiar tropes of feminist rhetorics, sometimes examining historical traces and at other times considering contemporary manifestations. These feminist rhetorical tactics, like the rhetors' roles in the previous section, often function paradoxically, by disabling even as they are enabling women and other marginalized groups to express themselves and to construct subject positions. Or they may accomplish their rhetorical objectives mostly by distortion, dislocation, and circumlocution.

In the essay "Authorial Ethos, Collaborative Voice, and Rhetorical Theory by Women," Jane Donawerth traces how female rhetorical theorists between 1600 and 1900 disguised the fact that they were lone theorists by "collaborating" with the words of other writers to create paradoxical "single-authored conversations" rather than traditional public discourse. Women who wrote rhetorical theory during that extended period of time did so in genres quite different from those found in the treatises of male rhetorical traditions.

One reason for this difference stemmed from the difficulty women had in establishing an ethos with the authority to construct a theory and to persuade readers of its value. In those centuries, silence was commonly prescribed, echoing Sophocles, as a virtue for women. As a result, in theoretical writings on communication, women often employed a collaborative voice as a technique for establishing authority and for suppressing the obvious secret that a lone woman was daring to produce theory. Donawerth examines five such women's works: In mid-seventeenth-century England, in *Women's Speaking Justified,* Margaret Fell interwove scriptural language with scriptural quotation to argue that women have been and should be preachers—in other words, she collaborated with God. In seventeenth-century France, in *Conversations* and in *Conversations Nouvelles,* Madeleine de Scudéry revised the classical rhetorical dialogue into a vehicle for her theories of conversation and letter writing. In the late-nineteenth-century United States, in *Woman in the Pulpit,* Frances Willard wove together her own words, along with letters and essays from male and female preachers, to argue for the benefits of women preaching. In her brief preface to *Bits and Odds,* Hallie Quinn Brown discussed how the elocutionist collaborated with another author's words. And in her turn-of-the-century volume for the Women's Home Library, *Correct Writing and Speaking,* Mary Augusta Jordan slipped her theories on women's speech and letter writing in between huge quotations from learned progressive men. These women theorists grounded their theories in conversation rather than public discourse, building authority out of an imagined or real collaboration.

Karlyn Kohrs Campbell's essay, "Theory Emergent from Practice: The Rhetorical Theory of Frances Wright," examines the theoretical implications of the representations of self and others by nineteenth-century rhetor Frances Wright—rhetorical acts that worked both to her benefit and to her detriment. Many female rhetoricians in the past were unable to call themselves rhetoricians, let alone rhetorical theorists; however, by extrapolating from the traces of evidence that are extant, we can infer an implicit rhetorical theory in the work of some of these women. Campbell does exactly this in examining the coherent theory underlying the work Frances Wright produced in a variety of roles throughout her lifetime, including those of Utopian community founder, journalist, writer, and orator. She finds in these traces nothing less than the earliest humanist rhetorical theory, a nineteenth-century precursor to the twentieth century's consciousness-raising. Wright's theory was grounded in human equality and homogeneity and based on appeals to the audience's similar experiences. Accordingly, her ethos was not one of an authority but rather that of a fellow inquirer. Like so many other feminists who have assumed that the rhetoric of sisterhood would mask other differences, Wright's use of it was conflicted. Campbell considers the successes and failures of this theory put into practice and its effects on Wright's reputation.

Jane Gallop, in "Econstructing Sisterhood," critiques directly the problems of representing self and others through the "rhetoric of sisterhood." In this case she draws on her actual relationship with her own biological sister as it was captured in their email correspondence. The sisterhood metaphor, a decades-old cultural feminist fantasy of sameness among women, is shown, ironically, to divide Gallop and her sister. That is, if feminism purports to speak for all women, as if all women were the same—in other words, sisters—it excludes nonfeminist women, especially those who are not middle class, academic, or Western. Gallop concludes, paradoxically, that in order to construct a relationship, she must resist the fantasy of sisterhood, one of many handicapping, essentialist roles often expected of women.

In addition, Gallop illustrates an interesting facet of women's use of technology for new kinds of conversation and collaboration. However, it is important that her essay not be read as if that were her primary focus. If it were, a reader would be likely to look for references to recent work in gender and technology in it. These are not there—nor should they be. Rather this is a transcription of a lecture given at the 1999 Feminism(s) and Rhetoric(s) Conference in Minneapolis, Minnesota, on the occasion of her sister's birthday. With her sister actually present in the audience, Gallop reflected on the meaning of literal and figurative sisterhood, thus making us consider the barriers that we as academic women—and academic feminists—place between nonacademic women and ourselves. A contemporary rhetor, Gallop joins many historical rhetors who have experimented with new social relationships.

In "Exceptional Women, Expert Culture, and the Academy," Lois Cucullu rereads Virginia Woolf in order to consider the implications for women's rhetorical representations when, in imitation of Woolf, women privilege their professional roles over their private ones. Virginia Woolf, in her 1931 essay, "Professions for Women," promulgates the complex figure of the modernist writer, professional expert, and feminist intellectual who was subsequently taken up by second-wave feminists. Not only did Woolf's narrative encourage the dismantling of the private site of domestic authority, but it also furthered her desire to replace it with professional power- and status-carried terms that have since riddled the course of the women's movement. One in particular is the impasse of Woolf's feminist discourse over the issue of class. Critics have long recognized, and academic feminists have apologized for, Woolf's inability to hurdle class barriers, but on the assumption that the failure arose from cultural values she inherited. She knew better but could not do better—or so the story has gone. How different her position and that of second-wave feminists become once we understand that she actively erected class barriers as part of her professionalism, and that these very barriers, aesthetic ones among them, made possible her ascent as a feminist intellectual and modernist artist.

5

Authorial Ethos, Collaborative Voice, and Rhetorical Theory by Women

Jane Donawerth

Women who wrote rhetorical theory between 1600 and 1900 did so in forms quite different from the textbooks and treatises of the men's rhetorical tradition.[1] One reason for this difference is audience: men's theory instructed boys in school or college; women's theory instructed women reading at home, or addressed a mixed public audience and argued for women's education in some branch of rhetoric.

A second reason that women wrote theory in forms different from men's, however, is the difficulty women had—and still have—in establishing ethos with the authority to construct a theory and persuade readers of its value. European and American culture of the seventeenth to nineteenth centuries prescribed silence as a virtue for women and promoted a gender ideology that relegated women to a naturally inferior position.[2] As a result, in their theoretical writings on communication, women often employed collaborative voice to establish authority and to suppress the obvious secret that a lone woman was producing theory. This was especially true when the intended audience of the work was both men and women. By "collaborative voice" I mean not "group writing," as Lisa Ede and Andrea Lunsford define it in their study of collaboration (14–16), but rather something like "dialogic" rather than "hierarchical" collaboration as they describe it (133–36). I will return to this matter of definition in my conclusion. In this essay I examine works by four women who use collaborative voice: from seventeenth-century England, Margaret Fell; from seventeenth-century France, Madeleine de Scudéry; from nineteenth-century United States, Frances Willard; and from early-twentieth-century United States, Mary Augusta Jordan.[3]

Margaret Fell, presently known as "the mother of Quakerism," was an early convert of George Fox, and her house became the center for early Quaker meetings, correspondence, appeals to the king, rest and recreation for traveling preachers, and childcare for women preachers on the road (many of Fell's daughters were preachers). Fell wrote *Women's Speaking Justified* in prison in 1666 after being found guilty of holding church services in her home.[4] She interweaves scriptural language with scriptural quotation to argue that women have been and should be preachers—she collaborates with God.

We can see how this interweaving of biblical and authorial language works at the level of diction in the following passage:

> It was Mary Magdalene, and Joanna, and Mary the mother of James, and the other women that were with them, which told these things to the Apostles. *And their words seemed unto them as idle tales, and they believed them not.* Mark this, ye despisers of the weakness of women, and look upon yourselves to be so wise: but Christ Jesus doth not so, for he makes use of the weak: for when he met the women after he was risen, he said unto them, *All Hail,* and they came and held him by the feet, and worshipped him, then said Jesus unto them, *Be not afraid, go tell my brethren that they go into Gallilee, and there they shall see me* [Matthew 28:10, Mark 16:9]. And John saith, when Mary was weeping at the sepulchre, that *Jesus said unto her, Woman why weepest thou? what seekest thou? And when she supposed him to be the gardener, Jesus saith unto her, Mary; she turned herself, and saith unto him, Rabboni, which is to say master; Jesus saith unto her, Touch me not, for I am not yet ascended to my Father; but go to my brethren, and say unto them, I ascend unto my Father and your Father, and to my God, and your God* [John 20:16–17]. Mark this, you that despise and oppose the Message of the Lord God, that he sends by women; what had become of the Redemption of the whole body of mankind, if they had not believed the Message that the Lord Jesus sent by these women, of and concerning his Resurrection?[5]

Here Fell slyly points out that it is the women, the Marys who stayed with Jesus during the crucifixion while the men hid, who first preach the good news of Jesus' death for all.

In this passage Fell begins in her own words, and then inserts a scriptural quotation—"*And their words seemed to them as idle tales*"—to mark the men's misogynist assumption that women cannot be preachers.[6] She continues in her own words, but flavors them with biblical diction and allusion: the clause "Christ Jesus . . . makes use of the weak," for example, is an allusion to a scriptural passage from Paul's letters (1 Corinthians 1:27) about the reversal of low to high in Christian values. Fell ends her historical narrative in support of women's preaching by quoting Jesus' own words telling the women to carry the message (from Matthew 28:10, Mark 16:7, and John 20:15–17). Since the Word of God is irrefutable, her quotations buttress her own authority as speaker and become at the same time an extrinsic argument from testimony. She thus presents her very language as a summary of and collaboration with scripture.

In addition, Fell bases each of the major arguments in her pamphlet in favor of women's preaching on scriptural passages, a hermeneutic approach to argumentation common in sixteenth- and seventeenth-century Reformation Europe. Her overall argument is more a reinterpretation of scripture than a set of assumptions drawn out to conclusions (although it is also that). Fell begins by proposing, from scriptural examples, that God sees men and women as equal, citing the creation in Genesis 1:27–29, revising the story of Eve so that Eve and Adam are equal in blame and repentance, and referring to 1 Corinthians 1:27–28, where Paul proclaims that God chooses the weak to do his work. She then marshals instances in the Bible where the church is spoken of metaphorically as a woman, using them to argue that women are a God-ordained part of the church, citing an impressive array of passages from Isaiah, Jeremiah, the Psalms, the Song of Solomon, and Revelations. She also lists examples where Jesus speaks directly to women rather than through male intermediaries: the Samarian woman, Martha, Joanna, and the repentant prostitute usually assumed to be Mary Magdalene. Fell concludes, "Thus we see that Jesus owned the love and grace that appeared in women,"[7] using this recognition not only as support for her argument but also to build ethos.

In a long section Fell refutes the passages where Paul commands that women will not speak in church and that women will learn from their husbands (1 Corinthians 14 and 1 Timothy 2). To do this, Fell adopts a Protestant hermeneutic that requires scripture to be read in its historical context and according to the intent of its human speaker: Fell supposes that Paul means to exclude not *all* women, but only women not yet released from the law, who cannot yet trust in the inspiration of the Inner Light. It is these "indecent and unreverent women" who should be silent, she explains, not those women who "had union and fellowship with the Spirit of God."[8] Fell cites other passages from Paul where the Apostle welcomes or praises women: in quoting from 1 Corinthians 11:4–13, for example, Fell skips the verses that enjoin female subservience and cites only those verses that support her argument.

Fell demonizes the Catholic and Anglican Churches and their policy of excluding women from priesthood through interpreting the "Whore of Babylon" passages in Revelations as references to Catholics and nonreformed Anglicans (Revelations 17:6, for example). She returns to this refutative condemnation of priests in her postscript on the hypocrisy of blind priests who use women's words from the Bible as texts for their sermons, to get money, but then tell women that they may not preach. In a final passage, Fell lists almost every woman in the Bible who speaks—Aquilla and Priscilla, Deborah, Huldah, Sarah, Anna, Martha and Mary, Miriam, Esther, Judith, and even Mary, Jesus' mother—as preachers and prophets, inventing (Fell would see it as recovering) a Judeo-Christian history of women preachers. Fell can do this because the Quakers have redefined preaching more democratically, to include the testifying and witnessing on which they center their church services (rather than only formal public speaking). As Fell explains, again using scriptural words, and as she carries out in the collaborative form of her pamphlet, "your sons and daughters shall prophesy" (Acts 2:27 and Joel 2:28).

While Fell's collaboration with scripture in *Women's Speaking Justified* is hierarchical in the sense that she appeals to a superior authority, it is collaborative in the sense that she feels free to adapt and appropriate scriptural language, and to argue with the pronouncements of men in the Bible by citing their own words against them (especially Paul). In other of her pamphlets, she explains further the basis for her and other women's authority to preach. The biblical scripture is not itself the authority, but rather "the Word that is nigh, in the Heart, which is the Word of Faith which we preach" ("An Epistle to Convinced Friends" 95). And this Word is available to all who have true faith: "The word in *Davids* heart was a light unto him, and so it is unto all, whose heart is upright, who is guided by the light, which is the word, which is the Spirit" (*A Loving Salutation* 15). Thus Fell's hermeneutic justifies her adopting scriptural language to her own ends, for scriptural authority does not end with the printed text, but rather resides in the conscience of each believer.

A very secular version of collaboration appears in Madeleine de Scudéry's rhetorical works contemporary to Fell. Madeleine de Scudéry was born into an impoverished gentry family and made her own way (and that of her brother, Georges) through her education and writing after they were orphaned. Their conversational skills at Mme. de Rambouillet's salon, as well as their writings, gained Georges a diplomatic post and, later, Madeleine her own household and salon in Paris and a pension from the king.[9] In dialogue essays published in the 1680s in France (some adapted from dialogues taken from her romance novels published in the 1650s), Scudéry constructs a rhetoric for salon conversation that models the advice she gives, adapting the classical rhetorical dialogue as a vehicle for her own theories of domestic discourse—conversation and letter writing. She provides dialogues on conversation, speaking too much or too little, invention, and wit in her 1680 *Les Conversations sur Divers Sujets* and "The Manner of Writing Letters" in her 1684 *Conversations Nouvelles sur Divers Sujets.*[10]

Following Plato in the *Gorgias* and the *Phaedrus,* Cicero in *De Oratore,* and Augustine in *De Magistro,* Scudéry uses the dialogue to promote her rhetorical theory. In the essays in her first volume, she appropriates classical principles to establish standards for salon conversation. In "Of Conversation," for example, she adapts the conception of speech as civilizing, which Cicero had imported from the Sophists, and the sophistic idea that the goal of speech is pleasure (which she renames "*l'agréable*") to conversation. In another dialogue, "Of Speaking Too Much or Too Little, and How to Speak Well," Emile lists the major qualities of the ideal speaker as those possessed by Plotine, and the list Scudéry gives him runs through the Roman five divisions of oratory adapted to conversation: invention is spontaneous, arrangement is clear, style is "noble and natural," and memory and delivery, with "no hesitation," are at the service of invention. In these dialogues Scudéry further adapts Aristotle's twofold division of sophistries into those of words and those of matter to an analysis of mistakes in conversation, and offers advice on wit and the relation of art versus nature that she appropriates from Cicero and Quintilian. She is thus using a standard Renaissance technique for establishing authority by working within tradition, by alluding to the classics, and by recovering ancient knowledge for contemporary uses, the knowledge itself helping to establish the authority of the speaker.

Now let us look closely at one dialogue, "On Wit," to see how Scudéry performs collaborative ethos. This dialogue begins as a narrative, but we never learn who the "I" is, male or female, and so both male and female readers may identify with the speaker's point of view. In addition, the group holding the discussions is almost exactly gender balanced: the speaker is traveling with two gentleman cousins and two ladies; the family they visit is a Spanish count, his newly returned son, and the sea-captain friend who has just brought him home, but the count has invited several ladies from the area as local guests to help make his visitors feel welcome. The dialogue is addressed to "Madame," as if telling a travel story. So the dialogue frame, which encloses several conversations, is also set as a dialogue, but a dialogue in which the reader is free to take the positions of speaker and listener.

The dialogue pays detailed attention to the ceremonious luxury of its setting, sounding very much like the famous Versailles entertainments, although with far fewer guests. The guests are treated to a symphony during the carefully arranged themed dinner, cannons and trumpets when they toast the king, cedar-wood caskets perfuming the air, formal gardens, and an outdoor opera in an arbor.

The dialogue is staged as an elaborate collaboration, a conversation among the elegant guests, and falls roughly into three sections: a friendly debate between Clarice and Melinta about the topic of conversation, Clarice voting for an account of the son's travels and Melinta despising such stories; a discussion of the nature of wit; and an epideictic portrait of a judicious king. In the first debate most of the guests participate, choosing sides between Clarice and Melinta about the value or interest of travel stories, and the outcome is a negotiated compromise: Clarice will get her travel story only after Melinta gets a discussion of wit, and Melinta gets to choose the form—a portrait of a famous person, not simply a list of waterfalls and rivers.

The discussion on wit arises out of a digression from this debate, a guest asking the travelers whether or not wit is the same in all places and countries. The travelers (and of course the author, Scudéry) give a sophisticated, materialist answer: wit "varies according to the diversity of nations, of temperaments, and of customs. . . . For according to the temperament of a people and the customs of nations, wit is rude or tactful, nasty or agreeable; it is mocking among some people and among others a simple playfulness that makes society more pleasant." But even this answer, accommodating to all people, is turned over and examined: Clearchus refutes with the example that some individuals don't joke, but Melinta defends the universality of wit by analogy to reason—some people are stupid, but we still say that all humans have the faculty of reason. Clarice, a sore loser in the debate about travel stories, gets in a dig at Melinta, suggesting that she carries her teasing to the point of injustice at times, Melinta defends herself, and the rest of the group line up, not around liking or disliking Melinta, but around the nature of wit. Melinta proposes that wit must include "agreeable malice" and some agree, while Clarice and Euridamia suggest that there is no innocent teasing and that even "gallant teasing" is like "walking along a precipice—you may fall into the pit of rude insult."

At this point the group moves to sorting out a position of consensus by proposing and agreeing to the kinds of behaviors that do not belong in witty conversation: one should not mock friends, enemies, oneself (because immodest), inferiors or superiors, crimes, evil, or foreigners, and one must always pay attention to decorum (occasion and audience); one must avoid vulgarity, repetition, long stories, proverbs, and joking about everything; one should follow only the court as a model for wit; and one must never say terrible things about someone as if it is a joke. After reaching this negative consensus, the group appoints Euridamia to set up a list of rules for wit,[11] since by this point she has won over even Melinta to her side. Euridamia, however, refuses the role of judge and states the principle of consensus that the group has been working under all along: "I wish only to tell you my opinion and to submit it to your judgment." The group, led by Euridamia, agrees that wit is brief, original, not too cruel, "bold familiarity," and has a twist at the end; wit speaks the "language of well-bred people," avoids satire or cutting remarks, and a true wit never says anything to friends that amuses the speaker more than the person being made fun of. Antigene astutely adds the social purpose of wit: with wit one may tell the truth to people whom one cannot politely criticize.

The long praise of the king, although viewed as a model of elegant language during Scudéry's own time, is actually an example of wit that breaks some of the rules the group has agreed upon. It is a very long praise of the speaker's king but disguised as a character sketch of a famous long-dead Egyptian monarch; consequently, it is a joke at Clarice's expense, not the travel story she desired. The speaker signals that he is teasing Clarice with this story by warning the group, "Do not laugh at this," and by his exaggeration of the evidence for the story's authenticity. While the story is too long and too much a travel story to be counted as wit by the terms of the dialogue, it has a twist at the end, and it allows the speaker (and Scudéry herself) to tell a truth without offending: she praises the monarch—and so Louis XIV, her own king—for never allowing his ministers too much power, which is actually a warning against trusting too much in ministers. Finally, Clarice is as pleased by the trick, the shift to praise of her current monarch, as the speaker is himself, so he does not offend his friend.

So this dialogue is not only truly collaborative, representing a group coming to a consensus through debate and accommodation, but also multilayered in its collaboration: a conversation, framed by a conversation, and finally, a joke at the author's expense—Scudéry has written a long travel story as her example of wit, which is forbidden as dull in the dialogue. Scudéry moves to this self-mockery near the end, by suggesting that no proper courtier of her time would read the dialogues of Plato or Xenophon, and "if he should come upon a book in which the natural manner of living of well-bred people is painted, . . . he could hardly be made to open the volume . . . [after he found out] that it was printed by Barbin or Courbé." Scudéry thus concludes with a joke she and the reader share: Barbin and Courbé were the printers who published Scudéry. Scudéry's witty self-mockery establishes herself-as-author in ironic collaboration with the reader, both knowing what the characters in the dialogue do not.

Frances Willard, for a while Dean of Women at Northwestern University, was a nineteenth-century social reformer and suffragette, who helped organize and eventually headed the Women's Christian Temperance Union (WCTU). With other women in the WCTU, Willard helped to invent techniques of social protest and public demonstration that we still use, and promoted public speaking for women, training them in parliamentary procedure.[12] Willard published *Woman in the Pulpit* in 1888. Weaving together her own words with letters and essays from male and female preachers, she argues for women's right to preach. Whereas Fell had adopted collaboration with scripture to achieve authority, Willard drew on the republican authority of testimony by the best citizens, quoting long passages from twenty-one men and eleven women in defense of women preaching.

Willard introduces her topic through the words of men praising her defense. T. De Witt Talmage agrees with Willard's defense of women's preaching, because women's voice, he claims, will bring tenderness, pathos, and sympathy to religion. Joseph Cook, in a second letter, himself provides testimony from a woman, quoting a letter from a woman missionary whose teaching has gradually moved from women's meetings in her parlor to public speaking in church. He further argues that if the women who wrote *Uncle Tom's Cabin* and *Aurora Leigh* can preach so notably in print, there is no reason women should not preach orally in churches; that he does not name these writers (Harriet Beecher Stowe and Elizabeth Barrett Browning) increases the force of his argument, for he expects every reader to know these texts. He concludes with an analogy linking the nineteenth-century conception of women's domestic sphere to men's public roles: "Hand in hand, man and woman build the home; hand in hand they ought to build the state and the church" (Willard 14). Again, he expects his readers to collaborate with him in constructing his argument, for "Hand in hand" is an allusion to the end of Milton's *Paradise Lost*, thus also an interpretation of that poem and of Genesis to suggest divine approbation for equality between men and women. A third letter, by Joseph Parker, makes the standard essentialist argument, but with irony: men, Parker suggests, have the ability to make scripture difficult to understand, but women bring pathos and sympathy to its interpretation and dissemination. These prefatory letters, like the epideictic poems at the beginning of Renaissance books, or the blurbs from reviews on the front pages of our own culture's paperbacks, advertise the contents through approval of famous men. Willard shows herself, through this means, in conversation and collaboration with the famous divines of her day.

Willard also constructs her own argument in support of women's preaching. Chapter 1 of *Woman in the Pulpit* is a refutation of Paul's proscriptions against women speaking or teaching in church. Willard argues that the "rules" of Paul and of scripture in general are culture bound, demonstrating that current pastors follow only a selection of these rules: Protestants don't require celibacy of the clergy or unleavened bread at communion, for example. Thus, she concludes, scripture should *not* be taken literally, and she sets out a table that juxtaposes the strictures restricting women against words by Paul or Jesus to show that even these early Christians did not really require silence of women. Like Fell, Willard reinterprets biblical women who are prophets, judges, or who record their prayers as preachers, listing Miriam, Deborah, Hannah, Esther, Judith, and the Marys. Willard ends with a bold reversal: "The whole subjection theory [of women being subject to men's governance] grows out of the one-sided interpretation of the Bible by men" (37). Men and women need to collaborate to get the interpretation right.

In chapter 2 of *Woman in the Pulpit,* Willard sets up a positive argument for women's preaching: women demonstrate their faith as apostles in the scriptures, so there is historical precedent for women preaching; preaching is particularly appropriate to women, who by their natures appeal to moral sentiment; with proper training, women's voices are physically sufficient to be heard; motherhood fits women for a life of spiritual guidance of others; and God calls women as well as men to preach—women are already preaching as missionaries and in the WCTU. Here Willard steps back from the social constructionist argument she uses for scriptural interpretation, relying on an essentialist view of gendered spheres: "Men preach a creed; women will declare a life. . . . Men's preaching has left heads committed to a catechism, and left hearts hard as nether millstones. . . . [But] Religion is an affair of the heart" (47).

But the bulk of Willard's argument is founded on testimony from many supporters. Chapter 3 is a refutation of the argument that women cannot be preachers because their vocation must be "mother." While Willard frames the chapter with her own arguments, most of the chapter is lengthy quotation, first from an anonymous woman preacher and then from Senator Henry Blair. The woman argues that motherhood as a spiritual state prepares women to be preachers if we just relieve them of the irrelevant jobs of "cook, laundress, seamstress, and nurse-maid" (68); Senator Blair, in his book on temperance and the right to vote, suggests that motherhood prepares women to be good citizens and to vote in the best interest of their children. Chapters 4 and 5 offer testimony from male and female preachers (each in their own chapter). From the men we hear that one has been "converted" from his "bitterest prejudices" against women's preaching by his more enlightened reading of Saint Paul (73–74); that the Bible cannot be fully understood until "men and women work it out together" (76); that since men have successfully converted many women, we should allow women to convert the men (76); and that there exists insufficient evidence that God has *not* called women to preach to refuse them this right (82). From the women we hear that it is right for women to preach because "it is surely right for a messenger to give a message of truth" (96); that women are natural preachers because of their "sympathetic and intuitional nature, . . . [and their] high moral sense" (97); that raising well-cared-for children does not prevent women from being available and effective ministers (from twenty-five years' experience by a woman preacher) (98–99); and that women have the "reason," the "voice," the persuasive "eloquence," and the "religious sense" to give them an "advantage in winning souls" (133). Willard concludes with a debate between two men resulting from a shorter defense she had published in a journal.

Willard thus recapitulates her society's gendered spheres in the design of her book, allowing men and women to make different but equally well-reasoned arguments in support of women's preaching (and even one argument against it), demonstrating the consensus of a multivoiced community. She assumes an audience that is hostile to the practice of women's preaching. She constructs her argument in collaboration with her audience, both hostile and supportive, interweaving refutation and what Aristotle calls "inartistic proofs"—testimony from witnesses. She lets other voices speak along with her in order to be heard. Willard separates men and women into their own chapters—creating quite literally in her book the separate spheres of nineteenth-century Anglo-American social life. Yet she argues against this doctrine for preaching, demonstrating a tension between her commitment to social change, and an essentialist view of women's gender as naturally nurturant.

Mary Augusta Jordan was educated at Vassar College and was a professor of English at Smith College from 1884 to 1921. Influenced by ideals of progressive education, she stood against the turn-of-the century trend in favor of correctness.[13] In 1904 Jordan published *Correct Writing and Speaking* in the Woman's Home Library series, and her book seems to be based on her lectures from Smith College rhetoric courses.

Whereas the other theorists I have talked about adopted collaboration as a means to gain the authority to address a public audience, Jordan is ostensibly addressing an audience of women. Yet she inserts her theories on women's speech and letter writing in between lengthy quotations from learned progressive men. Jordan has imported this collaborative technique that previous women theorists used for mixed audiences for a different purpose—to address the issue of what type of education women should have. In the late nineteenth century, as women colleges were created, educators debated what should constitute college education for women—should women be taught men's learning, or should they be taught knowledge appropriate for women?[14] Jordan chooses to do both, by "collaborating" with men.

Jordan "collaborates" with men by including long quotations from men—men in their own voices—in her textbook. She is thus offering men's knowledge to women students, showing she is certain that women are capable of understanding such knowledge. But she is not so certain that this knowledge is "correct" or that it is appropriate to women students. We see these reservations in the dialogic ways she uses her male collaborators, and in the knowledge she adds in her own voice.

Jordan does use quotations from male experts to establish authority, quoting approvingly A. J. Ellis, Robert Louis Stevenson, and H. G. Wells.[15] But she criticizes the "great man" theory of the history of English language (14), and in most instances she modifies or even perverts the original intentions of the great man she quotes. Quoting John Walker's against Richard Sheridan's views of English pronunciation, then A. J. Ellis's against Sheridan's (34–35), she sets experts against each other so that she can reinforce her thesis—that there is no single "correct" English, since great men cannot agree on a standard. She quotes Matthew Arnold only to critique him: "The weakness of this description [of criticism] is the weakness, however, of Arnold's entire conception of the relation of human beings to culture . . . [for this] false distinction [between what is known and what is thought] opens the door to all sorts of intellectual tyranny" (74). And she makes fun of Sir Thomas More, quoting him not only for his argument in favor of the common reader's good sense but also for his nonstandardized English: "The most superficial examination of this fearless expression of opinion," mocks

Jordan, "makes it clear that the bold champion of the freedom of the reader allowed himself extensive liberty of grammar and construction" (23). Jordan introduces men's voices into her textbook in order to discuss the matters of language, rhetoric, and literary criticism with them, not simply as authority. She thus creates for herself a kind of dialogic ethos, depending partly on the authority of these male experts, but partly, also, on overturning this authority.

The knowledge Jordan adds in her own voice is the kind of rhetorical theory that women had been writing for the two hundred years before Jordan's textbook: advice on conversation and letter writing.[16] Jordan examines the requirements for conversation and presents it as a collaborative venture, where the speaker is more interested in furthering other speakers' goals of self-expression than her own (229–37). Jordan treats letters as the most frequent literary expression of the common person, and especially addresses the faults that her "girl" students might succumb too—fancy paper and colored ink. She is especially interested in letters as gifts, establishing a conversation between people, especially women, over long distances (60–64, 237–42). Finally, Jordan also adds, to the tradition of women's rhetoric, advice on public speaking for women—assuming that what most women are required to do is after-dinner speaking for social or moral causes. She is especially concerned that the public speaker should not impose ideas on her audience but instead should gather up the spiritual forces of the audience and express them (64–71). "The audience is not to be dominated, cajoled, or bullied," Jordan instructs: "It is to be interpreted, and made to know its own self in terms of something else than prejudice, or passion, or lazy self-indulgence. . . . The successful speaker of the present will use all his art to enable him to discern the signs of the spiritual forces coming into action in his presence. His aim will be to conserve them, to let as little as possible real energy go to waste" (69).

These women theorists center their theories on conversation rather than on public discourse. Like all Quakers, Fell believes that preaching should be replaced by testimony from the Inner Light by all Friends, a conversation with each other and God. Scudéry is a founder of the *précieuse* salon culture in France and offers a theory adapting classical dicta on effective persuasion and style to conversation. Willard advocates the public speech of preaching for women, but does so within the women's club movement and the WCTU, based on parlor entertainment and conversation circles. And Jordan includes advice on conversation in her textbook on "correct" speaking and writing. Basing their theories conceptually on conversation, these women also make a conversation in their writings, building authority out of imagined collaboration.

Having traced the construction of imagined collaboration in four instances, we can now return to Ede and Lunsford's definitions in their study of collaboration. None of the women examined in this essay seem to have published as authorial collaborators in the works we examined, although Frances Willard comes closest to it, with her collection of letters from other people. Margaret Fell frequently collaborated with other Quaker Friends in other pamphlets. But all of these women did use what I have been calling "collaborative voice." In their conclusion, Ede and Lunsford declare that their "study of collaborative writing has led [them], finally, to embrace the full complexity of collaborative acts and, as a result, to dissolve the traditional boundaries between collaborative writing and writing" (137). At the very least, they discern two modes of collaboration. "Hierarchical collaboration" is a mode of efficiently completing writing tasks in the professions, where each participant is assigned a portion; it is a highly structured form, where goals are specific and each person's task explicitly limited, under the leadership of a senior group member. This form of writing works because the goal is limited to pragmatic problem solution or information delivery (133). A second mode, however, "dialogic collaboration," involves more fluid roles and less structured process, according to Ede and Lunsford. In this mode all group members participate in defining goals, and one goal is often the production of knowledge (rather than the simpler delivery of information). This mode, Ede and Lunsford claim, can be "deeply subversive" (133) because it can better acknowledge the reality of "a plurality of voices" in any cultural production of knowledge (135).

This mode, "dialogic collaboration," is quite close to the "collaborative voice" employed by the women I have studied in this essay. They complicate the definition of collaboration yet further, however, because their collaboration is imagined and constructed rather than a result of multiple authors. Even in the case of Frances Willard, who includes whole letters, the structure is an imagined written dialogue of collected pieces rather than a hierarchical process of multiple authors writing to order—it is Willard's means of demonstrating the consensus of her community in favor of women's preaching. In addition, the arguments of all of these women then become layered: the words of others are embedded in their own arguments, creating an ethos based on self-in-relation-to-others rather than a self-sufficient authorial self. Such an ethos is not an essentialist reflection of women's gendered role, but is instead a carefully constructed rhetorical implement, depending on the ironic complexity resulting from the juxtaposition of diverse voices.

Notes

1. For more information on women rhetorical theorists, see Patricia Bizzell and Bruce Herzberg, *The Rhetorical Tradition;* Joy Ritchie and Kate Ronald, *Available Means;* and Jane Donawerth, *Rhetorical Theory by Women before 1900: An Anthology.*

2. On silence as a requirement of the ideal woman in Renaissance and nineteenth-century conduct books, see Suzanne W. Hull, *Chaste, Silent & Obedient, English Books for Women, 1475–1640;* and Nan Johnson, "Reigning in the Court of Silence: Women and Rhetorical Space in Postbellum America," and *Gender and Rhetorical Space in American Life, 1866–1910.*

3. Although not much work has been done on women rhetorical theorists, a great deal has now been accomplished on the history of women's rhetoric. See especially Karlyn Kohrs Campbell, ed., *Man Cannot Speak for Her;* Carole Levin and Patricia A. Sullivan, eds., *Political Rhetoric, Power, and Renaissance Women;* Andrea Lunsford, ed., *Reclaiming Rhetorica: Women in the Rhetorical Tradition;* Molly Wertheimer, ed., *Listening to Their Voices: Essays on the Rhetorical Activities of Historical Women;* Christine Mason Sutherland and Rebecca Sutcliffe, eds., *The Changing Tradition: Women in the History of Rhetoric;* Cheryl Glenn, *Rhetoric Retold: Regendering the Tradition from Antiquity through the Renaissance;* Catherine Hobbs, ed., *Nineteenth-Century Women Learn to Write;* Lucille M. Schultz, *The Young Composers: Composition's Beginnings in Nineteenth-Century Schools;* Shirley Logan, ed. *With Pen and Voice: A Critical Anthology of Nineteenth-Century African-American Women,* and Logan, *"We Are Coming": The Persuasive Discourse of Nineteenth-Century Black Women;* Carla Peterson, *"Doers of the Word": African-American Women Speakers and Writers in the North (1830–1880);* Jacqueline Jones Royster, *Traces of a Stream: Literacy and Social Change among African American Women;* Nan Johnson, "Reigning in the Court of Silence" and *Gender and Rhetorical Space in American Life, 1866–1910;* Carol Mattingly, *Well-Tempered Women;* Susan Kates, *Activist Rhetorics and American Higher Education, 1885–1937;* Bizzell and Herzberg, eds., 2nd ed. *The Rhetorical Tradition;* and Janet Carey Eldred and Peter Mortensen, *Imagining Rhetoric: Composing Women of the Early United States.*

4. On Fell's life, see Isabel Ross, and Bonnelyn Young Kunze. On Fell as a rhetorical theorist, see Donawerth, "The Politics of Renaissance Rhetorical Theory," 261–63, and Bizzell and Herzberg, 748–52.

5. The quotations from Fell are taken from my edition of Margaret Fell, *Women's Speaking Justified, Proved and Allowed of by the Scriptures . . .* (London, 1666), Folger Shakespeare Library F642 (copy 1), in my anthology, *Rhetorical Theory by*

Women before 1900; I modernize spelling and punctuation, but not grammar—in this passage there are very few changes.

6. See Luke 24:11. Fell follows the King James Version, the version that Fell and other Quakers generally used, but here and elsewhere she seems to be quoting from memory, for her quotations are slightly off—one preposition substituted for another, verb tenses changed, phrases transposed. See my essay "Margaret Fell's Reading and Writing Practices."

7. In Donawerth, *Rhetorical Theory,* 63.

8. Ibid., 65.

9. On de Scudéry's life, see Nicole Aronson. On de Scudéry as a rhetorical theorist, see Elizabeth Goldsmith, 41–76; Donawerth, "'As Becomes a Rational Woman to Speak'"; and Bizzell and Herzberg, 761–66, as well as the introduction to the March 2004 edition of Scudéry's rhetorical writings, translated by Donawerth and Strongson.

10. All quotations from Scudéry's work are the translations from *Letters, Orations, and Dialogues of Madeleine de Scudéry,* translated by Julie Strongson and me, from the University of Chicago Press in March 2004. For more on Scudéry's theory, see my essay in *Rhetorica.*

11. As Elizabeth Goldsmith observes, the group dynamic in de Scudéry's conversations moves from a negative survey of what other speakers do wrong to positive praise of one of themselves as a model for speaker; see ch. 2, pp. 41–75.

12. On Willard's life, see Ruth Bordin. On Willard's rhetoric, see Bonnie J. Dow; Richard W. Leeman; Carolyn DeSwarte Gifford; Carol Mattingly; and Martha Watson. On Willard as a rhetorical theorist, see Donawerth, "Poaching on Men's Philosophies of Rhetoric" and "Conduct Book Rhetoric by Women."

13. On Jordan's life, see Kathleen Perkins. On Jordan as a rhetorical theorist, see Donawerth, "Textbooks for New Audiences," and Susan Kates, "Subversive Feminism" and *Activist Rhetoric.*

14. On issues in women's higher education during Jordan's tenure at Vassar, see Solomon, esp. ch. 6, pp. 78–93.

15. Jordan quotes A. J. Ellis, for example, 54–56; H. G. Wells, 113–18; and Robert Louis Stevenson, 91–97.

16. See my essay on nineteenth-century conduct book rhetoric by women.

Works Cited

Aronson, Nicole. *Mademoiselle de Scudéry.* Trans. Stuart R. Aronson. Boston: Twayne, 1978.

Bizzell, Patricia, and Bruce Herzberg, eds. *The Rhetorical Tradition: Readings from Classical Times to the Present.* 2nd ed. Boston: Bedford/St. Martin's, 2001.

Bordin, Ruth. *Frances Willard: A Biography.* Chapel Hill: U of North Carolina P, 1986.

Campbell, Karlyn Kohrs, ed. *Man Cannot Speak for Her.* 2 vols. Contributions in Women's Studies #101. New York: Greenwood Press, 1989.

Donawerth, Jane. "'As Becomes a Rational Woman to Speak': Madeleine de Scudéry's Rhetoric of Conversation." Wertheimer 305–19.

———. "Conversation and the Boundaries of Public Discourse in Rhetorical Theory by Renaissance Women." *Rhetorica* 16.2 (Spring 1998): 181–99.

———. "Nineteenth-Century United States Conduct Book Rhetoric by Women." *Rhetoric Review* 21.1 (2002): 5–21.

———. "Poaching on Men's Philosophies of Rhetoric: Eighteenth- and Nineteenth-Century Rhetorical Theory by Women." *Philosophy and Rhetoric* 33.3 (2000): 155–62.

———. "The Politics of Renaissance Rhetorical Theory by Women." Levin and Sullivan 256–72.

———. *Rhetorical Theory by Women before 1900: An Anthology.* Lanham, MD: Rowman and Littlefield, 2002.

———. "Textbooks for New Audiences: Women's Revisions of Rhetorical Theory at the Turn of the Century." Wertheimer 337–56.

Dow, Bonnie J. "The 'Womanhood' Rationale in the Woman Suffrage Rhetoric of Frances E. Willard." *Southern Communication Journal* 56.4 (Summer 1991): 298–307.

Ede, Lisa, and Andrea Lunsford. *Singular Texts/Plural Authors: Perspectives on Collaborative Writing.* Carbondale: Southern Illinois UP, 1990.

Fell, Margaret. "An Epistle to Convinced Friends" (1656). *A Brief Collection of Remarkable Passages and Occurrences . . . With Sundry of Her Epistles.* London, 1710. 95–97.

———. *A Loving Salutation to the Seed of Abraham among the Jewes.* London, 1656.

———. "Women's Speaking Justified, Proved and Allowed of by the Scriptures (1600)." Donawerth, *Rhetorical Theory* 59–72.

Hobbs, Catherine, ed. *Nineteenth-Century Women Learn to Write.* Charlottesville: UP of Virginia, 1995.

Gifford, Carolyn DeSwarte. "Frances Willard and the Woman's Christian Temperance Union's Conversion to Woman Suffrage." *One Woman, One Vote: Rediscovering the Woman Suffrage Movement.* Ed. Marjorie Spruill Wheeler. Troutdale, OR: NewSage Press, 1995. 117–33.

Glenn, Cheryl. *Rhetoric Retold: Regendering the Tradition from Antiquity through the Renaissance.* Carbondale: Southern Illinois UP, 1997.

Goldsmith, Elizabeth C. *"Exclusive Conversations": The Art of Interaction in Seventeenth-Century France.* Philadelphia: U of Pennsylvania P, 1988.

Hull, Suzanne W. *Chaste, Silent & Obedient: English Books for Women, 1475–1640.* San Marino, CA: Huntington Library, 1982.

Johnson, Nan. "Reigning in the Court of Silence: Women and Rhetorical Space in Postbellum America." *Philosophy and Rhetoric* 33.3 (2000): 221–43.

———. *Gender and Rhetorical Space in American Life, 1866–1910.* Carbondale: Southern Illinois UP, 2002.

Jordan, Mary Augusta. *Correct Writing and Speaking.* The Woman's Home Library. New York: A. S. Barnes, 1904.

Kates, Susan. *Activist Rhetorics and American Higher Education, 1885–1937.* Carbondale: Southern Illinois UP, 2001. 27–52.

———. "Subversive Feminism: The Politics of Correctness in Mary Augusta Jordan's *Correct Writing and Speaking* (1904)." *College Composition and Communication* 48.4 (December 1997): 501–17.

Kunze, Bonnelyn Young. *Margaret Fell and the Rise of Quakerism.* Stanford, CA: Stanford UP, 1994.

Leeman, Richard W., ed. *"Do Everything Reform": The Oratory of Frances E. Willard.* New York: Greenwood, 1992.

Levin, Carole, and Patricia A. Sullivan, eds. *Political Rhetoric, Power, and Renaissance Women.* Albany: SUNY Press, 1995.

Logan, Shirley. *"We Are Coming": The Persuasive Discourse of Nineteenth-Century Black Women.* Carbondale: Southern Illinois UP, 1999.

———, ed. *With Pen and Voice: A Critical Anthology of Nineteenth-Century African-American Women.* Carbondale: Southern Illinois UP, 1995.

Lunsford, Andrea, ed. *Reclaiming Rhetorica: Women in the Rhetorical Tradition.* Pittsburgh: U of Pittsburgh P, 1995.

Mattingly, Carol. *Well-Tempered Women: Nineteenth-Century Temperance Rhetoric.* Carbondale: Southern Illinois UP, 1998.

Perkins, Kathleen. "Mary Augusta Jordan." *American National Biography.* Ed. John A. Garraty and Mark C. Carnes. New York: Oxford UP, 1999. Vol. 12: 274–75.

Peterson, Carla. *"Doers of the Word": African-American Women Speakers and Writers in the North (1830–1880).* New York: Oxford UP, 1995.

Ritchie, Joy, and Kate Ronald, eds. *Available Means: An Anthology of Women's Rhetoric(s).* Pittsburgh: U of Pittsburgh P, 2001.

Ross, Isabel. *Margaret Fell: Mother of Quakerism.* London: Longmans, Green, 1949.

Royster, Jacqueline Jones. *Traces of a Stream: Literacy and Social Change among African American Women.* Pittsburgh: U of Pittsburgh P, 2000.

Schultz, Lucille M. *The Young Composers: Composition's Beginnings in Nineteenth-Century Schools.* Carbondale: Southern Illinois UP, 1999.

Scudéry, Madeleine de. *Les Conversations sur Divers Sujets.* Amersterdam, 1686. Folger #171523. Volume I.

———. *Conversations Nouvelles sur Divers Sujets, Dedie'es Au Roy.* La Haye, 1685. Folger #171523. Tome II.

———. "On Conversation," "Speaking Too Much or Too Little, and How to Speak Well," and "On the Manner of Writing Letters." *Letters, Orations, and Dialogues of Madeleine de Scudéry.* Trans. Jane Donawerth and Julie Strongson. Chicago: U of Chicago P, 2004.

Solomon, Barbara Miller. *In the Company of Educated Women: A History of Women and Higher Education in America.* New Haven, CT: Yale UP, 1985.

Sutherland, Christine Mason, and Rebecca Sutcliffe, eds. *The Changing Tradition: Women in the History of Rhetoric.* Calgary: U of Calgary P, 1999.

Watson, Martha. *Lives of their Own: Rhetorical Dimensions in Autobiographies of Women Activists.* Columbia: U of South Carolina P, 1999.

Wertheimer, Molly Meijer, ed. *Listening to Their Voices: Essays on the Rhetorical Activities of Historical Women.* Columbia: U of South Carolina P, 1997.

Willard, Frances E. *Woman in the Pulpit.* Boston: D. Lothrop, 1888.

6

Theory Emergent from Practice

The Rhetorical Theory of Frances Wright

Karlyn Kohrs Campbell

Feminist scholarship in rhetoric has several goals. One important but difficult aim is to identify the rhetorical theories that informed the practices of women activists in the past. Another is to identify the distinctive characteristics of early women's rhetorical practices, including the strategies they preferred and the representations of themselves as rhetors and of others as audiences that emerge out of these practices. In what follows I attempt to describe a template that might be used to identify implicit rhetorical theory, which I illustrate by applying it to the discourse of Frances Wright.

Some noteworthy efforts have been made to identify women's rhetorical theory, in particular, Krista Ratcliffe's *Anglo-American Feminist Challenges to the Rhetorical Traditions,* which attempts to extract rhetorical theories from the works of Virginia Woolf, Mary Daly, and Adrienne Rich.[1] Ratcliffe's book is an excellent introduction to this area, but her use of the five canons (invention, disposition, style, delivery, memory) underscores the need for an approach better adapted to the discourse of women. This essay builds on my earlier scholarship, which attempted to create a kind of template for extracting rhetorical theories from the works of thinkers who had not written anything that they understood to be a theory of rhetoric.[2] That template had the form of a three-legged stool, a nice, womanly metaphor, composed of an ontology or a definition of humans that explains how and why we are open to and capable of influence; an epistemology or a conception of the nature, sources, and limits of human knowledge; and an axiology or conception of the sources and dynamics of human values, including how they are validated and challenged.

Ontological assumptions often are part of a theorist's definition of rhetoric. Perhaps the most obvious example is Francis Bacon's definition of rhetoric as the "application of reason to imagination for the better moving of the will," which reflects the faculty psychology for which is he well known.[3] Aristotle's analysis of the conditions under which emotions are aroused and his views of the proclivities of those of different ages, classes, and socioeconomic status are additional examples.[4] An epistemology determines what constitutes expertise and how differing views of what is "true" can be resolved. Nietzsche's view of truths as social constructions, "illusions that we have forgotten are illusions,"[5] for example, echoes the assumptions of such ancient Sophists as Gorgias and Protagoras. Those who have authored what are recognized as rhetorical theories tend to hold either that there is some absolute truth (e.g., Augustine's view of truth as residing in Scripture and known through faith and by grace as a result of a hermeneutic process[6]); or that truth is socially constructed (the Nietzschean view); or, like Aristotle or Francis Bacon, they divide the realm of knowledge into areas in which absolute truths can be known and areas in which such truths are impossible or are socially constructed. Finally, an axiology or system of values provides warrants or premises for arguments or the assumptions underlying dominant narratives. Aristotle refers to such shared beliefs or values as *endoxa;* Kenneth Burke refers to the shared experiences that constitute the consubstantiality that permits identification to be evoked symbolically;[7] cultural theorist Stuart Hall refers to shared conceptual maps that constitute a culture and permit the communication of meaning.[8]

This template is particularly significant because it enables critics to extract the elements of a rhetorical theory from the practices of those who never discuss rhetoric directly or make explicit comments about persuasion. Moreover, the template allows a critic to scrutinize the practices of writers and speakers in order to infer the theory underlying their actions, particularly as evidence of consistent behavior emerges. This work is particularly important in the case of women who were among the first to enter the public sphere. Because their rhetoric often did not fit the categories of or assumptions underlying traditional theory, it may be deemed unworthy of attention or study or be denigrated as atheoretical.

Here I hope to illustrate the way that theory can be extracted from practice by looking at the rhetoric of Frances Wright, the first woman to lecture on social and political issues all across what was then the United States; Robert Connors refers to her as the first female civic orator.[9] Briefly, Wright was born in Scotland in 1795; she first visited the United States in 1819; she returned in 1824, became a citizen, and made this country the center of her activities until 1830. Her life included three key rhetorical efforts: her defense of Nashoba,[10] her editorship of the *Free Enquirer*, and her career as a lecturer.[11]

Nashoba

In 1825 Wright bought a tract of land in Tennessee and ten slaves and established Nashoba, a socialist community designed to educate former slaves so they and their children could become free and productive citizens. In 1827 an article was published in the *Genius of Universal Emancipation*, edited by Benjamin Lundy, revealing that free love principles governed relations between the sexes, including relations between those of African and non-African descent, and Wright was attacked for sanctioning "the formation of illicit sexual connexions [*sic*], without the obligations of marriage."[12] She responded in "Explanatory Notes," which appeared in installments in the *New-Harmony Gazette*.[13] Biographer Celia Morris calls this document "the most powerful . . . and the most revealing" statement she ever made,[14] but instead of allaying controversy, it fueled intense hostility that would affect everything she attempted thereafter.[15]

Initially, Wright explained that Nashoba was an experimental attempt to combine theory with practice. In the second installment of "Explanatory Notes," she detailed the conditions of membership, which were consistent with the principles of liberty and equality; specifically, "The marriage law existing without the pale of the institution, is of no force within that pale. No woman can forfeit her individual rights or independent existence, and no man assert over her any rights or power whatsoever, beyond what he may exercise over her free and voluntary affections" (132–33).

Wright grounded these comments in a view of human nature in which human passions were central:

> Prejudice and fear are weak barriers against passions, which, inherent in our nature . . . are maddened into violence by pernicious example and pernicious restraint, varied with as pernicious indulgence. . . . Let

> us not teach that virtue consists in the crucifying of the affections and appetites, but in their judicious government. Let us not attach ideas of purity to monastic chastity, impossible to man or woman without consequences fraught with evil. . . . Let us teach the young mind to reason, and the young heart to feel, and instead of shrouding our bodies, wants, and desires, senses, affections and faculties in mystery, let us court enquiry, and show that acquaintance with our own nature alone guides us to judicious practice, and that in the consequence of human actions, exists the only true test of their virtue or vice. (132)

Finally, she turned to "the topic most offensive to the American public," slavery and its attendant attitudes. She claimed that those familiar with U.S. slavery would probably agree with her that "the emancipation of the colored population cannot be *progressive thro' the laws.* It must and can only be *progressive through the feelings;* and through that medium be finally complete and entire, involving at once political equality and the amalgamation of the races" (133). Her belief in the centrality of the passions in human life is reflected here, a view linking prejudice to intense personal feelings; accordingly, such attitudes, she believed, could be changed only through altered circumstances and experiences, particularly conditions in which children of varying ethnic backgrounds would be reared and educated together.

In support of her claims, Wright offered examples of the behavior of white Americans, which showed that there was "no natural antipathy" between whites and nonwhites—for example, the white Louisianan who makes the "graceful quadroon his mistress" (133). If such acts were contrary to nature, they could not happen; thus she concluded, "the only question is whether it shall take place in good taste and good feeling,..or whether it shall proceed, as it now does, viciously and degradingly, mingling hatred and fear with the ties of blood." She ended the second installment by enunciating clearly the goal of the experiment, "to educate his [the man of color's] children with white children, and thus approaching their minds, tastes and occupations, to leave the affections of future generations to the dictates of free choice."[16]

"Explanatory Notes" was an astonishing document. In a period and in a nation deeply influenced by Enlightenment rationalism, Wright asserted the primacy of the passions in human affairs, and she defined virtue, not as suppression of desire, but as free choice based on an evaluation of consequences. She envisioned racial integration in all aspects of life as the only possible solution to the problems of slavery and the attitudes it engendered. Consistent with her view of virtue as practice, she proposed integrated, equal education for all—white and black, male and female—and expected that the affections and mutual interests developed in that process would lead naturally to the sexual and ethnic blending of all who formed this nation.

Reaction was swift and sharp. Former President James Madison called her views on amalgamation, as well as her notions on religion and marriage, "universally obnoxious"; Benjamin Lundy, the abolitionist editor who had revealed the principles underlying the experiment, wrote that the practices at Nashoba were "averse to the nature and general opinions of mankind."[17] In June of 1828 Wright left Nashoba and traveled to New Harmony, Indiana, where she joined Robert Dale Owen as coeditor of the *New-Harmony Gazette,* later the *Free Enquirer,* beginning a new career as a journalist and, shortly thereafter, as an orator and lecturer.

The New-Harmony Gazette/The Free Enquirer

In August of 1828 Wright and Robert Dale Owen issued a prospectus for the *New-Harmony Gazette,* stating that their goal was "to promote the cause of human improvement" and pledging to conduct themselves with courtesy, moderation, and good taste, and, of particular importance, to publish any letters written in the same spirit. Unlike other newspapers of that period, which were financed by political blocs and edited by those they hired, the *Free Enquirer* encouraged and facilitated open public deliberation. In its pages, readers encountered an array of voices offering views on virtually every controversial public issue. Of special rhetorical interest is how these editorial policies empowered readers. In analyzing its content, Christine Oravec writes: "The overall effect is an intertextual conversation in which speakers, critics, and audiences exchange positions, at times criticizing, at times becoming the object of criticism." By including "multiple critical voices" and by "providing a forum for the audience's response," Oravec comments, "Wright violated most of the social and critical standards that were established, or rapidly were being established, in her day."[18] The journal is remarkable for its willingness to print opposing views, including highly critical reactions to Wright's lectures. Admittedly, the voices that emerged were male; the voices of female readers would be heard some years later in the *Una,* the *Lily,* and other women's rights publications.[19] Just as Nashoba put into practice her beliefs about what was needed to effect social change and to erase the ravages of slavery, these editorial policies enacted the principles of free inquiry that Wright would espouse and explain in her lectures.

Orator and Lecturer

Wright first spoke on July 4, 1828, at New Harmony, Indiana, an experience that enabled her to recognize her skills as a speaker and performer who could hold and win an audience. She now set out to provide audiences throughout the nation with the kind of instruction she believed they desperately needed. She next spoke at the Cincinnati courthouse, delivering the first in a series of three lectures on successive Sundays.[20] Because of the large size of the audiences, each lecture was repeated in a local theater. The English writer Frances Trollope witnessed these lectures and wrote:

> That a lady of fortune, of family, and education,..should present herself to the people in this capacity would naturally excite surprise anywhere . . . but in America, where women are guarded by a sevenfold shield of habitual insignificance, it has caused an effect that can scarcely be described. . . . I shared the surprise but not the wonder; I knew her extraordinary gift of eloquence, her almost unequalled command of words, and the wonderful power of her rich and thrilling voice . . . [but] all my expectations fell far short of the splendour, the brilliance, the overwhelming eloquence of this extraordinary orator. . . . Her tall and majestic figure, the deep and almost solemn expression of her eyes, the simple contour of her finely formed head, unadorned, excepting by its own natural ringlets; her garment of plain white muslin, which hung around her in folds that recalled the drapery of a Grecian statue, all contributed to produce an effect, unlike any thing I had ever seen before, or expect to see again.[21]

Trollope mentions Wright's height, which was close to six feet, her short hair, and her exceptional clothing; in fact, she wore the costume of the New Harmony community, which was made of muslin and "consisted of bloomers, with a dress or jacket over them that came to the knees."[22] In an era when women's average height was below the current average of five feet, four inches, when women typically wore dresses of silk and taffeta shaped by tight-laced corsets with huge skirts billowing over crinolines and brushing the floor, and when cutting one's hair was daring, her appearance must have been as shocking as her views.

Trollope's admiring comments were echoed by others. Henry Rogers, who later helped to found the Massachusetts Institute of Technology, attended all five of her lectures in Baltimore. He was "wonderstruck" at her eloquence: "A prodigy in learning, in intellect and courage, she awes into deference the most refractory bigots." Of the series, he wrote, "there were throughout such clearness and reach of thought, sublimity of diction, and often such powerful philippics against the clergy, that every mind seemed spell-bound throughout the term of her lectures."[23] Wright's lectures were clearly organized, philosophical disquisitions that reinforced none of the conventional views of women. They espoused highly controversial positions, but these were developed clearly and supported with explanation, argument, and evidence. Each lecture developed concepts that became the premises underlying the arguments in those that followed. The first discussed the nature of true knowledge; the second, free inquiry as a means to knowledge; the third, the divisions and essential parts of knowledge; and the next three concerned religion, morals, and opinions.[24] Her overall argument was that true knowledge has nothing to do with the supernatural or with faith but comes only through sensory experience; by the end of the series, that claim logically led to an outright attack on the churches as the most formidable enemy of human progress.

Wright was assailed in part because of her successes in attracting substantial audiences. One historian summed up her appeal as follows:

> Franny Wright's lectures generally filled the largest theatre in town. In New York, her popularity kept the Park Theatre open in February, 1829, after all others had closed for lack of trade. . . . The following August, in Boston, the Federal Theatre was "filled in every part" for her address, which means that some twelve hundred persons were exposed to her influence directly. Her farewell oration, delivered in New York in June, 1830, drew "probably three thousand persons" to the Bowery Theatre.[25]

When she repeated the Cincinnati lectures in New York, "curious crowds flock[ed] to hear her—'thousands,' as Robert Dale [Owen] remembered, 'sometimes going away unable to find even standing room.'"[26]

Wright's audiences grew as she moved east from Cincinnati, and those who came were not just the curious, the radicals, and the freethinkers. They included a substantial group of Quakers and respectable but serious progressive women, the foremothers of the fight for woman's rights.[27] Such key figures as Elizabeth Cady Stanton kept Wright's works, along with those of Thomas Paine, on her library table; Susan B. Anthony owned her *Biography, Notes, and Political Letters;* and Paulina Wright Davis delivered an encomium to her at the twentieth anniversary of the National Woman Suffrage Association.[28] In her first lecture, as repeated in New York City, Wright said:

"It is with delight that I have distinguished, at each successive meeting, the increasing ranks of my own sex. Were the vital principle of human equality universally acknowledged, it would be to my fellow beings without regard to nation, class, sect, or sex, that I should delight to address myself. But until equality prevail in condition, opportunity, and instruction, it is every where to the least favoured in these advantages, that I most especially and anxiously incline" (20).

When Frances Trollope heard Wright in Philadelphia in 1829, she reported seeing more women in the audience than she had ever seen in a U.S. theater, and she described the event in some detail: "Miss Wright came on stage surrounded by a body guard of Quaker ladies, in the full costume of their sect. She was, as she always is, startling in her theories, but powerfully eloquent, and, on the whole, was much applauded."[29] Over the next year and a half, she spoke at venues from Boston to New Orleans. According to the *Free Enquirer,* her last speech in New York on June 19, 1830, was crowded with three thousand people, half of them women. Boston's influential Reverend Lyman Beecher wrote that regrettably she won over educated, refined women, "females of respectable standing in society," and, worst of all, women who had been friends to his own children.[30]

Substance and style meshed in Wright's lectures as she attempted to enact, within the constraints of the lecture format, the educational principles that she advocated as the solution to the problems of social inequity, including slavery. The principles that informed her rhetorical choices and the style of her public discourse as well as her commitment to education as the primary instrument of social change were those of Swiss educator Johann Heinrich Pestalozzi (1746–1827), who in 1805 at Yverdon, Switzerland, founded a boarding school with students from every country in Europe. Educators came to Yverdon to study "the method" and carried Pestalozzi's ideas throughout Europe and the United States, establishing scores of Pestalozzian schools. Among those who visited Yverdon was Robert Owen, who adopted Pestalozzi's methods for the education of workers and their children at New Lanark in England. The Pestalozzi method was also adopted generally in 1861 by the Oswego Normal School in New York and became the guiding principle in some of the foremost U.S. teacher-training institutions.[31]

According to Pestalozzi, "the beginning of all knowledge is *observation;* the last point to be attained, a clear notion,"[32] the stance of a radical empiricist. In emphasizing the senses and sensations as the primary sources of knowledge, empiricism is an epistemic position singularly suited to Wright's views that feelings or passions are integral parts of knowledge and key elements in the formation of attitudes. Information derived from our senses—from taste, touch, sight, sound, and smell—is intimately personal, suffused with the vivid connotations of lived experience. Understood in that way, an empirical approach to knowledge, perhaps more than any other, integrates the conative and the conceptual. Accordingly, Wright's understanding of the bases of prejudice and the remedies needed to eliminate racism described in "Explanatory Notes" were at one with the epistemology that she detailed in her lectures. That epistemology also was the basis for her attack on religion as a form of superstition based on opinions that lacked foundation in experience.

Wright referred to Pestalozzi and his method in her lectures (49, 58); however, she was an empiricist of long standing. Perhaps the first declared empiricist was Epicurus,[33] whose ideas were the subject of Wright's Platonic-style dialogue *A Few Days in Athens,* penned initially in Glasgow and later published serially in the *New-Harmony Gazette.*[34] In one sense Wright's lectures are examples of rational persuasion, because each is structured to unfold systematically, and each builds on and assumes what has been set forth in those preceding. However, characterizing them in that way can lead to the mistaken assumption that the lectures develop deductively from premises asserted authoritatively by a speaker who assumes the role of expert. On the contrary, Wright's lectures develop inductively as the speaker engages in a simulated dialogue with members of the audience, facilitated by questions, with self-references that identify the speaker's positions, feelings, and the limits of her authority.

Wright began by claiming that "*all real knowledge is derived from positive sensations*" (10). In the opening lecture in New York City, her pedagogical intentions were clear: "I have consented to redeliver my elementary course on the nature of all knowledge, physical and moral" (3). In a preview she said: "My object will be simply to take with you a survey of the field of human inquiry; to ascertain its nature, its extent, its boundaries, its limits; to discover, in the first place, what there is for us to know; secondly, the means we possess for acquiring such knowledge as is of possible attainment, and thirdly, having satisfied ourselves as to what can be known, and as to what we know, to seek in our knowledge the test of our opinions" (5). Wright addressed her problems of credibility as a woman speaking in two ways. She described her motives, saying that "stimulated in my early youth, by I know not what of pitying sympathy with human suffering, and by I know not what persuasion, that our race was not of necessity born to ignorance, and its companion, vice, but that it possessed faculties and qualities which pointed to virtue and enjoyment; . . . I applied myself to the discovery of the causes of the one, and of the means for effecting the other" (15). She also attacked the credibility of those paid by the public who, she said, "dare not speak that which, by endangering their popularity, would endanger their fortunes. They have to discover not what is true, but what is palatable" (16). She used the failure of public officials to condemn slavery as an example to demonstrate that paid public servants dare not espouse controversial positions. Accordingly, her independence became an asset.

Wright's tone was direct and conversational; she treated the audience as peers; she denied that she was an authority but presented herself as a fellow inquirer. She asked many questions to induce audience participation in the development of the ideas, and she stated her purposes and conclusions clearly.[35] Although they developed inductively, each lecture was carefully structured so that each conclusion became a premise for the argument that succeeded. Presumably, she gained and held attention through structural clarity and simple language that included familiar analogies, pertinent and homely examples, and personal material. She tried to convince her listeners that they had as much access to knowledge as anyone, and by implication, she empowered them to challenge "pedants" and "hired public servants."

Because the second lecture concerned equality and liberty, Wright devoted more time to the rights of women. She made a strong plea for equal education for women, based on analogies with powerful appeal for Americans: "There is a vulgar persuasion, that the ignorance of women, by favouring subordination, ensures their utility. Tis the same argument employed by the ruling few against the subject many in aristocracies; by the rich against the poor in democracies; by the learned professions against the people in all countries. And let us observe, that if good in one case, it should be good in all" (32). Wright was sometimes confrontational because she defended unpopular and controversial positions, but lecture three illustrates her efforts at audience adaptation. Before she began its central argument, she said: "I must pause a moment to conciliate the feelings of my audience: I know the influence exercised by religious teachers, and I know the sway yielded to them" (42). She entreated the audience's "patience" and "gentle hearing," saying: "I am not going to question your opinions. I am not going to meddle with your belief. I am not going to dictate to you mine. All that I say is, examine, inquire" (45). She described her role as that of "a scholar, not a teacher," and her attitude toward the subject: "Anxiously, therefore, would I temper my words to the timid, and, if possible, the truths themselves, which we are met to search out and investigate" (54).[36]

Near the end of the lecture, she offered this confession of faith:

> [A]ll my studies, reading, reflection, and observation, have obtained for me no knowledge beyond the sphere of our planet, our earthly interests, and our earthly duties. . . . Whenever you shall come to the same conclusion, you will probably think the many spacious edifices which rear their heads in your city, are somewhat misapplied. . . . you will then doubtless perceive that they who wish to muse, or pray, had better do it after the manner designated by the good Jesus, namely, by entering their closet and shutting the door [Matt. 6:6]; and farther perceive, that the true Bible is the book of nature, the wisest teacher he who most plainly expounds it, the best priest our own conscience, and the most orthodox church a hall of science. (67–68)

The obvious question now was, if religion is not their source, what is the basis for morals?

Lecture six addressed the formation of opinions; Wright claimed that "Persecution for opinion is the master vice of society" (85), and as examples, she referred to religious persecutions and religious wars through history.

The final lecture concerned "existing evils and their remedy" (101–16). In this case Wright spoke in a different persona, as a foreigner "unblinded by local prejudices or national predelictions; a friend to humanity" (104). In light of U.S. problems, she asked: "What, then, is wanted here?" She answered: "What Sparta had—*a national education.* And what Sparta, in many respects, had not—*a rational education*" (106). She proposed national boarding schools funded by taxes for all children, not just the children of the poor, with limited visits from parents, who would be prohibited from interfering with their children's education. This lecture carried the views foreshadowed in defense of Nashoba to their logical conclusion with proposals for a system of education that may have been realized only in some of the kibbutzim of the modern state of Israel. As one might imagine, this immodest proposal was rejected out of hand.

Wright's ideas for social change were particularly disturbing to powerful interests, because they were addressed to the lower classes. "An Address to Young Mechanics" (198–205) or ordinary workers, delivered in the Hall of Science in New York, on June 13, 1830, began: "In addressing myself this evening to the young mechanics of our city, I would not be understood as considering their interests distinct from those of other classes in the community. The interests of the whole human family, in nature and in reason, are ever present to my mind as one and the same" (198). Of particular interest is that Wright urged them to study public speaking!

As this analysis makes clear, I do not share the criticisms of Wright's rhetoric made by Robert Connors, just as I do not approach her rhetoric using the broad categories of ethos, pathos, and logos, which William Grimaldi argues in his commentary on Aristotle's *Art of Rhetoric* are an integral part of and emerge out of enthymematic argument in the Aristotelian system.[37] As one might infer, Wright's ethos was damaged by her defense of the principles underlying Nashoba and generally by her espousal of unpopular positions. On the other hand, the competence and sympathetic concern for her audiences that are revealed in her lectures would have counteracted such reactions. Connors writes that "she did not know how to approach moving the emotions of an audience or, more likely, she did not believe in doing so."[38] As the lectures reveal, Wright fused the conative and the cognitive in her views of the role of human passion in generating belief and in claiming that all knowledge came from observation and sensation. She did not make the kinds of blatant emotional appeals typical of male rhetors of this period, but readers may judge from quoted material whether her lectures were appealing to or capable of moving her audiences. Finally, I am wary of judgments that do not praise women rhetors who have outstanding argumentative skills, which Wright clearly had, and that demand that praiseworthy discourse by a woman must evidence traditional qualities of femininity, such as appeals to emotion.

Rhetor and Rhetorician

What is noteworthy is that Wright's ideas and her rhetorical practices reflect a unified theory of rhetoric. In her defense of Nashoba, Wright sets forth a human ontology based on the role of the passions that ground the practice of equality and on a culture of freedom in the identification that becomes possible when people live, work, and learn together, what Kenneth Burke called *consubstantiality.* Her lectures describe and explain the epistemological and hermeneutic bases through which such experience permits human beings to judge the validity and credibility of evidence presented in support of claims. The values represented by Wright's practices as an editor and a lecturer are radical illustrations of deliberation based on human equality, the capacity of each and every person, whatever his or her background, class, or ethnicity, to evaluate evidence, test claims, and reason systematically about issues that are important for the community.

In viewing the work of early, modern, and contemporary women, I am struck again and again by their tendency to espouse a rhetoric that mimics key elements of what we have come to recognize as consciousness-raising.[39] Consciousness-raising presupposes participant homogeneity based on shared or similar personal experiences, which enable egalitarian exchanges. Those exchanges, winnowed through criticism and comparison, can generate a systemic analysis of the conditions of the group that, in turn, points toward actions, whether individual or group, that are needed to alter those conditions. Moreover, that her style imitates that of consciousness-raising may explain Wright's special appeal for female audiences for whom such a style would be particularly suited.

Wright is remarkable in her ability to see the human race as a homogeneous unity and to recognize that prejudice, discrimination, and hatred grow out of mystery, based on the absence of shared personal experience of others. Moreover, she stands out as one who proposed solutions that would amalgamate Americans educationally and socially in order to overcome the appearance of difference. Obviously, Wright did not use such modern rhetorical terms as identification, consubstantiality, mystery, or consciousness-raising, but her rhetorical practices and the content of her lectures suggest numerous similarities. In developing a human ontology emphasizing passion, an empirical epistemology grounded in the senses, and an axiology rooted in the equality of all humans, Wright's public discourse constitutes what is surely the earliest humanist rhetorical theory advanced in the United States.

Notes

1. Krista Ratcliffe, *Anglo-American Feminist Challenges to the Rhetorical Tradition.* (Carbondale: Southern Illinois UP, 1996).

2. Karlyn Kohrs Campbell, "The Rhetorical Implications of the Philosophy of Jean-Paul Sartre." Unpublished doctoral dissertation. University of Minnesota, Minneapolis, 1968; Karlyn Kohrs Campbell, "The Ontological Foundations of Rhetorical Theory," *Philosophy and Rhetoric* 3 (1970): 97–108.

3. Francis Bacon, *The Advancement of Learning,* in *The Rhetorical Tradition: Readings from Classical Times to the Present,* ed. Patricia Bizzell and Bruce Herzberg (Boston: St. Martin's, 1990). 625–31; cited material on 629.

4. Aristotle. *Rhetoric,* Bk. II, cc.2–17.

5. Frederick Nietzsche, "On Truth and Lies in a Non-Moral Sense," in Bizzell and Herzberg, *The Rhetorical Tradition,* 888–96.

6. Augustine, *On Christian Doctrine,* trans. and intro. D. W. Robertson Jr. (New York: Liberal Arts Press, 1958).

7. Kenneth Burke, *A Rhetoric of Motives* (Berkeley: U of California P, 1969), 20–23.

8. Stuart Hall, "The Work of Representation," in *Representation: Cultural Representations and Signifying Practices,* ed. Stuart Hall (London: Sage/Open University, 1997), 15–74.

9. Robert J. Connors, "Frances Wright: First Civic Rhetor in America," *College English* 42 (1999): 30–57. As is evident from my analysis, I disagree with Connors's conclusions about Wright's rhetorical skill and appeal.

10. Nashoba was the Chickasaw name for what others called the Wolf River, which ran through the property in Tennessee.

11. All biographical information is drawn from Amos Gilbert, *Memoir of Frances Wright: The Pioneer Woman in the Cause of Human Rights* (Cincinnati, 1855); Margaret Lane, *Frances Wright and the "Great Experiment"* (Manchester, Eng.: Manchester UP, 1972); Celia Morris [Eckhardt], *Fanny Wright: Rebel in America* (Urbana: U of Illinois P, 1992); Alice J. G. Perkins and Theresa Wolfson, *Frances Wright, Free Enquirer: The Study of a Temperament* (New York: Harper and Brothers, 1939); William Waterman, "Frances Wright," *Studies in History, Economics, and Public Law* 256 (1924): 205–306.

12. Morris, 143–44.

13. *New-Harmony Gazette* (January 30, February 6 and 13, 1828): 124–25, 132–33, 140–41. Subsequent references to "Explanatory Notes" are in parentheses in the text.

14. Morris, 155.

15. Lori D. Ginzberg explores the sources of resistance to Wright in "'The Hearts of Your Readers Will Shudder': Fanny Wright, Infidelity, and American Freethought," *American Quarterly* 46 (1994): 195–226.

16. As readers will be aware, the long history of lynching, based on the alleged rapes of white women, is a horrendous tale of white efforts to deny what Wright treated as obvious and factual.

17. Cited in Morris, 159, 166.

18. Christine Oravec, "Madwomen in the Balcony: The Female Audience, Fanny Wright, and the Rhetorical Criticism of Nineteenth-Century America." Unpublished manuscript, 1990; available from author, Department of Communication, University of Utah, 27, 29. See also Christine Oravec, "The Democratic Critics: An Alternative Rhetorical Tradition in the Nineteenth Century," *Rhetorica* 4 (1986): 395–421.

19. Martha M. Solomon, ed. *A Voice of Their Own: The Woman Suffrage Press, 1840–1910.* (Tuscaloosa: U of Alabama P, 1991).

20. There is some dispute about the dates of these first lectures; Perkins and Wolfson indicate that the original series was delivered on three successive Sundays

in July (211); Morris dates them as beginning on August 10 (316 n.10) based on a reference to Sunday the tenth in the *New-Harmony Gazette.*

21. Frances Trollope, *Domestic Manners of the Americans* (Gloucester, MA: Peter Smith 1832/1974), 70–73.

22. Morris, 128.

23. Emma Savage Rogers, ed. *Life and Letters of William Barton Rogers,* 2 vols. (Boston: Houghton, Mifflin, 1896), 1: 69–70.

24. Frances Wright, *Life, Letters, and Lectures, 1834/1844* (New York: Arno Press, 1972) 2–101. All subsequent citations from her lectures are from this source and are in parentheses in the text.

25. Sidney L. Jackson, *America's Struggle for Free Schools: Social Tension and Education in New England and New York, 1827–1842* (New York: Russell & Russell, 1965), 160.

26. Robert Dale Owen, "An Earnest Sewing of Wild Oats," *Atlantic Monthly* 31 (July 1874); cited in Lane, 32.

27. Lane, 34.

28. Morris, 282.

29. Trollope, 262–63.

30. Lyman Beecher, *Lectures on Political Atheism* (Boston: 1852), 93, cited in Morris, 199.

31. "Primary Instruction by Object Lessons," in Henry Barnard, *Pestalozzi and His Educational System* (Syracuse, NY: C. W. Bardeen, 1881), 405–28.

32. Ibid., 406.

33. "Epicurus," *The Encyclopedia of Philosophy,* ed. Paul Edwards (New York: Macmillan, 1967), I & II: 499.

34. Serialized in the *New-Harmony Gazette* beginning on October 4, 1826.

35. The research studies summarized in Richard E. Petty and John T. Cacioppo, *Communication and Persuasion: Central and Peripheral Routes to Attitude Change* (New York: Springer-Verlag, 1986), 200–03, detail the beneficial effects of rhetorical questions in inducing audience members to elaborate issue-related arguments.

36. These comments do not support Connors's assessment of Wright, who argues that she failed as an orator because she was "almost completely insensitive to the feelings and predispositions of many of her hearers, even the most liberal, and she eventually alienated most of her friends and supporters" (32–33).

37. William M. A. Grimaldi, S.J., *Studies in the Philosophy of Aristotle's Rhetoric* (Wiesbaden: Franz Steiner, 1972). Bizzell and Herzberg represent this in a diagram on p. 147.

38. Connors, 50.

39. Karlyn Kohrs Campbell, "Consciousness-Raising: Linking Theory, Criticism, and Practice," *Rhetoric Society Quarterly* 32 (2002): 45–64.

Works Cited

Aristotle. *Rhetoric,* Bk. II, cc.2–17.

Augustine. *On Christian Doctrine.* Trans. and intro. D. W. Robertson Jr. New York: Liberal Arts Press, 1958.

Bacon, Francis. *The Advancement of Learning. The Rhetorical Tradition: Readings from Classical Times to the Present.* Ed. Patricia Bizzell and Bruce Herzberg. Boston: St. Martin's, 1990.

Barnard, Henry. "Primary Instruction by Object Lessons." *Pestalozzi and His Educational System.* Syracuse, NY: C. W. Bardeen, 1881.

Beecher, Lyman. *Lectures on Political Atheism.* Boston, 1852.

Burke, Kenneth. *A Rhetoric of Motives.* Berkeley: U of California P, 1969.

Campbell, Karlyn Kohrs. "Consciousness-Raising: Linking Theory, Criticism, and Practice." *Rhetoric Society Quarterly* 32 (2002).

——. "The Ontological Foundations of Rhetorical Theory." *Philosophy and Rhetoric* 3 (1970): 97–108.

——. "The Rhetorical Implications of the Philosophy of Jean-Paul Sartre." Unpublished doctoral dissertation. University of Minnesota, Minneapolis, 1968.

Connors, Robert J. "Frances Wright: First Civic Rhetor in America." *College English* 42 (1999): 30–57.

"Epicurus." *The Encyclopedia of Philosophy.* Ed. Paul Edwards. New York: Macmillan, 1967.

Gilbert, Amos. *Memoir of Frances Wright: The Pioneer Woman in the Cause of Human Rights.* Cincinnati, 1855.

Ginzberg, Lori D. "'The Hearts of Your Readers Will Shudder': Fanny Wright, Infidelity, and American Freethought." *American Quarterly* 46 (1994): 195–226.

Grimaldi, William M. A. *Studies in the Philosophy of Aristotle's Rhetoric.* Wiesbaden: Franz Steiner, 1972.

Hall, Stuart. "The Work of Representation." *Representation: Cultural Representations and Signifying Practices.* Ed. Stuart Hall. London: Sage/Open University, 1997.

Jackson, Sidney L. *America's Struggle for Free Schools: Social Tension and Education in New England and New York, 1827–1842.* New York: Russell & Russell, 1965.

Lane, Margaret. *Frances Wright and the "Great Experiment."* Manchester, Eng.: Manchester UP, 1972.

Morris [Eckhardt], Celia. *Fanny Wright: Rebel in America.* Urbana: U of Illinois P, 1992.

Nietzsche, Frederick. "On Truth and Lies in a Non-Moral Sense." Bizzell and Herzberg, *The Rhetorical Tradition* 888–96.

Oravec, Christine. "The Democratic Critics: An Alternative Rhetorical Tradition in the Nineteenth Century," *Rhetorica* 4 (1986): 395–421.

———. “Madwomen in the Balcony: The Female Audience, Fanny Wright, and the Rhetorical Criticism of Nineteenth-Century America.” Unpublished manuscript, University of Utah, 1990.

Owen, Robert Dale. “An Earnest Sewing of Wild Oats.” *Atlantic Monthly* 31 (July 1874).

Perkins, Alice J. G., and Theresa Wolfson. *Frances Wright, Free Enquirer: The Study of a Temperament.* New York: Harper and Brothers, 1939.

Petty, Richard E., and John T. Cacioppo. *Communication and Persuasion: Central and Peripheral Routes to Attitude Change.* New York: Springer-Verlag, 1986.

Ratcliffe, Krista. *Anglo-American Feminist Challenges to the Rhetorical Tradition.* Carbondale: Southern Illinois UP, 1996.

Rogers, Emma Savage, ed. *Life and Letters of William Barton Rogers.* 2 vols. Boston: Houghton, Mifflin, 1896.

Solomon, Martha M., ed. *A Voice of Their Own: The Woman Suffrage Press, 1840–1910.* Tuscaloosa: U of Alabama P, 1991.

Trollope, Frances. *Domestic Manners of the Americans.* 1832. Gloucester, MA: Peter Smith, 1974.

Waterman, William. “Frances Wright.” *Studies in History, Economics, and Public Law* 256 (1924): 205–306.

Wright, Frances. *Life, Letters, and Lectures, 1834–1844.* New York: Arno Press, 1972.

7

Econstructing Sisterhood

Jane Gallop

The paper you are about to read was presented at the English Institute, in Cambridge, Massachusetts, on October 3, 1999. I tell you this at the outset because the paper still bears the marks of the occasion for which it was written. While it did begin as a piece of writing, it was not written for the temporally diffuse audience of publication.

You reading this now are not quite the "you" the text addresses. But in that you are in fact not so different from the original audience in Cambridge that Sunday morning. Although the English Institute was where this paper first saw the light of day, the talk was not written for that occasion either; my reading it there was a dress rehearsal. The real event, the event that "caused" this piece of writing, came six days later, in Minnesota.

The temporality of writing is, to be sure, incurably odd. You are reading this in some present moment that I, in what is now for me the present of writing, can only imagine, anticipate, and pretend to join you in with my direct address, my present-tense verbs and second-person pronouns, as if we were talking, as if we were in some here and now together. While writing is in this way generally off-kilter and belated, this paper will make you specifically aware of an event you missed (unless you happen to be one of the three hundred people who were present in Minnesota on that Saturday evening). Not the moment of writing, which is nearly always an event missed by the reader, but the moment for which the paper was written.

The paper is very much about how reading and writing might allow us to connect across distance, to bond in some mediated way rather than in the romantic immediacy of the here and now, to connect across time and space rather than in the intimacy of presence. Thus can I hope that the awkward framing, the various times and spaces of my writing and its audiences, will successfully "forward" the paper and its effects to you. (When you reach the end of the paper, you will know why I put "forward" in quotation marks, what I am referring to here, in anticipation of your reading and in retrospection of my writing.)

This paper is written to be presented next Saturday at a conference on Feminism(s) and Rhetoric(s) at the University of Minnesota. Without that event, at that place and time, it would never have been written, never even have been conceived. The paper is so dependent upon that event that I was not able to produce a version of it for you that sublimates the context. A year and a half ago when I received the invitation to speak at the conference in Minnesota, I read the date—October 9, 1999—and immediately thought "that's my sister's fiftieth birthday!" Because my sister lives in Minnesota, I fantasized giving a talk in honor of her on her birthday with her in the audience. So "sisterhood" in my title is first of all not figurative sisterhood, i.e. feminism, but literal sisterhood. This paper is about my relation to my sister.

Because it is written as a sort of present to my sister, I had to package it for the moment I will give it to her. I had to put her first, before you, my esteemed colleagues at the English Institute. So I wrote it very much imagining her there.

The paper begins like this: "Today, October ninth, 1999, is my sister's 50th birthday. Judi lives in St. Paul and is here with us this evening. This paper is dedicated to her: Happy Birthday, Judi."

Although I felt I must put Judi first, I hope of course that the paper will be of value to a more general audience. In fact, it explicitly treats the problem of my double address (to my sister and to my academic colleagues), but my double address is for me most anxiously embodied by the double scene of my delivering this paper. A scene in which the "original" moment, the one for which it is written, comes second.

Aside from my hope that the paper will have value beyond its occasion, I take solace in the fact that our topic here at the English Institute is in fact "Literature, Anxiety, Temporality." I do in fact literally feel anxious about the relation between my writing and temporality as I sit here before you this morning. I can at least hope that you will see the odd "present" of my paper as, if not a theorization of anxiety and temporality, at least a telling case.

The possibility of my being "a case" reminds me of an old joke, a favorite in my family, to which my sister has alluded several times in the last couple of weeks. The joke runs: "My sister is at Harvard.—Oh, what's she studying?—She's not studying anything; they're studying her."

Although I sort of enjoy becoming an old family joke about academia, I also hope we can take the strange absent present of my paper, its anticipatory temporality, as matter for our discussion of the present, and especially of that strange present that is the present of writing.

In any case, my apologies for not being completely here.

When I received my invitation to speak in Minnesota, I began to fantasize about dedicating my talk to Judi, as a sort of birthday toast. The more I thought about it, the more intricate the fantasy became, the more seriously my thought of Judi became intricated with the conference topic. I want to do more than just dedicate this paper to Judi; I want the dedication to my sister to be more than an extrinsic gesture; I want the dedication to be inseparable from the main point of my words. This paper is about my relation to my sister, about the rhetoric of my relation to my sister, and, by focusing on the specific case of my relation to Judi, it is an attempt to think through a major rhetorical problem of feminism—a problem we might call "sisterhood."

My topic here arose, thus, coincidentally. I wouldn't have thought to write this paper if not for the temporal and spatial coincidence of an invitation to speak in the Twin Cities on this particular date. However, I stress the "occasional" nature of my talk not for you to dismiss it as minor, as tangential embellishment, but because I believe in the fertility of the specific as the site of productive thinking. This foregrounding of my talk's "occasional" status has everything to do with the question of rhetoric. Dedications and occasional pieces are classic rhetorical stock; they are rhetorical sites where discourse is knotted to the extra-discursive, to the here and now, to real life. Call me a deconstructionist if you like, but personally I don't take rhetorical gestures as frosting spread on top of thought; I take rhetoric to be the very place where thought happens. I don't want the dedication to be a mere flourish laid "on top of" the real paper; I want the address to my sister to be central to the paper, essential, intrinsic.

My rhetorical situation in this paper is complicated—actually, is fraught—because of the peculiarity of my address. I am speaking at an academic conference as a feminist theorist about my relation to my sister; I am also speaking to my sister, my sister who is neither an academic nor a feminist.

That double address seems a tightrope walk without a net. If I speak simply as an academic theorist about my sister, not only will I be using her, exploiting her, alienating her, but I will be doing so in her presence and will thus have to answer to her. If, on the other hand, I speak simply to Judi, staying within the terms of her and my conversation, I will exclude the rest of the audience and fail to produce the more generally applicable knowledge that would justify my taking your time and attention here.

Although I don't think I can mend this divide, can't pull this odd double address together and unify what I have to say, I would like at least to put it on the agenda, to bear it in mind. I need to keep both my audiences in mind—both you, my academic feminist colleagues, and you, my only sister. It is, I think, precisely that awkward double address that I would call the rhetoric of sisterhood, the uncomfortable, fraught rhetorical situation that feminists must negotiate when we speak about and to other women, women who don't already participate in our discourse.

Sisterhood is not a tangential rhetorical problem for feminism; it is one of feminism's central rhetorical problems. Thirty years ago, in the first flush of "women's liberation," when the second wave was just cresting, "sisterhood" was pretty much a synonym for "feminism." Cozier, less philosophical, it connoted not so much the long history of women's bondage but a more optimistic emphasis on women bonding. Robin Morgan's 1970 anthology, *Sisterhood Is Powerful*, can serve as the landmark here.

Fourteen years later, Morgan published another anthology, this one called *Sisterhood Is Global*. The title's "Global" betokens the hard lesson that U.S. feminism was by then trying to learn about our own ethnocentrism; the title's "Sisterhood" is an attempt to stretch that all-too-domestic term to incorporate feminism's new range. It is indeed, as we say, "a stretch." The idea of "sisterhood" was in fact based upon the very same domesticating blind spots that the move toward the global attempts to get beyond. By 1984 the term "sisterhood" was an anachronism; Morgan's attempt to update it was an embarrassment.

I know it's tacky to say "I told you so," but, personally, I had always found the term "sisterhood" problematic. Even in the heady days when I was a proud women's libber, I was nonplussed by the celebration of "sisterhood" around me. Not, to be sure, because I was in any way worried about ethnocentrism. Rather it was because "sisterhood" could not help but recall my relation to Judi, and that did not seem at all like the female bond idealized under the term; my relation to Judi did not seem at all like feminism.

What it did seem like was sibling rivalry. Judi is two and a half years older than me; we shared a room, sleeping in twin beds in the girlie white furniture set. I was named Jane because at the time there was a radio show called "Judy and Jane": we were meant to be a matched set. And in our slotted similarity and felt difference, we did not bond, we competed. We competed for privileges, for our mother's love and attention, for our little brother's love once he was born, and for the love and attention our father could never much afford to show us.

It is through this structure of rivalry that I understand the contrast between Judi and me—as if our rivalry meant we had to become different sorts of girls, contrasting types of girls. Since neither of us wanted to be second best, we adopted differing ideals, opposing models and goals. Competing on different terms, we might avoid definitive comparison.

When still a teenager, Judi took over the cooking in our family home; down at the University of Minnesota she majored in home economics; cooking has always made me anxious, and I actually haven't done it at all for more than a decade. Judi said she was going to college to "get her MRS degree"; I wanted to get a PhD even though I didn't really know what it was. At the age of twenty-five, Judi had a wonderful big wedding in a beautiful white dress, preceded by a season of wedding showers—an event and a season that were the high point of her life, a dream come true. I never married. She wagered everything, bet her life, her happiness, on normative femininity; I was trying to win at a different game.

Feminism is not irrelevant to the difference between us; feminism might in fact name the difference between us. She never stopped trying to reap the benefits promised to good girls; I embraced feminism as the critique of the femininity at which I never could excel.

Within feminism, I heard rosy tales of the closeness between sisters, sisters bonding together against abusive parents, against an abusive world. But Judi and I were not close. It was not just that we were different—different interests, different values—it was that we each had a tremendous stake in our difference. Our differing choices about femininity mattered to us a lot: once they had been our strategies to compete against each other for the love we both wanted; now they were our dearest identities. It was not a matter of indifference to either of us whose choice was best.

Feminism told me that my choice was best, that Judi was wrong, that she had chosen the losing path. It was not just that Judi wasn't a feminist, that we didn't have that in common; it was that my investment in feminism was an investment in doing it better than Judi. Feminism was not a standpoint outside our sibling rivalry; it was a move within it.

And yet feminism wants to be for *all* women. Feminism derives its authority from the rhetorical claim to speak for the interests of women in general, rather than only for a restricted group of women, rather than only for self-identified feminists. In relation to that claim, feminism has always found the nonfeminist woman a thorny problem, a gnawing contradiction. Does feminism speak for those women who don't identify as feminists? Are they our constituency, or our adversaries? If we speak for them in disregard of what they themselves would say, how then can we speak to them?

As a feminist theorist I found myself abstractly pondering this philosophical and rhetorical knot; at the same time, though without seeing any connection, I also struggled with the ongoing personal problem of my relation to my sister. It wasn't that we had no relation whatsoever, but we had never found a relation in which we could both be comfortable.

Thirty-two years ago Judi moved from our home in Duluth down to the Twin Cities to attend the University of Minnesota; since that time we have always lived in different cities. Over those years, we have tried to connect in various media. We visited each other a couple of times, even had a few nights out drinking (those were the most successful, lubricated by alcohol; I discovered over a pitcher of margaritas that Judi could drink me under the table, something I admire in a woman). There was a brief period about a dozen years ago when we spoke on the phone regularly. At the time we both had young sons, and that seemed momentarily to give us a common ground. But neither the face-to-face meetings nor the phone calls ever managed to establish a relation we knew how to be in together; we kept bumping up against the awkwardness of our differences.

Two years ago Judi and I happened upon a new medium. We started writing email to each other. Since then we've been writing regularly: Judi writes me pretty much every day; I write her a little less often, but still with a dailiness. She has become the person in my birth family to whom I am closest, the one who knows most about my present life. Judi and I now have a relation, a real live relation; we now have something I might want to call "sisterhood." And we have it on and through email. (Pretty much exclusively in fact: we have not been able to transfer this email connection either to face-to-face or even to the phone.)

The title of my paper, "Econstructing Sisterhood," refers to our email relation. The title is meant to suggest that "sisterhood" is not something given, but something we build, and that I'm going to tell you the story about how the specific medium of email allowed Judi and me together to construct a bond.

Some would say that email is a paltry bond and that the fact that we cannot transfer the connection to a more live medium cheapens it, points to its limitation. Well, I'm not denying its limitations, but I want instead to insist that the very constraints of email, its forms and modes—in short, its "rhetoric"—enabled a relation where there wasn't one before.

The idea of a "sisterhood" constructed through such highly technological means is surprising. By referring to a familial, biological or domestic bond, "sisterhood" tends to suggest a relation that is natural, intimate, less mediated. When we use it figuratively (as in the rhetoric of feminism), it suggests something natural and cozy. And those connotations do not jibe with email—the computer, technology, writing, the disembodied connection—writing without the hand (without a signature to mark bodily presence). An econstructed sisterhood is a technologically dependent bond. And our romantic notions—which tend to be particularly strong around issues of women, family, feminism, and bonding—make us suspicious of such an obviously technologically mediated form.

The usual connotations of "sisterhood" clash with the connotations of email. Worse yet, my title introduces the horrid neologism "econstructing" because in its awkwardness, unfamiliarity, and shorthand it carries a lot of the graceless, unromantic style of email. The two words in my title embody the clash between two different sets of connotations, two different rhetorics. The two words of my title can also serve to figure the relation itself. Like those two words, Judi and I have not merged our differences into an overarching unified style. Like my title this morning, our email remains awkward, but it manages to mean and to communicate.

Feminism has spent the last twenty years working on an ethics that respects the differences between women. I'm beginning to suspect that, even more than an ethics, what we need is a rhetoric. In light of that, I'd like to propose this email correspondence as a model for communicating across difference. My point is not that we should all start finding nonfeminist, nonacademic pen pals. Rather I want to present this email relation as an example of a bond that negotiates limitation.

Judi writes to me pretty much every day. In fact when I'm out of town and can't check my email, she still writes to me every day. She says that writing to me functions like a diary, and so she wants to do it daily even if I'm not reading it daily. I write a bit less often, around five times a week, but my messages are also "daily" in the sense that I generally talk about things I've done in the last day and things I will do in the next day or two, as well as some reflections on how I feel about those things. The daily format allows us to cover a wide range of topics. Both of us write about things that happen at work, about our children, about purchases, household chores, sex, social events, bodily events (illness, weight). Although our lives are in many ways not similar, the daily format provides an organizing device that can include widely dissimilar things.

But these messages are not just a double-entry diary. Both of us respond to things the other says about her life. Not to everything, but to whatever happens to prompt response. And it is these responses that are, to my mind, the most valuable part of the email.

To convey the value of these responses, I need to contrast them with another relation, because we appreciate our email in contrast to that other relation: Judi and I enjoy how our email differs from phone conversations with our mother. We both talk regularly on the phone with Mom: Judi speaks to her at least once a day (Mom also lives in the Twin Cities now); I call her every Saturday morning. Although Judi talks to Mom a lot more often than I do, in both cases telephone is the major mode of contact: both of us talk to her much more often than we see her. And both of us find our phone calls with Mom frustrating, in pretty much the same way.

Judi and I complain to each other that Mom doesn't listen to us. We give each other the kind of attention we find hard to get from our mother. I imagine we know how to be attentive in just the right way because we were both schooled by our frustration with the same style of inattentiveness.

There are two different ways in which Mom "doesn't listen." Sometimes she talks at length about herself and her life and literally does not listen when I try to tell her something about my life. While that is her at her worst, it is a not uncommon telephone event, as if it were something about the phone. The other way she "doesn't listen" is that sometimes in response to things I say about my life or feelings, she jumps in too fast with ready-made advice, with solutions that are inattentive to the particular situation. In other words, sometimes she literally does not listen; other times when she hears what I say, she responds in a way that makes me feel like she isn't "really listening."

In order to appreciate my sister here, I find myself criticizing my mother. In terms of the general concept of "sisterhood," of bonds between women, that is certainly worth noting, and a complicated thing it is indeed. The complications are hardly just theoretical. My mother too will be there, sitting right next to Judi, listening to me. If this talk is a birthday gift to Judi, I fear it might be Mom who's paying for it.

On the other hand, maybe the problem is not so much Mom but rather the phone. As I said, the basic medium of my relation to Mom is the telephone, and what I prefer about my relation to Judi may well have to do with the difference between email and phone. As part of an attempt to think of an econstructed sisterhood as a relation in which the email is not extrinsic, not a mere carrier of the relation, but is in fact intrinsic, literally constitutive of the bond, I would like for a moment to focus specifically on the media, to consider why email might be better than phone as a means of communicating across difference.

Although the phone is a distance technology, it is one that feels immediate: you talk in synch time; you hear the other's voice. Perhaps most importantly, you are talking, not writing. I think the main thing that allows Judi and me to be attentive to each other, to "listen" to each other, is that we are in fact not "listening," we are reading.

I always reread Judi's emails at least once before I write back. I know she prints mine out and refers to them in writing her response. This is not spontaneous communication: it is an exchange of pause, consideration, thoughtfulness; it is a technology of reading and writing. Call me a deconstructionist if you like, but personally I suspect reading and writing to be more respectful of difference than can be the illusion of immediacy we have on the phone.

Of course, there is a downside to writing—one I believe Derrida called "dissemination"—writing's propensity to stray outside the intended scene of address. Some months after Judi and I started emailing regularly, I discovered that Judi printed up my emails and gave them to Mom. I don't know if that began as a sporadic practice, but now she always passes my emails on. This was not what I had in mind. I imagined Judi and I had a private one-on-one relation, which I valued because it was outside the family system. When I discovered that Judi put our private relation into general circulation, I felt a bit betrayed; later, I decided it didn't really matter. (As I write this, I wonder what relation there is between Judi's showing our email to Mom and my "showing" our email to all of you here. I mean who, after all, is "putting our private relation into general circulation"?)

I should say that Judi does not in fact circulate every word I write her. She edits my emails for Mom's eyes, taking out anything she doesn't want Mom to know, anything she thinks I wouldn't want Mom to know, and anything she thinks Mom wouldn't want to know. Although occasionally I will say, "Oh, I guess you'll have to edit out this paragraph," generally I submit myself to her editing without comment. Judi does not circulate the email she writes.

Although I never directly asked her, I have wondered why she would want to show Mom the emails. I have to admit that I thought about her tattling on me when we were kids, her running to Mom and getting me in trouble. Her circulating my emails has not, however, gotten me into trouble (that awaits this talk). Her showing Mom has in fact done the opposite of get me into trouble: Mom has told me (on the phone of course) that she values my emails, not only because she learns about my life, but because from my responses she learns more about what's going on in Judi's life.

These phone conversations with Mom about my emails suggest a much more complicated circuitry than the simple opposition between phone and email, Mom and Judi, I posited a bit ago. These two different relations do not only exist in contrast with each other; they actually affect each other. I know that I have had some good phone conversations with Mom precisely because of her reading my emails to Judi.

Whatever the complications of this sister/mother circuit, Judi and I bond quite comfortably around how we feel about Mom. Dad, however, is another story. I am pretty angry at Dad and feel he was not a good father to his daughters; Judi, on the other hand, seems largely uncritical of him and generally takes his side. Ironically, I often feel my anger at Dad most sharply when I think of Judi: I tend to blame him for her difficulties, her unhappiness, her insecurity. Although my anger at Dad makes me feel close to Judi in my head, in reality it produces distance between us: it is the thing we can least agree on, least share.

I fantasize that Judi and I could bond in our common suffering at Dad's hands. I see in her so much that resembles my own plight as a daughter wounded by her father's preference for his son. I imagine that if only Judi, too, could get angry at Dad, then she would be happy, could claim her right to what she desires.

My anger at Dad, my sense that he's to blame for my sister's suffering, we might want to call that "feminism." I think my fantasy here is very much the feminist fantasy of "sisterhood": a fantasy of "saving" my sister by making her more like me, a fantasy rooted in my belief that she really is like me but doesn't know it.

In reality, however, Judi and I are able to keep talking, are able to bond by letting our opposed views of Dad stand, by agreeing to disagree. Ironically, in order to construct our sisterhood, I must resist my fantasy of "sisterhood." This is a "sisterhood" across feminism rather than within feminism.

Before concluding, I'd like to consider one more aspect of my correspondence with Judi, an aspect that may well seem trivial. For more than a year now, I have been reporting weekly to Judi on my weight. Every Monday I weigh myself at the gym and then report what I call my "official weigh-in" on email. While I actually weigh myself every day—usually several times a day on a couple of different scales—what makes this weighing "official" is only that this is the weight I report to Judi. I have taken Judi as authoritative witness in my relation to my own weight. I should specify that Judi does not in fact know what I weigh (I imagine she would be horrified to know how large the number is, and I'm certainly not going to reveal it here). I don't report my weight but rather how much I have gone up or down from the week before.

To explain the significance of this ritual gesture, I need to gloss the history of my relation to my weight. I think eating/dieting has long been a central register of the opposition between Judi and me, perhaps even the central register. I remember a moment from our adolescence when Judi, dieting, was prodding me to eat the chocolate chip cookies she had baked, cookies she was not eating.

The centrality of this register is no doubt attributable to its centrality in my family of origin. I think all the moral and psychological issues—questions of good and bad, of pleasure and control—are in my family most densely clustered around eating.

Judi is thin, and I'm not; this opposition is undoubtedly constructed, not given. (In fact, as young children, Judi was chubby and I was thin.) Judi controls her weight, does not allow herself to gain weight, eats a very low-fat diet. I, on the other hand, have resisted controlling my weight for my entire adult life, feel militant about my right to eat fat, and like to define myself as the kind of woman who does not diet, who eats as much as she wants. Embracing the right to eat fat, I have defined myself not only differently than Judi but precisely as not the kind of woman my sister is.

Despite this opposition, or maybe in some way because of it, a little more than a year ago I found myself wanting to deliver my relation to my weight up to Judi's gaze. I had decided I wanted to lose weight, and admitting that to myself, I went on to admit it to Judi. It seemed a step beyond opposition, a moment of admitting that I was more like her than I liked to pretend. It felt like some form of giving in, of giving up a resistance. It also felt like giving Judi the power to criticize me, the power to feel superior. I took her as witness to my attempt to do something I knew her to be better at than me. I was asking for her help.

Her response has surprised me. I thought I was giving her the power to put me down; I expected a superior, withering gaze; I found instead an unforeseen generosity. Reporting my weight to Judi has become important to me: I often rush home from the gym on Mondays to write to her right away; I feel proud when I can report a loss and am always gratefully relieved when she forgives my lapses and encourages me not to give up.

Last Monday, September 27, 1999, at 6:32 P.M., I wrote to Judi: "Excellent weigh-in to report today. I lost three and a half pounds since last week. Last week I was up two, but that still means a loss of a pound and a half from my low of two weeks ago. This is my last weigh-in before my trip. I'll try not to gain too much during the trip so you can be proud of how I look (course compared to you I will always look fat . . .)"

A paragraph break and then my email continues: "Wish I had as good news on my writing. I'm trying to write an ending to *EcoSis.* I wrote two stinking pages which I will throw away tomorrow. I felt dead in the head. I feel like I just wish it were done, but I have to have a great ending."

Judi wrote to me at 7:10 P.M.: "Nice weight loss. . . . Keep it going for the next month and you could be at a ten pound loss by Halloween. [new paragraph] Hope you found an ending to me. . . . .[ellipsis Judi's]"

Then at 7:18 P.M., she sent me another email. This one was not "written to me," but was "forwarded." It had been sent to her by Shawna, a woman she used to work with, a woman who used to French-braid Judi's hair during breaks at work. Shawna had not written it but was likewise "forwarding" it, not just to Judi but to a whole list of people.

This forwarded email, circulating quickly among so many people—surely some of you have received it—is not only a quintessential email (by being so rapidly and widely circulated) but is in fact a meta-email. It is not just an email message but a message *about* emails. Its content is: "Eleven reasons why email is like a penis."

Reason 10: "Those who have it think that those who don't are somehow inferior." Reason 9: "Those who don't have it may agree that it's neat, but think it's not worth the fuss that those who have it make about it." Reason 6: "In the distant past, its only purpose was to transmit information vital to the survival of the species. Some people still think that's the only thing it should be used for, but most folks today use it mostly for fun."

It is rare for Judi to send me this sort of email, a forwarded, generally circulating email; this may in fact be the first time. Given the timing, I'd like to take it as Judi's response to my telling her I needed an ending to my paper.

While Judi probably sent me this message "mostly for fun," I'd like to take the equation of email and the penis way too seriously, to treat it as a theoretical contribution to the topic of feminism and rhetoric. I'd like us to read its rhetoric seriously. By its rhetoric I mean everything from its dissemination, to its tone, to the odd fact that it is a list not of ten but of eleven reasons why email is like a penis. (Eleven seems to me a very odd number, one that screams "one too many," one that's asking for the reader to lop one off.)

As "Reason 6" tells us, email today is more likely to be used for dissemination than insemination. Whatever my fantasies of a private relation, one of the things that characterizes email is the ease with which writing can be put into wide and speedy circulation. The "ending" Judi sent us, this example of a widely circulating message, can remind us that an econstructed sisterhood is one inevitably disseminated beyond my fantasies of a cozy closed circuit.

This multiply-forwarded email recalls another important sense of "sisterhood," one that picks up, forwards, and transforms the feminist rhetoric. "Sisterhood" was always meant to be a broad relation, one that was not private, restricted to either our natural or even our chosen sisters, an open rather than a closed community. Sending me this message, just in time to get it included in this paper, Judi makes me see our relation as part of a larger econstructed circuit.

The message is quasi-feminist in tone. Its playful, critical relation to the penis suggests a female perspective, not just female but with a critical distance on phallocentrism ("Those who have it think that those who don't are somehow inferior"). The message could be taken as an assertive, playful feminist statement that bonds a circuit of women.

But the message is also ironic. While the content is distant from and critical of an investment in email, the fact that it is itself an email message means that writer and reader bond in a contradictory relation. This combination of ironic distance notwithstanding continuing investment may well be the rhetoric of women bonding over and through our ambivalent relation to men.

Although Judi did not author this email she sent me, although she literally did not add anything to the message, there nonetheless is something of hers to read there—not in the message itself but in the address. The "To:" line of the heading contains three e-addresses: at the same time Judi forwarded this message to me she also sent it to two other women—her best friend, and her ex-husband's girlfriend, who happens also to be named Jane (Judi sometimes refers to her as "the other Jane"). Judi has developed quite a nice relationship to that Jane, a relationship that in fact developed and largely exists on email. Judi's ex-husband is troubled by this bond.

I am of course Judi's literal sister; best girlfriends are often figured as "sisters"; but what sort of sister is "the other Jane"? To answer that question, I turn to an esteemed feminist theorist. Gayatri Spivak once told me that women who have slept with the same man are called cocksisters.

Now, I have to confess that I don't know where Gayatri got the term nor what all it is meant to imply. But with a message telling me that email is like a penis, I am prompted to speculate that there may well be a connection between what I'm here calling econstructed sisterhood and what Spivak calls cocksisters.

Judi's relation to the other Jane is literally "econstructed": they got close by writing email. Judi has, it turns out, econstructed two relations, one with me and one with this other Jane. These two econstructed sisterhoods have something in common beyond the coincidence of name: both relations involve women connecting across rivalry. Judi and I, literal sisters, negotiate sibling rivalry; Judi and the other Jane bond across sexual rivalry.

Back in the days of cozy "sisterhood," "sisters" (who later became cultural feminists and lesbian separatists) were valued not only because we were alike but also and importantly because we were different than men, a difference implicating technology and the phallus. The phallus, technology, theory, and rhetoric were all male, and the fantasy of sisterhood was a fantasy of unmediated connection. "Econstructed sisterhood" demands a way of thinking about women bonding beyond the cultural feminist fantasy of women's antiphallic, natural sameness.

I said earlier that I thought what we needed in feminism was not so much an ethics of difference between women but a rhetoric. At the end of this paper, I'm still at the beginning of that question. In view of that as yet unimaginable rhetoric, I've posted the example of my email correspondence with my sister. And in lieu of a conclusion, I've brought the message my sister forwarded last Monday as a theorization of email and gender.

While it may be only coincidental that Judi and the other Jane have an econstructed relation, Judi's meta-email suggests a stronger, more theoretical connection. The complicated tone of ironic distance, despite real attachment for both penis and email in that message, bonds its circuit of readers in an econstructed sisterhood that may also be an instance of a rhetorical bond I am amused to call cocksisterhood.

Thus ends the paper proper. After I presented it at the English Institute, about a dozen people said they wanted me to write and tell them what happened in Minnesota the next week. Here's what happened:

Reading the paper with my sister and mother in the audience was really scary. I delivered the entire talk without once looking in their direction. I was afraid that if I looked at them I would not be able to continue reading; I was more afraid of what I would see on their faces. While I generally deliver papers slowly, wanting the audience to catch every word I have written, I read this one hyper-slowly: I was stalling. I took a sip of water between each paragraph, because I was afraid to go on.

The audience was stunningly quiet. Someone who was there later told me that she thought the audience was afraid of what I might say, what might happen. It was as if the audience saw me at the precipice and held its breath, expecting me to jump.

It was in fact an event; it felt live. In the paper I had written of a tightrope walk without a net, and that was how I felt—as if at any moment I could plunge. The risk did not seem academic.

So, you may be wondering, how did they take it? What did they think? ("They," of course, are Judi and Mom.)

Judi loved it. I felt my gift to her was a great success. She seemed expansive and looked radiant afterward. She asked me for a copy of the paper, told me she liked it even better upon reading it, circulated copies to friends, including Shawna and the other Jane. (She forwarded to me the email Shawna wrote her after reading the paper; so I know that while a bit put off by the academic vocabulary, Shawna thinks Judi fortunate to have a sister like me.) Judi also confirmed that she did indeed forward me the "email is like a penis" list because she hoped it might help me write the conclusion.

Mom, on the other hand, seemed tense after my talk. We embraced awkwardly when I returned to my seat, and she left shortly thereafter. I spent the next day at her house, and it was as if nothing had happened, which was both a relief and demoralizing.

The next Saturday, during our first phone call since the talk, Mom and I had a fight, the worst fight in years. Having taken the risk of complaining publicly about her phone calls, I could not bear finding myself in a call where nothing seemed to have changed; so I criticized her directly. Whereas in writing the talk I had carefully composed my criticism of her, editing out as much of my angry excesses as I could, in the call I said everything I had edited out of the talk, and more. We found ourselves in an increasingly bitter exchange of reciprocal accusations. The call ended with us both still in full anger. Mom said that she was hanging up and that I had better call next week.

The following Saturday Mom was exemplary in her attentiveness, asking me questions about my life, questions she seemed to have jotted down upon reading my latest email to Judi. As I write this afterword, that is my most recent contact with Mom.

If this seems too cozy an ending, it probably means I am once again closing the circuits of sisterhood. So let me end by speaking of another member of my family who was present at that event, someone I have not yet mentioned.

While I told you that Mom was sitting next to Judi, I didn't tell you that on the other side of Judi sat Stacy, my brother's wife. In retrospect it seems remarkable that in a discussion of various forms of sisterhood, of mediated, and tense, and rivalrous sisterhoods, of women bonding across their relations to men, I neglected to mention my sister-in-law.

Whereas Judi and I now have different family names (she has kept her ex-husband's name), Stacy has become a Gallop. When I said Judi was "my only sister," was I intentionally excluding Stacy? Am I trying to reduce my family to a cozy, childhood version of it, only counting the "blood relatives"? Am I rejecting the constructed sister-in-law for the natural sister, by only counting the latter?

It is not, believe me, because I don't like Stacy. I like Stacy enormously, think she's wonderful, appreciate her sensitivity and wisdom. I often say that Stacy is my favorite person in my family, feeling this a rather clever if pointed joke. Right now I'm realizing that I don't really understand the joke.

I am realizing that I have some resistance to counting her as a "sister." I suspect that over the nearly twenty years she's been part of my family, I have often slighted Stacy in just this way. And as I close this paper, I'd like to begin thinking about what that means.

Works Cited

Morgan, Robin. *Sisterhood Is Global: An International Women's Movement Anthology.* Garden City, NY: Anchor Press/Doubleday, 1984.

———. *Sisterhood Is Powerful: An Anthology of Writings from the Women's Liberation Movement.* New York: Random House, 1970.

8

Exceptional Women, Expert Culture, and the Academy

Lois Cucullu

It bears remembering that Shakespeare's sister, Virginia Woolf's mythical female progenitor of *A Room of One's Own,* was a woman with a past. By that I mean a cultural past, for Judith Shakespeare's genesis cannot be credited solely to the reproach of an obscure bishop as Woolf's essay suggests.[1] Female Shakespeares were in fact part of a much larger cultural debate over women's aptitude at the turn of the last century. Indeed, some twenty years before Woolf set her Judith in print, Elizabeth Robins posed the question "Where's the woman Shakespeare?" in her two works on the British suffrage movement—the drama *Votes for Women* (74) and the novel adaptation *The Convert* (265). Hurled at a Trafalgar Square rally of suffragettes by a hostile male art student in play and novel, the taunt attempts to undermine women's political competence by tying it to artistic success. The questioner implies that the absence of exceptional women—a female Shakespeare or Plato or Michelangelo or Beethoven or Raphael, as this provocation was also framed—offered proof positive of women's disqualification from citizenship.[2] Rising to the bait, Robins's suffragette activist, Miss Levering, rebuffs the student's affront and affirms women's capabilities, demanding to know how many prodigies are present in the audience, and further: "How many Shakespeares are there in all England to-day? Not one. Yet the state doesn't tumble to pieces. Railroads and ships are built—homes are kept going, and babies are born. The world goes on! (*bending over the crowd*) It goes on *by virtue of the common people*" (*Votes* 74–75).[3]

Although the suffragette's ennobling of "the common people" is clearly aimed at repulsing presumptions of male superiority, it also included in its broadside a rejection of female superiority. As Robins made clear in a suffrage address the following March, female Shakespeares were the chimera of women's liberation. What she called "[t]he deadening illusion entertained about, and shared by, the 'Exceptional Woman'" was "*a Drug in the Market*" that deludes women into putting individual pursuits before collective interests and the common good ("Feministe Movement" 53, 70). However, her conclusion "that women are less disposed in these days to over-estimate their individual value" ("Suffrage Camp" 73) discounted the currency that the figure of the exceptional woman continued to gain over the next decade with, among others, Woolf and her peers.

Indeed, in 1911 the exceptional woman provided the raison d'être for the creation of the protomodernist journal *The Freewoman, A Weekly Feminist Review,* which advocated in its premier issue a feminism that would be above all "self-conscious and introspective." "For the first time," its editorial asserted, "feminists themselves make the attempt to reflect the feminist movement in the mirror of thought" ("Notes" 3). Significantly, this same inaugural issue also demoted franchise reform to "a rough and ready expedient" (3).[4] And when outraged suffrage activists and sympathizers vigorously objected, the feminist weekly responded by taking an even stronger stand: "To be a freewoman one must have the essential attribute of genius," the second issue proclaimed. "Last week we implied it, and this week we state it" ("Commentary" 21). "[I]t is the work of the Suffragist women to guard the rear," it declared, "it is that of the Freewomen to steer the van" (22).[5] In the following issue, cofounder Mary Gawthorpe addressed the suffrage movement directly, maintaining her support of female franchise but stressing the critical importance of *The Freewoman*'s editorial policies in support of knowledge creation. "[I]t is most essential," she wrote in "To the Women's Social and Political Union," "that a vehicle for the expression of uncompromising and sincere opinions should exist" (42).

Some eighteen years later, Woolf joined the debate and covered over the divide by making the lowborn genius Judith Shakespeare the focal point of her 1929 polemic and proleptically the starting point for a genealogy of exceptional women writers. The effects of this symbolic genesis were to deflect suffrage's rhetoric of equality and to grant the exceptional woman hailed by *The Freewoman* the instant name recognition of a Shakespeare and a prefab literary lineage for Woolf's own and future generations. Nor should her canny elevation of the exceptional woman entirely surprise. Even before the outcast Judith Shakespeare's literary debut, before even the postbellum limited extension of the national franchise mollified suffrage reformers on the British and U.S. sides of the Atlantic, Woolf and fellow female modernists Dorothy Richardson, Katherine Mansfield, Gertrude Stein, Djuna Barnes, H.D., and Mina Loy had already subscribed to some version of the exceptional woman and detached themselves from franchise activism.[6] Like the founders of *The Freewoman,* they espoused an antiwoman sentiment in their criticism of the cult of domesticity and were decidedly more quiescent about suffrage reform as the primary means of emancipation. Yet they took these positions even as they denounced, often stridently, a male monopoly of the arts. Critical of male privilege and ambivalent about female suffrage, these early modernists enjoyed the dubious status of being classed by turn as hostile to men and thus suspected of being unwomanly, and at the same time as disloyal to women and thus accused of masculine hubris. In consequence, their appearance on the literary scene further complicated the egalitarian foundation of feminist ideology and the identitarian politics inherent in the binary of male versus female.

I begin with this brief recitation of the cultural debate surrounding female Shakespeares and their generic equivalent, exceptional women, and the different and complex paths female intellectuals such as Woolf chose for liberation as a means to underscore tensions apparent in the opening decades of the last century that should strike a familiar, albeit dissonant, chord today. The disagreement then by feminists over extraordinary versus ordinary women, intellectual engagement versus political reform, "steering the van" as opposed to "guarding the rear" brings to mind the dissension that flared in the 1990s over the direction of feminism, present and future, especially as this dissension arises from disparate accounts of feminism's recent past and its current status in the academy.

One powerful installment of the debate over feminism's prospects occurred in issues of *Critical Inquiry* in 1998 and 1999 between Susan Gubar and Robyn Wiegman, in which Wiegman countered Gubar's elegizing of the halcyon days of feminism's institutional ascent through the practice of literary scholarship by calling for another stage in knowledge production. She charged the movement, as she had enjoined an introductory class of women's studies students, "[to] resist the impulse to reproduce only what it thinks it already knows; it must challenge," she insisted, "the impulse to repeat" ("What Ails Feminist Criticism?" 371). Where Gubar bemoaned the replacement of feminist literary scholarship with the recondite methodologies of a new generation of academic feminists that pushed her own and other literary critics' work to the sidelines, Wiegman saw feminist discourses in the 1990s constructively "preoccupied with narrating the history of feminism as both a political movement and an intellectual discourse" (367). This preoccupation was a necessary one, according to Wiegman, who argued that "the academy is not a place outside or separate from the political, nor is its dedication to intellectual labor insignificant in the reproductive practices of a whole host of social dominations" (371).

Despite Wiegman's assurances, Gubar's objections to feminism's espousal of highbrow esotericism were repeated that same year by Martha Nussbaum's censure of what she termed feminism's new insularity. Disputing, like Gubar, its institutional vitality, Nussbaum, in the *New Republic* review "The Professor of Parody," criticized academic feminism's new disciplinary interests, best exemplified by the works of Judith Butler, that had led to an abandonment of feminism's founding values. In Nussbaum's review, Butler's social constructionism amounted to little more than a "hip quietism" that was conducting a rising generation of academic feminists into the cul-de-sac of empty politics and away from the real-world political commitment of social justice for all women. "It tells scores of talented young women," Nussbaum chafed, "that they need not work on changing the law, or feeding the hungry, or assailing power through theory harnessed to material politics. They can do politics in the safety of their campuses, remaining on the symbolic level, making subversive gestures at power through speech and gesture" (45). Spoiled by feminism's institutional success and under the thrall of hyperintellectualism, in Nussbaum's view, Butler and her theory cohorts threatened to dispense not with simply literary criticism and the prestige of a founding generation of university feminists, as Gubar had protested, but with political activism and, worse still, the very category of woman itself. In the aftermath of Nussbaum's appeal for a return to an old-style/real-world feminism centered on women, a thoughtful Wiegman coolly observed in "Feminism, Institutionalism, and the Idiom of Failure" that "to conjoin academic to feminism today is almost always a distinct insult, an accusation that draws its blood precisely because politics and academics have come to be so firmly opposed" (108). Here she tellingly surveyed the divide of feminist doers and knowers along a fault line that, not surprisingly, was located with the academy. That academic success should mark a crisis, she explained this way: "It is this opposition between the political as a set of social movement ideals and the institutional as a project of academic transformation that underlies to a great extent the mood swing in academic feminism in the 1990s, where feminist articulations of the political agenda that impelled it into the academy have been held in check by a diagnostic analysis that seeks to understand the tenor of bad feeling (and hurt feelings) of feminism's current institutional success" (108). As Wiegman subsequently noted in "Feminism's Apocalyptic Futures," such distinguished feminists as "Linda Gordon, Susan Gubar, Nancy K. Miller, Tania Modleski, Martha Nussbaum, Naomi Schor, among others—have expressed their regret about the failure of feminism's present tense. For some of these feminist thinkers, failure is defined by measuring the present according to the ethos, intentions, and critical dimension of a purportedly more activist feminist past, a time prior to both the academic institutionalization of feminism and its public-sphere decline" (807).

Complicating the dispute over feminism's vigor both inside and outside the academy has been the axial disquiet about the resiliency of the humanities and, what's more, of the university as an intellectual institution. Gubar's worry over the humanities' downsizing that "discourages feminist critics from assuming that we will have successors and what successors mean—a future" ("Critical Response II" 392) and Wiegman's concern with the fragile status of any resistant knowledge or knowledges in institutions increasingly under transnational and corporate mandates have been shared by Joan Scott. In the special issue of *differences* she edited on the future prospects of women's studies, Scott situated the uncertain fate of feminist knowledge within the larger context of forecasts over the humanities' decline.[7] With the ongoing restructuring of the university, not only has feminist knowledge been put at risk, but also the humanities mission overall has come under siege—and this at a time when women comprise 56 percent of student populations in U.S. colleges and universities, a figure predicted to rise still higher—and when the new century's vista of digital literacy and transgenic technologies fast approaches. At a moment in which feminist interventions appear particularly acute, Gubar's requiem for the movement's earlier activism and Nussbaum's rebuke of its new ultraintellectualism assume even greater significance and make more urgent the institutional support Wiegman deems vital for disciplinary robustness.

The present friction, therefore, over political commitments and institutional accomplishments, over the worth of recent feminist knowledge, over the breach between the agent and object of feminist practice, and, aggravating this, the question of the absolute ontological status of the category "woman," not to mention the bad feelings the foregoing have occasioned, makes the former debate over exceptional women and Woolf's answering persona two decades later more than an intriguing parallel. In fact, if we take Nancy Cott's point in her study of modern feminism that exceptional women were decisive in the elaboration of twentieth-century women's liberation, then the disagreement of a century ago, excised from the cultural memory of feminism's more recent instantiation, may be seen to signal a divisiveness that has dogged metropolitan feminism from its inception.[8]

Accordingly, to respond to the current debate over "whither" or "withering" feminism, I suggest going further back than the meager temporal allowance of the last thirty years. This is especially the case if among the objectives are, as Wiegman has persuasively argued, to understand and decouple "the discipline's continued commitment to British intellectual and geopolitical colonialism" and "[to] disarticulat[e] the history and meaning of academic feminism from the prototypical plot of white women's subjectivity" ("What Ails Feminist Criticism?" 375, 379). To grasp the changing circumstances that feminism along with the humanities and the university face at the beginning of a new century, we need to understand more fully feminist accreditation at the opening of the last century, by which I mean the process and logic through which feminist intellectuals became agents of knowledge, empowered to reproduce experts like themselves. For those of us whose disciplines are centered in literature departments, this means disturbing the corpus once again of what to Wiegman would be that dead white woman of the British canon, Virginia Woolf, already much in evidence on these pages. Exhuming Woolf, however, gains fresh impetus from Catherine Gallagher's claim of late in "A History of the Precedent: Rhetorics of Legitimation in Women's Writing" that it was the writer's charismatic rhetoric in *A Room of One's Own* and, specifically, her invention of the female precursor, Judith Shakespeare, that fueled feminism's advance over the course of the last century (323–27). Germane to my interests are the content and logic of Gallagher's argument, not the least its recovery of a female writer that not only illustrates again the persistence of the debate over exceptional and ordinary women but also points to the process of accreditation at the heart of disciplinary practice.

Taking Woolf as exemplar, I shall argue in what follows that female literary modernists, with their claims to unique knowledge and with the cultural and intellectual capital these obtained, helped fashion a distinct paradigm of feminist reformation around the arts that has had far-reaching consequences for academic feminism as a mode and practice of knowing. This paradigm, decisively shaped by Woolf's discursive deployment of the exceptional woman, once heralded by *The Freewoman* as indispensably "steering the van," gave to the movement a singularly modern inflection from which reverberates the current discord over the value of its intellectual and institutional achievements. In making this argument I shall attempt to place the modernist movement, a key intellectual component that has on the whole been absent from historicizing feminism, into the amalgam of feminism and its profession.

Crosshairs

It remains more than a passing cultural curiosity that Virginia Woolf was installed as lightning rod and icon of feminist ideology in the closing decades of the twentieth century as she was concurrently being enshrined in the high modernist canon.[9] This seemingly contradictory investiture—snooty Bloomsbury author as feminist high priestess on one hand, and women's champion as high-brow modernist on the other—was precisely the doubled position she sought with "Shakespeare's Sister" and the rudimental one from which she urged women to join her in the professions in her now-famous 1931 speech, "Professions for Women."[10] Woolf's talk in effect bestowed on women aspiring to the professional class the ready-made tradition that Judith Shakespeare conferred on the modern woman writer. The peroration of *A Room of One's Own* and the 1931 speech suggested that both novelist and professional were Judith Shakespeare's rightful heirs. As Woolf declared to her audience at the London Society for Women's Service, professional ascension was as vital an avenue to women's intellectual and economic liberation as had been her ascent as a novelist. Her address notably gave voice to the growing recognition that the accessibility of university education had made professional accreditation increasingly attainable by women. With professional standing, women could broker knowledge and culture, support themselves financially, participate more fully in public life, and thereby tender the model and means for succeeding generations of spirited women to follow. Her talk thus confirmed two trends visible by 1931: one was the crescent of the professional class, and the other was the unprecedented number of women seeking admission to it. Recollecting these should call to mind as well that Woolf's invitation marked the zenith of female professional participation in these decades rather than further increase.

Revisiting this earlier site of metropolitan feminism's ideological formation—the cultural moment of Woolf's literary modernism and her incitement to professionalize—I suggest that her essay and speech served not simply as a rallying cry for female inclusion in the 1920s and 1930s. They also came to serve feminism's subsequent revival and, more particularly, its ascent in the academy and the professions. From the 1970s forward, *A Room of One's Own* and "Professions for Women" functioned in tandem as a master narrative of feminist progress, of a feminist teleology if you will.[11] One unmistakable mark of the narrative's growing prestige was the inclusion of "Shakespeare's Sister" and "Professions for Women" in the fourth edition of *The Norton Anthology of English Literature* (1979) and soon afterward in *The Norton Anthology of Literature by Women: The Tradition in English* (Gilbert and Gubar). The lone representation of "The Mark on the Wall" in the 1968 *Norton Anthology* and its tepid allowance of Woolf as a "brilliant minor figure" (Abrams et al. 1379) gave way in the 1979 edition to selections of fiction and nonfiction, to include her feminist polemics, all capped by this consummate display of intellectual doublespeak: "Virginia Woolf now becomes," hailed the 1979 cover note, "the major author she has always been" (Abrams et al.)[12] Academic publishing's "major author" upgrade acknowledged the literary modernist's new cultural stature and by default the feminist ideology woven into her coattails. Although women scholars in literary and language fields were most immediately advantaged by this notice, it also played a key role in galvanizing and legitimating female intellectuals to write and to speak with authority across academic and professional disciplines. It is no exaggeration to state that Woolf's model and her utopic community of women had broad application outside the practice of literary studies.

Yet feminists' endorsement of Woolf's utopic narrative obscured, to lengthen the above conceit slightly, the modernist ideology lining these same coattails. Here we might take up Gallagher's reassessment of the novelist and of feminism's process of accreditation that discloses the import of neglecting the alliance of feminism and modernism. Though Gallagher's declared purpose in "A History of the Precedent" is to identify the different rhetorics by which women of various epochs have authorized themselves as writers, she conspicuously chooses Woolf as her last example and makes her the prime exemplar of feminism's rise in the twentieth century. However, that her model also proceeds from an expressly modernist ethos merits only this passing remark: "*[L]ike most modernist authors,* [Woolf] derives rhetorical power from the idea of *her singularity,* her inability to proceed comfortably along the normal routes of either reason or custom" (324, emphasis added).

Slighting Woolf's modernist attachments turns out to be a telling omission. Allowing that the charismatic precedent of *A Room of One's Own* "is so familiar to us that we sometimes have difficulty grasping the specifics of its authorization" (323), Gallagher owns having once dismissed in the 1970s such early women writers as the sixteenth-century's Margaret Tyler for their lack of charisma. Her justification reads like a summary of *A Room of One's Own* and "Professions for Women." "Certain as I was that early modern women were afraid to write, that they felt the lack of antecedents and encouragements, that their writing must therefore be interpreted as resistant or rebellious," Gallagher goes on to concede that she had rejected Tyler's writing because of a rhetoric that was traditional, ordinary, "doing nothing new" (310). Without the "new," a quality famously linked to the modernist authors Gallagher casually references, Tyler's rhetorical style lacked, by 1970 feminist critical standards, the generative potency and cachet of Woolf's self-proclaimed singularity and, hence, authority and value. By contrast, armed in 2000 with the understanding that Woolf's singularity is only one of several available modes of legitimation, Gallagher can now correct Tyler's previous omission and admit her to the elect. The changing context is instructive. By identifying with Woolf's charismatic model, "so familiar to us that we sometimes have difficulty grasping the specifics of its authorization"—specifics that included its modernist underpinnings—and rejecting Tyler's ordinary model, Gallagher reveals the exclusionary logic at work in legitimating female writers in the 1970s but without attending to the full implication of its operation. "Like most modernist authors," Woolf, and in her footsteps Gallagher, adopted singularity over reason or custom and chose antecedents accordingly. Beyond certifying predecessors, however, this same logic was employed in authorizing and rejecting contemporaries—other women writers or female scholars or their fields of inquiry or communities of women. To insist of the selection process, as Gallagher then does, that "a rational-legal universalist concept of individual rights underlay it" (326) is to ignore the restrictive terms and turns of her own argument and, by extension, of the larger movement of feminist professionalization.

The consequences of privileging singularity become clearer with Gallagher's final admission. Tyler's belated election is not a felicitous illustration of feminism's increasing inclusiveness but yields instead the sobering conclusion of charismatic feminism's demise. The loss of charisma and its coeval, the loss of exclusion, is apparently of greater moment to feminism than any progress toward the "rational-legal universalist concept of individual rights underl[ying] it." In withholding a progressive outcome, the exclusion pulled off in the 1970s is effectively replicated in 2000. Surely this inference must adhere in Gallagher's closing grievance that the downfall of Woolf's founding charisma spells the limit of academic feminist success: "Its long march though the institutions, especially those of the American academy, have resulted in what [Max] Weber called 'the routinization of charisma'" (326). Feminism's apotheosis is tied to charismatic practice, and its attenuation to postmodern decline: herein, evidently, lies the root of feminism's doldrums.

Yet what Gallagher's earlier disparagement and reappraisal point to is not simply the range of rhetorical precedents available to women writers or more complexly their diminution in the present. Rather, they demonstrate the process of feminism's disciplinary accreditation at the heart of its institutionalization. Without attending to the logic and history of Woolf's modernist interpellation and second-wave feminism's adoption of it, her argument lacks the capacity to disentangle its own enmeshment in modernism's exclusionary practices and, along with it, the ability to discern that possibly only its implementation has become enervated, and not academic feminism or the movement more generally.

For a more productive mechanism by which to understand the function of the charismatic mode and its consequences for Woolf and feminism, we might turn instead to Pierre Bourdieu's analysis of "the fields of cultural production" and his broader explanatory category of "charismatic ideology." When applied to modernism's miscellany of charismatic authors associated with Woolf, Bourdieu's analysis usefully describes the process by which these writers used declarations of their own uniqueness or manifestos of their work's technical or aesthetic mastery to distinguish themselves from rival contemporaries and styles and, even more, to challenge outright the prestige of those dominant in a field that lacks the obvious institutional controls, legal guarantees, and hereditary legacies—all gatekeeping protocols—by which election may be bestowed and acknowledged (*Field* 61–76).[13] Bourdieu's analysis is particularly well suited to literature as a field because the boundaries that separate it from other disciplines and from its lay audience tend to be, as Terry Lovell has so cogently explained, highly porous, such that its expertise is continually being absorbed—and no more so than when it is the most compelling, at which point it is transformed from special knowledge of the expert into the common knowledge of the laity, a point I return to below (Lovell 143–44). Bourdieu's approach to the frisson between generations, contemporaries, and experts provides a means to read Gubar's and Nussbaum's elegies for the feminists of their generation and their special knowledges, and at the same time to pursue Wiegman's entreaty "to challenge the impulse to repeat" in a way that Gallagher's charismatic rhetoric does not allow.

Here I propose that the conjunction of feminism with modernism and the professions that opened this section and that subtends Gallagher's recent analysis is neither mere happenstance nor anomaly but is fundamental to Woolf's ascription as both modernist and feminist, and thus bears significantly, perhaps even fundamentally, on academic feminism. As the "exceptional woman" par excellence, Woolf not only helps explain the logic informing the neglected alliance of metropolitan feminism, modernism, and expert culture but also helps make sense of the contentious setting and precarious circumstances in which feminism finds itself today. At stake, I suggest, is the agency of social reproduction and the model and knowledge this agency empowers. For one key to this understanding, I turn to the modern expert with this all too brief disquisition on the professions.

Cult Status

The now critical commonplace that the expert class became increasingly necessary by the end of the nineteenth century and ultimately indispensable in the twentieth owes much to the work of, among others, Magali Sarfatti Larson, Alvin Gouldner, Burton Bledstein, Harold Perkin, Barbara and John Ehrenreich, and the aforementioned Bourdieu. As their genealogies of modern professionalism imply, the old bourgeois model ideal for producing a national polity of hard-working, God-fearing, law-abiding, thrifty-in-expenditure, and prolific-in-offspring citizens was gradually challenged by another model. This emergent model was, in contrast, decidedly secular and worldly in outlook, more prodigal in spending habits and considerably less sedulous about propagation, and increasingly acculturated to urban technologies and markets to realize the material and cultural progress we now collapse under the idiom "lifestyle."[14] In short, the nineteenth-century model best equipped to spit out, as it were, the propertied and conjugal bourgeois couple or its wannabes was slowly superseded by one that made the dominant classes (industrialists, statesmen, merchants) more and more reliant on expert knowledge for governance, a dependency that the professional classes were only too happy to accommodate with their special know-how.

Yet the intervention of specialists was felt decisively in the one area that those who study the sociology of the professions have only recently begun to accredit as a critical anterior site of expert production. Their studies' oversight became the very insight that Woolf's experimental works of the twenties register: experts came to power in no small measure by supplanting the social order that had become reliant over the Victorian century on the autonomous bourgeois household under the domestic woman's regulation.[15] As feminist literary scholars Nancy Armstrong, Mary Poovey, and Anita Levy—and more recently, Elizabeth Langland and Monica Cohen—have demonstrated, the domestic woman's immediate supervision of everything from the mundane matters of daily life to the complex affective and kinship relations was as instrumental as any public policy or state institution in outfitting the industrial and imperial nation-state with the very citizens and social stability it required.[16] Middle-class women presided over a domain that secured procreation and regulated the affective relations of courtship, domestic romance, monogamous marriage, and the family. What they administered in aggregate enabled the reproduction of a labor force, the transfer of property between families and generations, and the social stability necessary for industrial development, imperial expansion, and national unity. Cashier the domestic woman, and the net effect is to jeopardize the social fabric that held the nation together. Nonetheless, this is in essence what transpired. The social knowledge that once accumulated in the middle-class household and left through its portals as a kind of affective literacy by the end of the nineteenth century was brought increasingly into the home by outside experts from such diverse disciplines as domestic science and sexology, transforming it and the social, subjective, and conjugal reproduction that was once its near-exclusive office.[17] The class of specialists that materialized within a professional and not a strictly social or religious or commercial milieu, that arose in response to the epistemic and economic transformation of the Victorian epoch, nonetheless took the private arenas of home and human consciousness as prized loci of its disciplinary mandate.

It is with this paradigmatic displacement by expert culture of the bourgeois household's authority to include its cultural envoy, the domestic novel, that literary modernists and their technical innovations ought also to be located. Not only did writers and artists have to embrace an aesthetic version of "professional" expertise or forfeit their cultural standing to such disciplines as psychology, anthropology, sociology, medicine, and law, but they also had to bring the social matrix of the home into their cultural orbit if their literary knowledge was to continue to carry any import. In other words, they had to claim the arts as the special province of their expertise or relinquish their positions as social interpreters and cultural mediators. Thus it was against domestic jurisdiction and the professionalization of knowledge that the literate culture that literary modernists came to dominate defined itself.

Although she was a latecomer to the literary avant-garde, Woolf grasped the predicament in which she and her fellow artists found themselves better than any of her contemporaries. Thus in her celebrated domestic novels of the mid-twenties, *Mrs. Dalloway* and *To the Lighthouse,* Woolf returns to the familiar terrain of the Victorian drawing room to modernize the novel with a new model of affective literacy, encased in the eminently portable and highly reproducible technology of consciousness. Here she effectively incorporates the household's affective sensibility within an aesthetic of consciousness that renders the emotional realm subject to her stylistic and disciplinary innovations. In successive steps she first puts upper-class party hostess Clarissa on the streets and then the faculty wife Mrs. Ramsay on canvas, marketing both as aesthetic objects of high art that disguise the novelist's arrogation of domestic ideology and expiate her culpability in usurping it.

In aestheticizing the consciousness of her characters in a distinctly poetic language, Woolf rewrote affective relations and, in so doing, provided a new mechanism by which readers would come to view fictional characters and, more significantly still, to recognize themselves as discrete individuals and as a modern social aggregate. Not only does Woolf's technology of aesthetic interiority, what she called in her diary "dig[ging] out beautiful caves" (*Diary* 2: 263), help to secularize the household, but this technology, in pulsing along apparently unfettered through London streets in *Mrs. Dalloway,* also hollows out an imaginary public space as the authentic private space of consciousness for the laity to read in novels such as hers. This portable technology, ideally suited for what one critic has termed "the homeless mind," operates as a kind of black box of consciousness, ever ticking away, in daydreams and sleep, recording that innermost babble, that ineffable hum of the psyche.[18] It is thus held to record our most secret desires and fantasies, hidden motivations and fears, innermost ambitions and inhibitions—and to this apparatus, literary modernists have given a distinctive, if esoteric, language that functions as an innovative form of emotional literacy. As such, this consciousness contraption came to instruct educated and common readers alike, both male and female, on how to make silent determinations about their fellow pedestrians of the metropolis and, of even greater consequence, to make silent determinations of themselves, suggesting that they no longer need, nor can they rely on, the Angel in the House whispering in their ears what they should or should not feel or do or think. The Victorian woman's social knowledge was, in short, rendered obsolete. In its place, modernist technology hardwired us all. So naturalized has this technology become, an example of Lovell's insight, that we are hardly cognizant of its history, much less able to recognize how our individual consciousnesses reproduce it on a daily basis.

My larger point here, however, is to draw attention to how the modernist Woolf undertook to displace a singular form of female social knowledge and the Victorian model it served with her own arguably unique knowledge and model. This appropriation of authority over a paradigm under stress should not be lost on us in the present moment, nor should the means by which it was accomplished. A highly lyrical prose and a technology for narrating consciousness masked Woolf's interests in replacing the material, affective, and ideological bases of the domestic household with her own: the social angel and Victorian novelist for the metropolitan subject and literary modernist, if you will. Of critical importance is this: just as the social model of the middle-class household screened the political interests of the propertied middle class and defused class conflicts under the cover of emotional truth, so too does this literary model under the cover of stylized emotional truth come to screen the evidence and political interests of its own ideological production, and with this end in view.[19] The erasure operates under the supervision and for the benefit of modernist experts such as Woolf. For it is their specialized knowledge that becomes a new mechanism of social reproduction and, inasmuch as the cognoscenti hail it as the primary means by which modern consciousness can be known, it also becomes a new standard of cultural accreditation. In asserting their uniqueness and autonomy, in deploying, according to Gallagher, not a traditional or rational but a specifically charismatic rhetoric, literary modernists appropriate the domestic woman's ideological con, I am suggesting, of shielding their social disciplinary apparatus of affect and emotion under the cover of innovative language and take it into new territory with their aesthetic of interiority. In lieu of the private household as the disciplinary locus of emotional truth, we have the aesthetic preserve of modern consciousness produced by literary artists—allegedly separate from other knowledges and professedly exempt from commercial taint, yet eminently mobile and universal—and this is for the edification of an elite literary constituency and, more broadly, for the laity. The end result is a versatile apparatus of social reproduction that relies on and legitimates literary modernists' expertise. Viewed from a metacritical vantage point, it suggests that modernism obeys the same logic as do those disciplines that formally professionalize themselves in order to establish its literary expertise as an autonomous and valuable domain of knowledge and its practitioners as the specialists who determine and dispense their esoteric knowledge as universal truth.[20]

In the process, literary modernists gain social standing and cultural capital for their intellectual and artistic labor. Of equal remark, the novelist Woolf's success effectually elevates female intellectuals and artists as exceptional practitioners on a par with their exceptional male counterparts. It is from this expert position and with the cultural capital of her critical and commercial successes from *Dalloway* to *Orlando* that Woolf can first entreat women to become independent writers in *A Room of One's Own* by proleptically constructing a genealogy based on her imaginary female predecessor Judith Shakespeare, and thereafter to enter the professions tout court in "Professions for Women." In other words, for Woolf it was a short step from the logic of the expert to the cult of the expert. As the stuff now of feminist myth, in "Professions" she baldly murders the Angel in the House, the personification of Victorian domesticity, and thereby bids farewell to domestic governance. In her next breath, she summons the educated daughters of the deposed matriarch to join her in the professions. Hence it is with these liberatory exploits that Gallagher can read "Woolf's rhetoric as an attempt to create an emancipatory alternative inside a charismatic trend," thus effectively doubling her singularity: Woolf is the exceptional writer who is also an exception to modernist charisma, or, by way of Weber's taxonomy of rhetorics, Woolf represents "the transformation of charisma in an anti-authoritarian direction" (Weber, *Theory* 386, qtd. in Gallagher 325). And to the extent that women have heard and heeded, Gallagher is, of course, quite correct, but as her belated rescue of Margaret Tyler suggests, some women were more directly summoned than others. So I return to the vexed problem of inclusion: who were hailed, and on whose terms?

Professional Syntax

To address these questions, let me return for a moment to the scholars who write on the expert class for a description of its logic and credential process. According to Alvin Gouldner, this new class is fundamentally antiegalitarian: "the special privileges and powers of the New Class [of professionals] are grounded in their *individual* control of special cultures, languages, techniques, and of the skills resulting from these" (19). For the Ehrenreichs, the logic of professionalism operates by the appropriation and suppression of the functions and knowledge of an indigenous or native group (319). Of this acquisitive practice, Mary Poovey's study of gender ideology in the Victorian epoch implies that the professional class recharacterized the separate sphere model into specialist versus nonspecialist as a means to consolidate its authority (*Uneven*). Describing this vetting process more bluntly still, Magali Sarfatti Larson calls it the structure of "modern inequality." In her view, "professionalization [is] the process by which producers of special services [seek] to constitute *and control* a market for their expertise" (xvi). While Larson's focus is the public and economic realms and not the cultural realm of artists and intellectuals per se, her insight is nonetheless relevant. She posits that expert culture "inaugurated a new form of structured inequality," the implementation of which "prefigure[d] the general restructuring of social inequality in contemporary capitalist societies." One singular outgrowth is "the achievement of socially recognized expertise" (xvii).

Antiegalitarian, monopoly of expertise, structured inequality, confiscation and suppression of local knowledges, such logic and terms surely describe literary modernism, not only by my calculation but by its own, with its elite ethos, its claims of uniqueness and aesthetic mastery, its insistence on autonomy and rupture with the past, and its experimental practice patterned on scientific inquiry.[21] Most of these criteria have, in fact, found a target in the modernist Woolf. They have thus made tenuous from the start any attempt to construct a firewall between her modernism and her feminism. The reason for the tenuity, I suggest, is that the logic of expert knowledge, which underlies her ascription as a charismatic modernist, is the same logic that informs her ascription as a charismatic feminist. She is the self-professed exceptional woman writer, the self-spawned issue of an imaginary female Shakespeare. Indeed, the speech "Professions for Women" provides a veritable *bildung* for such female progeny. With the reflexive overture "my profession of literature," Woolf breezily recounts to a rising generation of young British women of the educated bourgeoisie how she quit hack journalism, offed the Angel in the House, and opted for the higher caste and independence of creative novelist, backed, it should be noted, by an inheritance and the classy consumables of pedigree cat and private motor car ("Professions" 284–87). Her derogation of domestic ideology (local female knowledges), promotion of novelistic expertise (lyrical prose and technical innovations in the novel), and emphasis on income and quality objects (cats and cars) detail the process of professional accreditation whether in the service of authorizing her modernism or her feminism. Her peroration is simple and direct: social reproduction now rests with the expert class; either join it or become its object. Agent of knowledge or object of study appears to be the alternative. These moves indicate an awareness of where power resided and how professional ascription would function in the decades to come. Just as momentous, this charismatic speech, which details the mechanism of modernist investiture as a model to women of her educated class, became in the hands of second-wave feminists what I earlier termed a master narrative of feminist progress that helped authorize feminism in the field of literature and more broadly in the academy in the closing decades of the last century and in no small manner contributed to the success that is presently drawing fire.

Quo Vadis?

My points on the convergence of feminism, modernism, and the professions are several. To begin with, their convergence helps explain why Gallagher considers that "feminism's charisma [became] a victim of its own success" (326). With its institutionalization, "we bury the charismatic corpse," from which she extrapolates, with a perspicacity similar to Gubar's, that "critical reflection inside the academy repeats and reinforces fragmenting trends that have intensified the differences between women in the society at large" (326–27). Yet instead of burying the charismatic corpse or bemoaning fragmenting trends and the intensification of differences as unexpected or uncommon or debilitating outcomes, let me offer a different response and direction.

We would do well to acknowledge that professional and modernist ideology, out of which emerged the cult of the modern expert, helped empower feminist discourses in the academy and at the same time made them complicit with structures of domination active over the last century. These structures operate by producing specialists who suppress others as less knowledgeable and who selectively credentialize others to sustain, extend, and reproduce their expertise. In fact, we can trace this operation and its consequences in Woolf's neglect of her contemporaries, as Ann Ardis and Suzanne Clark have so lucidly demonstrated.[22] Or to pursue the earlier example, we find it in Woolf's deprecation of domesticity. Not only did the writer, along with her modernist peers, male and female alike, encourage the dismantling of household authority and the domestic woman's social knowledge, but her apparent desire as a feminist to replace it with literary and professional expertise carried new terms of exclusion. Making the household the universal measure of all women's oppression allowed educated white feminists of Woolf's time and of the 1970s to overlook the conditions of their own privilege. Ignoring the bourgeois household's historical and social specificity, they dismissed out of hand complex differences of class and race, ethnicity and sexuality that made for other equally compelling and contingent instantiations of the home. Thus, for example, as Harriet Jacobs's nineteenth-century liberation narrative *Incidents in the Life of a Slave Girl* instructs, slave and manumitted women's claims to marriage and children, to possessions and labor were not unequivocal evidence of their oppression in the ante- and postbellum United States. On the contrary, their ability to marry and to nurture their own children might function as clear manifestations of their emancipation. More than a century later, same-sex couples, in agitating for these rights (marriage, family, children, and property), plead a similar case. Despite these counterexamples, metropolitan feminists even in the present moment continue to cut their academic teeth, as it were, by acceding to the central orthodoxy that disparages domesticity.[23]

Moreover, despite efforts of greater inclusion and more nuanced historical narratives, there remains this impasse over Woolf's advocacy—and that is the problem of class, which is my second point. Critics long recognized and academic feminists apologized for the British novelist's inability to hurdle class barriers, but such apologies were based on the assumption that the failure arose from social values and a class standing that Woolf inherited and that they had subsequently expunged. She knew better but couldn't do better, or so the story has gone. How different both her position and that of academic feminists become once we understand that she actively erected exclusionary barriers as part of the ideology of the expert and that these very barriers, aesthetic ones among them, made possible her ascent as modernist artist and feminist intellectual. In essence, these same barriers have authorized female intellectuals after her, not the least feminist scholars and writers who, like myself, made her model theirs.

These barriers, be they ones of intellectual or aesthetic capital, institutional position, professional privilege, or academic pedigree, have ensured that whether the feminist teleological horizon is assimilation or absolute difference, uplift or solidarity, its limit would never be reached by all at once or even once and for all. For academic feminists whose lineage owes to the enfranchised elite of the educated bourgeoisie, this vista holds forth the promise of further interventions to achieve broader participation and the necessity of greater and updated knowledge, my third point. Both are characteristic of the professions and modernism and equally address Gubar's and Wiegman's very different responses. Gubar's complaint that the once feminist elect subsequently becomes its abjected is, in one sense, in line with Wiegman's encouragement of feminists to think anew, to resist repeating what is already known. Apparent opposites, they manifest the twin sides of professional ideology, what the modernist credo expresses in "*faire nouveau,*" out with the old and in with the new, the imperative of a modern culture driven by innovation and harried by obsolescence. This imperative, intrinsic to the expert classes, exerts significant pressure on them, according to Gouldner, who observes that because knowledges are not of themselves productive, experts must continually update, renew, and justify their specializations, or watch them be cast aside. This imperative has made for a kind of congenital transience for the professional class that appears to disturb academic feminism as well. Understood in the context of Bourdieu's analysis of "fields of cultural production," it suggests that "[i]n every field, the dominant have an interest in continuity, identity, and reproduction, whereas the dominated, the newcomers, are for discontinuity, rupture and subversion" (*Field* 340 n.15). So in a way, Gubar's feminist gothic, Nussbaum's theory lampoon, and Gallagher's charismatic corpse have got it right as they worry whether the chosen and what they know may well become routine, ordinary, or passé tomorrow. But such turnover is not unequivocally deleterious or, indeed, the entire story. Wiegman's incitement to make feminist knowledge new and relevant, though clearly not meant to be self-serving, alerts us to the dynamic pace of change we confront as intellectuals and must account for in our research, not the least of which is this: the knowledge production that made possible women's educational advances, to include academic success, vital as they have been, is contingent and will not necessarily answer for the future. As well, Wiegman's charge reminds us that knowledge is itself a commodity, and while the pressure to make it profitable or productive or useful has perhaps never been greater, its value cannot be so easily measured or predicted, a point Nussbaum neglects in her criticism of Butler's theoretical scholarship. Moreover, as knowledge requires capital to produce and sustain it, so also do resistant knowledges that challenge the dominant order, rendering them, as Wiegman noted, particularly fragile endeavors.

Which introduces a fourth point: by making clear the hegemonic mechanism of social reproduction that academic feminists have practiced from inside the academy when speaking and representing women on the outside with all the privileged nuances these Spivakian terms convey, I hope to put in some perspective the complexity of the mandates that informed this essay—the present antagonism over feminists' academic success, the generational rift between feminists, the disagreement over methodologies and objects of study, and the uncertain future of feminist discourse. To understand these tensions, it is not enough, I suggest, to decouple "the discipline's continued commitment to British intellectual and geopolitical colonialism" and to "disarticulat[e] the history and meaning of academic feminism from the prototypical plot of white women's subjectivity" (Wiegman, "What Ails Feminist Criticism" 375, 379) if these ignore the underlying exclusionary practices subscribed to irrespective of field or of any lingering Anglocentrism. Decoupling British hegemony and disarticulating white women's subjectivity, compelling and necessary objectives as they are, will remain insufficient as long as the professional ideology informing them is not also acknowledged.

Taking seriously Woolf's model and what it became for feminists, a master narrative of progress, with all its checkered history and results, we would do well to heed its logic of appropriation and displacement. And Joan Scott's and, more recently still, Mary Poovey's unease over the position of the humanities helps explain why. There is little argument that the United States (and not the United Kingdom) succeeded as an imperial nation-state in part by subsidizing knowledge production through the institution of the university in a way unprecedented over the last century.[24] Notwithstanding, every indication suggests, as Bill Readings's prescient study has proposed, that this project and the creation of the modern intellectual class within the university are being radically altered as are, along with them, the humanities.[25] In my view, we are witnessing the transformation of the professional model as it operated over the last century, and of those enfranchised by it, to include academic intellectuals. By now we can all parse the several trends in the academy that make this change appear inexorable: the decommissioning and corporatization of the research university, the emergence of brick-and-click hybrid institutions more attuned to markets than dedicated to research and teaching, the proletarianization of the professoriate, the replacement of faculty and their expertise in the classroom with digital technologies, the "free market" conversion of the humanities curriculum into a content industry and its instructors into content providers. As such, this restructuring of the university and the humanities' mission directly affects academic feminist scholarship and feminism's future efficacy. Yet to argue that the expert model, which helped to advance the profession of feminism in the academy, is changing is not to argue that feminist intellectuals and knowledge production won't be needed in the future or that the movement has surpassed itself. For academic feminism, given its historical contingency, is not synchronous with the feminist movement, nor can it be collapsed with the feminist movement, any more than could be Gubar's "literary" feminism. These are critical distinctions.

If the professional model as it functioned over the last century has reached its limit, then feminist knowledges and the movement writ large may be more necessary than ever. Here we might take our bearings from the 1911 editorial policy of the short-lived *Freewoman.* Its advocacy of "guarding the rear" as it urged on "steering the van"—risked at the highly contentious moment in which suffrage seemed all in all and Judith Shakespeare's name was yet unspoken—suggests that neither greater inclusiveness nor the creation of new knowledges is a cataclysmic sign of betrayal or of disintegration, even when such a move entails, as 1990s antagonisms register, a reduction of charisma for some methods or fields or practitioners or generations and an increase for others. Instead of the perspective that "critical reflection inside the academy repeats and reinforces fragmenting trends that have intensified the differences between women in the society at large" (327), which Gallagher proposes, we should perhaps attend to this greater one: the feminist movement was a partner to the most profound social change of the last century. How we answer this trust in a new century is most crucial, especially since in these extraordinary times, all we shall need to know, much less the models we'll confront and seize, is unclear.

Notes

The argument for this essay is drawn from the larger book project on modernism and expert culture entitled *Expert Modernists, Matricide, and Modern Culture: Woolf, Forster, Joyce* forthcoming by Palgrave Macmillan. I wish to thank Rita Raley and Dolora Wojciehowski for reading and commenting on drafts of the essay, and also the reviewers and editors at *Signs* for their very helpful comments. To the Huntington Library and its director of research, Robert C. Ritchie, I extend sincere thanks for the fellowship that enabled me to research and complete the essay. I presented an early version of this work at the Second Biennial Feminism(s) and Rhetoric(s) Conference in October 1999.

1. I am indebted to Lisa Tickner's work for introducing me to the history of this figure. In the famous gloss on George Macaulay Trevelyan's history, Woolf avers: "It would have been extremely odd, even upon this showing, had one of them [the women of the Elizabethan age] suddenly written the plays of Shakespeare, I concluded, and I thought of that old gentleman, who is dead now, but was a bishop, I think, who declared that it was impossible for any woman, past, present, or to come, to have the genius of Shakespeare" (*Room* 69–70). See also note 6 below, which details the 1920 debate between Woolf and Desmond MacCarthy over women's ability and Shakespeare's genius.

2. The play was staged in the spring of 1907 by Harley Granville Barker at the Court Theater of London and subsequently published as a novel that same fall. In 1909 the play also had a run of sixteen performances at Wallack's Theater in New York. In an essay for *Collier's Weekly* on June 29, 1907, titled "The Feministe Movement in England," Robins admitted: "I am one of those who, until comparatively recently, was an ignorant opponent of Woman Suffrage." The transforming event that led her to espouse the cause of women's suffrage appears very like the one dramatized in *Votes for Women* at Trafalgar Square: "But on that Sunday afternoon, in front of Nelson's Monument," Robins recounts, "a new chapter was begun for me in the lesson of faith in the capacities of women" (40).

3. In her 1905 essay collection, Marie Corelli answered the want of a female Shakespeare by declaring: "I do not think we shall ever have a female Shakespeare, for instance. But, at the same time, I equally do not think we shall ever again have a male one!" (174). A few years later in "Genius and Women Painters," Mary Lowndes would remonstrate: "How many times have women been reminded—in season and

out of season, in conversation, by platform speakers, in print—that their sex has produced no Michael Angelo, and that Raphael was a man?" (31).

4. It should be recalled that the founding editors of *The Freewoman,* Dora Marsden and Mary Gawthorpe, were themselves active in the militant Women's Social and Political Union; Gawthorpe was even imprisoned for her suffrage activism in 1906. While the fate of the weekly, in its morphing to *New Freewoman* and then to the *Egoist,* edited by Ezra Pound, is generally read as the capitulation of its feminist ideals (see Fernihough 491), its attachment to the critical values of the exceptional and creative intellect, which we now readily associate with modernism, remained intact.

5. Added to this cuff at women's equality, the journal declared: "Nor for one moment do we wish to support the view that all women will be free, any more than all men are free" ("Commentary" 21). It did concede, however, that the disparity between ordinary and exceptional women had social causes that could be ameliorated by greater cultural opportunities: "so many women appear ordinary, not because they are born ordinary, but because they are bundled pell-mell into a sphere in which they can show no special gift; and because they are expected to be so bundled, they are deprived of that training which would enable them to make their individual revelation communicable, that is, of their chance to become artists" ("Commentary" 21).

6. A duel in the press over the intellectual abilities of women, sparked by the publication of Arnold Bennett's *Our Women,* was also a likely antecedent of Woolf's later creation of Judith Shakespeare. Woman's intellectual endowment, according to Bennett and then to Desmond MacCarthy in his column in *The New Statesman,* was not only less than man's but was also resistant to improvement. "Some women undoubtedly have genius," MacCarthy allowed, "but genius in a lesser degree than Shakespeare, Newton, Michael Angelo, Beethoven, Tolstoi." Woolf took considerable offense at their remarks and spoke directly to the importance of the exceptional woman in her two responses under the title "The Intellectual Status of Women" (*New Statesman; Diary* 2: 342; see also Fox 145–47 and notes). See my discussion of Woolf's reticence about suffrage in "Retailing the Female Intellectual" (30–33, 56–57).

7. Scott expressed these concerns in "Women's Studies on the Edge. Introduction" (i–iv). In the same issue, see also Wendy Brown's "The Impossibility of Women's Studies."

8. "In contrast to nineteenth-century women's small likelihood of distinction except in women's rights or women-oriented activities," Cott contends, "twentieth-century women stood out as individuals, for pursuits not obviously determined by sex nor undertaken for the advancement of their sex" (239).

9. These two very different but related treatments of Woolf, as feminist and as

modernist, can be seen converging in Toril Moi's mid-eighties work *Sexual/Textual Politics.* Replying to what Elaine Showalter described as Woolf's equivocal feminism, Moi countered with a critical deconstruction of the traditional humanist aesthetics privileged by Showalter and concluded by glorifying Woolf the avant-garde modernist as feminism's "great mother and sister" (15). The referent is of course Showalter's chapter on Woolf, "Virginia Woolf and the Flight into Androgyny," in *A Literature of Their Own.* For a very helpful overview of the criticism on Woolf's feminism, see Laura Marcus, "Woolf's Feminism and Feminism's Woolf."

10. Woolf spoke along with Ethel Smyth, composer, writer, and suffrage activist, before the London Society for Women's Service, a professional women's group. The typescript appeared as "Speech Before the London/National Society for Women's Service, January 21, 1931," in *The Pargiters,* which Woolf first conceived as an experimental composite of essay and fiction. Her experiment gradually evolved into the novel *The Years,* with the speech published posthumously in a much-reduced state as "Professions for Women" in *The Death of the Moth and Other Essays.* This reduced version was later included in Woolf's *Collected Essays.*

11. See Joan Scott's query on the fate of such narratives in her introductory essay in *differences,* "Women's Studies on the Edge."

12. Not only was Woolf's work "signally increased" by editors and cofounders of the anthology, M. H. Abrams and David Daiches (Abrams et al. 1979, xxxviii), but also added for the first time was a significant portion of work by such writers as Mary Wollstonecraft and Mary Shelley. The sixth and now seventh *Norton* editions carry *A Room of One's Own* in its entirety. As Margaret Ezell has remarked of Woolf's essay, "No single theoretical text has had as much impact on shaping both the contents and the vocabulary of existing anthologies and teaching texts as Woolf's lecture series to the students at Newnham and Girton" (44). And no group of feminist scholars has employed Woolf's text more resolutely than Showalter, Gubar, Ellen Moers, and Susan Gilbert. Ezell credits them with collectively producing the linear historical narrative of female creativity that underwrote not only their own scholarly endeavors but also the development of the field known as women's studies.

13. As Bourdieu observes: "The history of the field arises from the struggle between the established figures and the young challengers. The ageing of authors, schools, and works is far from being the product of a mechanical, chronological, slide into the past; it results from the struggle between those who have made their mark (*fait date*—'made an epoch') and who are fighting to persist, and those who cannot make their own mark without pushing into the past those who have an interest in stopping the clock, eternizing the present stage of things" (*Field* 339–40). He describes this cultural circuitry in his dialectics of cognition (*connaissance*) and

recognition (*reconnaissance*) ("Intellectual Field" 22, 111) and in his introduction to *Distinction: A Social Critique of the Judgement of Taste* (1–7). For another complementary perspective on charismatic ideology as the modern professional ethos, see Bledstein (93–97).

14. Weber's distinction of classes and status groups merits quoting: "With some over-simplification, one might say that 'classes' are stratified according to their relations to the production and acquisition of goods; whereas 'status groups' are stratified according to the principles of their *consumption* of goods as represented by special 'styles of life'" (*From Max Weber* 193).

15. Peter Laslett's study of the family as a social organization argues that social scientists tended to view its history through the lens of "folk memory" and used contemporaneous family models of so-called primitive societies as the historical past of "advanced" Western ones. It is this very erasure of the immediate past of the Western family and its replacement with a primitive model that allowed social scientists to assert disciplinary control over the field of the family and household by denying their own historical context. As Laslett revealingly notes: "The very term *history* itself represents an earlier phase in their [social scientists'] development which probably had to be rejected if properly empirical and adequately comparative research was to get under way" (Laslett and Wall 2–4).

16. I refer of course to Armstrong; Poovey, *Uneven;* and Levy, *Other Women.* For refinements to these, see Langland and Cohen.

17. This premise owes much to Levy's *Other Women* and, in particular, her epilogue "Modernism, Professionalism, and Gender," which points specifically to the trespass on domestic governance by the expert knowledge of psychology and of social sciences and then links their expertise to literary modernism; see as well Levy, "Gendered Labor."

18. *Homeless mind* is the term, according to Hilde Heyen's *Architecture and Modernity,* that best captures the condition of the mobile and rootless indigene of modernity.

19. Poovey provides the clearest gloss on this operation: "One of the functions of the opposition between the private, feminized sphere and the masculine sphere of work outside the home was to mitigate the effects of the alienation of market relations. The illusion that freedom and autonomy existed for the man within the home therefore depended on the illusion that within the home no one was alienated—and this depended on believing that woman desired to be only what the man wanted her to be—that her reproductive capacity dictated her 'maternal nature' and this nature was not sexually aggressive but selfless and domestic" (*Uneven* 77–78).

20. As Bledstein describes expert culture more generally: "the culture of professionalism required amateurs to 'trust' in the integrity of trained persons, to respect

the moral authority of those whose claim to power lay in the sphere of the sacred and the charismatic. Professionals controlled the magic circle of scientific knowledge which only the few, specialized by training and indoctrination, were privileged to enter, but which all in the name of nature's universality were obliged to appreciate" (90).

21. For a more developed list of these criteria, see Huyssen 197. See also John Carey's study of the elitism of modernist intellectuals, in which he contends that "the spread of literacy to the 'masses' impelled intellectuals in the early twentieth century to produce a mode of culture (modernism) that the masses could not enjoy" (214).

22. See Ardis's study of Woolf's slighting of New Woman novelists and fiction and Clark's of sentimental affect.

23. I am not here advocating a return to the cult of domesticity of either the Victorian epoch or cold war era. Instead I suggest that to discredit domestic models out of hand is to ignore their contingency and specificity and also to overlook one central means by which modernists and feminists, as well as the professional classes, authorized themselves. Efforts to dismantle the separate sphere taxonomy, which has become a virtual cottage industry of feminist criticism, as had earlier efforts of uncovering it in every literary and historical text from Chaucer to Faulkner, testify to the importance of domesticity in the founding and elaboration of feminist discourse.

24. Poovey's account of government support of the university deserves quoting at length: "Between the 1940s and 1964, government investment in university science grew at an exponential rate, at which point it stopped increasing. The long history of the university's reliance on government funds means that the ideal of disinterested inquiry has always been more myth than reality. Nevertheless, and especially after World War II, government support for university science heavily favored research over the development of specific products, and guidelines that regulated the use of federal funds, like the provision for indirect costs, enabled universities to support programs not directly linked to the sciences. Paradoxically, then, the combination of government support for university science and provisions that allowed universities to redistribute this wealth beyond the sciences enabled universities to acquire a remarkable degree of relative autonomy in modern U.S. society. This autonomy is signaled by the universities' ability to foster programs that do not pay for themselves, to establish and maintain standards of academic freedom, and to successfully defend the institution of tenure, despite complaints that the latter violates the principles of a free market in labor" ("Twenty-First Century" 3–4).

25. Readings's work is only one of several examining the plight of the humanities. See also Nelson; Bérubé; Scholes; and Showalter, "Presidential Address."

Works Cited

Abrams, M. H., et al., eds. *Norton Anthology of English Literature.* Rev. ed. Vol. 2. New York: W. W. Norton, 1968.

———. *Norton Anthology of English Literature.* 4th ed. Vol. 2. New York: W. W. Norton, 1979.

———. *Norton Anthology of English Literature.* 6th ed. Vol. 2. New York: W. W. Norton, 1993.

———. *Norton Anthology of English Literature.* 7th ed. Vol. 2. New York: W. W. Norton, 2000.

Ardis, Ann L. *New Women, New Novels: Feminism and Early Modernism.* New Brunswick, NJ: Rutgers UP, 1990.

Armstrong, Nancy. *Desire and Domestic Fiction: A Political History of the Novel.* New York: Oxford UP, 1987.

Bérubé, Michael. *The Employment of English: Theory, Jobs, and the Future of Literary Studies.* New York: New York UP, 1998.

Bledstein, Burton J. *The Culture of Professionalism: The Middle Class and the Development of Higher Education in America.* New York: W. W. Norton, 1976.

Bourdieu, Pierre. *Distinction: A Social Critique of the Judgement of Taste.* Trans. Richard Nice. Cambridge: Harvard UP, 1984.

———. *The Field of Cultural Production: Essays on Art and Literature.* Ed. Randal Johnson. New York: Columbia UP, 1993.

———. "The Intellectual Field: A World Apart." *In Other Words: Essays towards a Reflexive Sociology.* Trans. Matthew Anderson. Stanford, CA: Stanford UP, 1990. 140–49.

Brown, Wendy. "The Impossibility of Women's Studies." *differences* 9.3 (1997): 79–101.

Carey, John. *Intellectuals and the Masses: Pride and Prejudice among the Literary Intelligentsia, 1880–1939.* New York: St. Martin's, 1992.

Clark, Suzanne. *Sentimental Modernism, Women Writers and the Revolution of the Word.* Bloomington: Indiana UP, 1991.

Cohen, Monica F. *Professional Domesticity in the Victorian Novel: Women, Work, and Home.* Cambridge: Cambridge UP, 1998.

"Commentary on the Bondwoman." *The Freewoman, A Weekly Feminist Review* 30.2 (1911): 21–22.

Corelli, Marie. *Free Opinions Freely Expressed on Certain Phases of Modern Social Life and Conduct.* London: Archibald Constable, 1905.

Cott, Nancy F. *The Grounding of Modern Feminism.* New Haven, CT: Yale UP, 1987.

Cucullu, Lois. "Retailing the Female Intellectual." *differences* 9.2 (1997): 25–68.

Ehrenreich, Barbara, and John Ehrenreich. "The Professional-Managerial Class." *Between Labor and Capital.* Ed. Pat Walker. Boston: South End Press, 1979. 5–45.

Ezell, Margaret J. M. *Writing Women's Literary History.* Baltimore: Johns Hopkins UP, 1993.

Fernihough, Anne. "'Go in Fear of Abstractions': Modernism and the Spectre of Democracy." *Textual Practice* 14 (2000): 479–97.

Fox, Alice. "Literary Allusion as Feminist Criticism in *A Room of One's Own.*" *Philological Quarterly* 63.2 (1984): 145–62.

Gallagher, Catherine. "A History of the Precedent: Rhetorics of Legitimation in Women's Writing." *Critical Inquiry* 26 (2000): 309–27.

Gawthorpe, Mary. "To the Women's Social and Political Union." *The Freewoman, A Weekly Feminist Review* 7.3 (1911): 41–42.

Gilbert, Susan, and Sandra Gubar, eds. *Norton Anthology of Literature by Women: The Tradition in English.* New York: W. W. Norton, 1985.

Gouldner, Alvin W. *The Future of Intellectuals and the Rise of the New Class: A Frame of Reference, Theses, Conjectures, Arguments, and an Historical Perspective on the Role of Intellectuals and Intelligentsia in the International Class Contest of the Modern Era.* New York: Continuum, 1980.

Gubar, Susan. "Critical Response II: Notations *in Media Res.*" *Critical Inquiry* 25 (1999): 380–96.

———. "What Ails Feminism?" *Critical Inquiry* 24 (1998): 878–902.

Heynen, Hilde. *Architecture and Modernity: A Critique.* Cambridge: MIT Press, 1999.

Huyssen, Andreas. "Mass Culture as Woman, Modernism's Other." *Studies in Entertainment: Critical Approaches to Mass Culture.* Ed. Tania Modleski. Bloomington: Indiana UP, 1986. 188–207.

Jacobs, Harriet [Linda Brent]. 1861. *Incidents in the Life of a Slave Girl: Written by Herself.* Ed. Lydia Marie Child; ed. and intro. Jean Fagan Yellin. Cambridge: Harvard UP, 1987.

Langland, Elizabeth. *Nobody's Angels: Middle-Class Women and Domestic Ideology in Victorian Culture.* Ithaca, NY: Cornell UP, 1995.

Larson, Magali Sarfatti. *The Rise of Professionalism: A Sociological Analysis.* Berkeley: U of California P, 1977.

Laslett, Peter, and Richard Wall, eds. *Household and Family in Past Time: Comparative Studies in the Size and Structure of the Domestic Group over the Last Three Centuries in England, France, Serbia, Japan, and Colonial North America, with Further Materials from Western Europe.* Cambridge: Cambridge UP, 1972.

Levy, Anita. "Gendered Labor, the Woman Writer, and Dorothy Richardson." *Novel* 25.1 (1991): 50–70.

———. *Other Women: The Writing of Class, Race, and Gender, 1832–1898.* Princeton, NJ: Princeton UP, 1991.

Lovell, Terry. *Consuming Fiction.* London: Verso, 1987.

Lowndes, Mary. "Genius and Women Painters." *Common Cause* (Apr. 17, 1914), 31.

MacCarthy, Desmond (pseud. Affable Hawk). "Books in General." *New Statesman* (Oct. 2, 1920).

Marcus, Laura. "Woolf's Feminism and Feminism's Woolf." *The Cambridge Companion to Virginia Woolf.* Ed. Sue Roe and Susan Sellers. Cambridge: Cambridge UP, 2000. 209–44.

Moi, Toril. *Sexual/Textual Politics: Feminist Literary Theory.* London: Methuen, 1985.

Moers, Ellen. *Literary Women.* Garden City, NY: Doubleday, 1976.

Nelson, Cary. *Manifesto of a Tenured Radical.* New York: New York UP, 1997.

"Notes of the Week." *The Freewoman, A Weekly Feminist Review* 23.1 (1911): 3–4.

Nussbaum, Martha. "The Professor of Parody: The Hip Defeatism of Judith Butler." *New Republic* 220.16 (1999): 37–45.

Perkin, Harold James. *The Rise of Professional Society: England since 1880.* London: Routledge, 1989.

Poovey, Mary. "The Twenty-First-Century University and the Market. What Price Economic Viability?" *differences* 12.1 (2001): 1–16.

———. *Uneven Developments: The Ideological Work of Gender in Mid-Victorian England.* Chicago: U of Chicago P, 1988.

Readings, Bill. *The University in Ruins.* Cambridge: Harvard UP, 1996.

Robins, Elizabeth. *The Convert.* New York: Macmillan, 1907.

———. 1907. "The Feministe Movement." *Way Stations.* New York: Dodd, Mead, 1913. 40–45.

———. 1908. "Suffrage Camp Revisited." *Way Stations.* New York: Dodd, Mead, 1913. 50–74.

———. [1907]. *Votes for Women: A Play in Three Acts.* London: Mills & Boon, n.d.

Scholes, Robert E. *The Rise and Fall of English: Reconstructing English as a Discipline.* New Haven, CT: Yale UP, 1998.

Scott, Joan Wallach. "Women's Studies on the Edge. Introduction." *differences* 9.3 (1997): i–v.

Showalter, Elaine. *A Literature of Their Own: British Women Novelists from Brontë to Lessing.* Princeton, NJ: Princeton UP, 1977.

———. "Presidential Address, 1998: 'Regeneration.'" *PMLA* 114 (1999): 318–28.

Weber, Max. *From Max Weber: Essays in Sociology.* Ed. and trans. H. H. Gerth and C. Wright Mills. New York: Oxford UP, 1946.

———. *The Theory of Social and Economic Organization.* Trans. A. M. Henderson and Talcott Parsons. New York: Free Press, 1947.

Wiegman, Robyn. "Feminism, Institutionalism, and the Idiom of Failure." *differences* 11.3 (1999): 107–36.

———. "Feminism's Apocalyptic Futures." *New Literary History* 31 (2000): 805–25.

———. "What Ails Feminist Criticism? A Second Opinion." *Critical Inquiry* 25 (1999): 362–79.

Woolf, Virginia. *The Diary of Virginia Woolf.* Ed. Anne Olivier Bell. 4 vols. New York: Harcourt, 1977–1984.

———. "The Intellectual Status of Women." *The New Statesman* Oct. 9 and 16, 1920.

———. 1925. *Mrs. Dalloway.* New York: Harcourt, 1953.

———. 1931. "Professions for Women." *The Collected Essays.* Ed. Leonard Woolf. Vol. 2. London: Hogarth Press, 1966–1967. 284–89.

———. "Professions for Women." *The Death of the Moth and Other Essays.* London: Hogarth Press, 1942. 149–54.

———. *A Room of One's Own.* London: Hogarth Press, 1929.

———. 1927. *To the Lighthouse.* New York: Harcourt, 1955.

———. "[Speech Before the London/National Society for Women's Service, January 21, 1931]." *The Pargiters.* Ed. Mitchell A. Leaska. New York: New York Public Library, 1977. xxvii–xliv.

Part 3

Representing Women's Contemporary Identities: Positions, Locations, Applications

By holding subject positions no longer largely circumlocutory, by experimenting with novel forms of feminist rhetorics, while now no longer dislocated but rather relocated within sites of traditional rhetorics in order to transform them, women rhetors today enjoy freedoms that were unimaginable in the past. In this section our contributors offer telling examples of how contemporary women are representing themselves with more pluralistic complexity than ever before and crafting new genres, strategies, and locations for feminist rhetorics. Even so, challenges still remain for women trying to negotiate the many complications and contradictions of contemporary subject positions. Establishing ethos at a time when postmodern critiques of "voice" threaten to re-silence women is in itself a central problem, if not the central rhetorical problem of our time. And, finally, promulgating new forms of rhetoric in both new and traditional locations still meets with predictable pockets of resistance. The women included here draw on the remarkable intellectual courage of their historical predecessors in order to forge ahead.

The concept of voice is certainly entwined with women and rhetoric historically, in times when women were often literally silenced, and struggled, therefore, to develop positions from which to speak and write. However, in contemporary times, too, voice has proven to be a powerful though problematic construct. In "Why Feminists Can't Stop Talking about Voice," Cindy Moore considers the consequences of the postmodern critique of voice, particularly as the term is used by cultural feminists. The postmodern view holds that the term "voice" inevitably suggests a stable unitary self located outside language and the community, a view of voice that is, in short, an impossibility. Moore maintains, though, that much that is powerful will be lost if it is abandoned altogether. Drawing on varied work on voice of the last thirty years and on her own work in research and teaching, she suggests ways we can use voice responsibly, retaining its cultural power, its linguistic possibilities, and its link between speaking and writing, but at the same time acknowledging important postmodern constructs and critiques. Ironically, she concludes that voice itself may have fallen out of favor because its own identity is shifting and unstable.

Kate Ronald and Joy Ritchie, in their essay "Pedagogy of Public Engagement: The Uses of Women's Rhetorics," consider examples of feminist rhetorics that appear so far outside the traditional boundaries of what we now call rhetoric that we may not yet have recognized or acknowledged them. Although an emerging body of women's rhetoric has been identified that fits with traditional conceptions of rhetorical theory, there may be other powerful examples that do not resemble these theories at all. Instead, these examples may emerge outside traditional contexts and may appear unruly, urgent, personal, and angry. They may defy traditional rhetorical relationships and suggest very different rhetorical tactics. Ronald and Ritchie describe the features of this "women's rhetorical theory" and provide examples such as the work of novelist Dorothy Allison. They also examine how a group of undergraduate students used these rhetorical principles for their own public rhetorical acts and how a group of graduate students applied the principles to teaching composition. Thus, in contemporary times, feminist rhetorics are being applied for new purposes in new locations. Moreover, Ronald and Ritchie envision these new genres occupying positions and transforming traditions within the academy—the same intellectual sites that historically branded women such as Lady Montagu a "literary slattern" and left Virginia Woolf standing, in her imagination, outside the locked Oxford library door.

Finally, one of these "unruly" rhetors, the writer Dorothy Allison, explores differences among women as she reflects on the class barriers that women and other marginalized groups still face, drawing on her own life and career and showing how she has used writing to represent her working class, "poor white," and "queer" experience. Throughout this reflection on work as existing "between fiction and real life," Allison is constantly aware not only of representing class and gender in her fiction and memoirs but also of the ways cultural receptions of class and gender have shaped her own identity in the first place. Unlike Virginia Woolf, who actively engaged aesthetic and class markers to establish herself as an intellectual and writer, Allison turns class status upside-down and proudly bares all to a world apparently more willing now to appreciate her as she is. This piece is a lecture she delivered at the Second Biennial Feminism(s) and Rhetoric(s) Conference in Minneapolis, Minnesota, in 1999. Here, more than in any of her published essays, we find Allison addressing the issue of class directly to a feminist audience and addressing it in a language that deliberately veers from that of formal academic prose. Since many of the historical rhetors considered in this volume spoke as well as wrote, we have chosen to include a speech from a contemporary speaking rhetor (along with Jane Gallop's speech mentioned earlier).

Allison recommends a twofold course of action. It is one that she herself has followed and one that enables her to speak from the interstices of gender, class, sexuality, and region, each of which comprised her own subject position, and to relocate herself while still preserving her own brand of feminist rhetoric. First, she suggests reading widely, so that one acquires a broader set of literacy experiences outside the boundaries not only of one's lived experience but also outside the ubiquitous constraints of media images. Simultaneously, one should begin writing about one's own class experience—telling the truth about it regardless of possible shame in its messiness or ugliness. The writing that results may have topics, strategies, and conventions that lie outside the boundaries of traditional discourse, but it will be no less—and perhaps more—energetic and compelling. Writing memoir also allows the writer to reflect on the way she or he has been defined. In this technique for "coming to voice," she encourages working-class rhetors and writers to write directly and boldly, without concern about whether this private work ever reaches a larger audience, for, she says, its true value is in what it does for the writer herself. Given the reputation she has achieved as a writer, which allows her the privilege of writing for herself, one might question whether this is practical advice for all women; nevertheless, Allison firmly believes that satisfying oneself comes first. And in her case, the breadth and depth of cultural analysis that she employs to satisfy herself offers an inspiration for others. Unlike the charges levied by and against Carolyn Heilbrun's *Writing a Woman's Life,* Allison does not write naive memoir. She knows full well that her stories must be shaped at the point (and place and medium) of utterance, as we have argued previously. She is generating her rhetorical theory, as well as her agency, out of lived experience. And perhaps this is an important message, after all, for women who hope to be heard.

9

Why Feminists Can't Stop Talking about Voice

Cindy Moore

When I was on the job market for the first time (roughly five years ago), I had an experience so impressive that it continues to influence the ways I think about teaching and writing. It occurred during an interview with members of a small communications department. Seated in an uncomfortable hotel desk chair with queen-sized beds behind me and a tenth-story view of a gray Toronto cityscape in front of me, I was discussing my dissertation project (an ethnographic study of a feminist writing course) and highlighting the importance of the voice metaphor for the (mostly female) students I had observed. Suddenly, one of the interviewers (a well-known rhetorician whose work I knew and admired) exclaimed, "*Voice*?! I thought we had stopped talking about that years ago. Are people still talking about voice?" I remember blushing, stammering something akin to "yes," and rattling off (in no particular order) names like Peter Elbow, David Bartholomae, and Gloria Anzaldua to save what felt like my rapidly sinking ship. I remember then outlining, carefully and calmly, the various ways the metaphor seemed to help students understand their struggles with writing and speaking and, in the end, to express themselves better and more confidently both in and outside of class. Finally, I remember the glazed faces of the interviewers, the uncomfortable shifting of chairs, how quickly we moved on to the next question.

Later, I realized that while I had interpreted my interviewer's question about voice quite literally, he probably had other intentions. More than likely, he wanted not so much an accounting of current scholars who discussed or employed the voice metaphor in their work, but rather to convey his doubts about any serious, up-to-date scholar talking about a concept that was popular in the 1970s. Whatever the case, I recognized that if *I* wanted to keep talking about voice, I would not only need to continue reading others who were interested in the subject (for personal confirmation and professional support), but I would also need to think more carefully about why voice was something that academics—especially feminist academics—*should* keep talking about.

When I considered my own experience with voice—particularly as it permeated my graduate studies in the late 1980s and early 1990s—it seemed an illustration of both the metaphor's historical importance to the academy and its variability. As an MA student, I pursued three areas of concentration: poetry writing, women's literature, and composition theory. I remember that in my poetry workshops voice had much to do with style. Poets were credited with having strong voices when they used words or rhythms in a manner that was "fresh," innovative. The promotional "blurbs" on the backs of the books we read reinforced this conception of voice. Carolyn Forché's second collection, *The Country Between Us,* for example, was promoted by Margaret Atwood as "poetry of courage and passion, which manages to be tender and achingly sensual and what is often called 'political' at the same time." "This is a major new voice," Atwood concluded. Similarly, Jorie Graham celebrated Jane Miller's work in *American Odalisque* with back-cover passages like the following: "She has developed a means by which to make chance contend with narrative; lyricism with cacophony and seriality. One of her instruments is an astoundingly supple voice, capable of shifting registers of diction and tone at a speed I'd call that of the *fast lane.* A voice as much song as scream, as much brazen as lusting for silence. A voice that, in fact, lets silence override it often enough—and with sufficient weight—as to make us hear silence again as if from scratch."

As I listened in class, read poetry, and worked hard at writing it, I remember wondering, along with some of the other less-experienced poets, when and how I would recognize *my* poetic voice. The consensus at the time seemed to be that we would know it when we found it; something would click between head and heart, between hand and page. Of course, it helped to write a lot. But it also helped to read widely and well, to develop what T. S. Eliot referred to as a "historical sense" (4)—an awareness that "the most individual parts" of any writer's work (e.g., Jane Miller's unique mingling of "lyricism" and "cacophony") are infused with the creative efforts of all the writers who came before him or her. As one of my professors explained it, "You find your own voice by reading and absorbing the work of others."

In women's literature courses (particularly those taught from an explicit feminist perspective), voice took on another meaning. Although it had something to do with individual style, with innovation, it had even more to do with expression of identity—and not just artistic identity, but gendered identity too. Approaching women's literature as feminists, we were less interested in how writers might situate their work within a tradition, and more concerned with how they asserted themselves by subverting or revising tradition. Works like *The Awakening* or "The Yellow Wallpaper," for example, were important—not for how they "conformed" to literary history (Eliot 5), but for how they didn't. Voice was used as a metaphor to capture the disruptions, the differences: the textual expressions of female authors intent on shaping their own creative destinies. Once again, our use of the metaphor in the classroom seemed reinforced by the reading we did outside of class. Commenting on early-twentieth-century literature, critic Elaine Showalter, for instance, persuaded us to see women writers' rejections of traditional "aesthetic techniques and narrative strategies" as a means of resisting "the pressures to abandon their own visions and voices" (125). With respect to *The Awakening,* in particular, Showalter discussed Kate Chopin's desire to revise not only masculine literary tradition but also the "didactic" feminist conventions of her day—"to record, in her own way and in her own voice, the *terra incognita* of a woman's 'inward life' in all its 'vague, tangled, chaotic' tumult" (71). Indeed, because of the effort on the part of Chopin and others (e.g., Charlotte Perkins Gilman, Zora Neale Hurston, Virginia Woolf) to link textual experiments with explorations of female psychology, voice seemed a convenient way to represent yearnings that were both artistic and emotional. And because artistic and emotional life was, for women writers, so inextricably linked to physical reality, it made sense that voice (a word defined in terms of physicality) would expand its metaphorical boundaries even further to encompass embodied experience—the physical isolation, illicit sexual attractions, postpartum depressions, and domestic abuses encountered by authors and characters alike. It made sense that critics like Sandra Gilbert and Susan Gubar would compare the artistic silencing of nineteenth-century women to chronic illness, anorexia, self-mutilation, and physical disability. A "lively" or "imaginative" girl of this period was especially "likely to experience her education in docility, submissiveness, selflessness as in some sense sickening," they write. "To be trained in renunciation is almost necessarily to be trained to ill health, since the human animal's first and strongest urge is to his/her own survival, pleasure, assertion" (54).

The composition theory courses offered another layer to voice, as here we talked not only in terms of style, self-expression, and social and political critique but also of how teachers inspire all of this. As a young feminist, I was especially attracted to feminist work in composition. I quickly found that just as voice had been an important metaphor for feminist literary critics, so it was among feminists in composition—particularly those who conducted classroom research. Joan Bolker, for example, had this to say about two of the women students she encountered at Ivy League schools in the late 1970s: "Each of these women describes a lack of personality in her papers, and her sense of non-ownership, and of disappointment at not being able to make herself heard . . . While [they] have both learned how to write papers, they have not yet learned to write—that is, to be able to communicate by expressing their own ideas, feelings, and voices on paper" (906). Drawing upon feminist work in linguistics and psychology, respectively, Pamela Annas and Elizabeth Flynn asked us to consider the relationship between discourse form and gender identity—something that Bolker had hinted at in her earlier essay. In "Style as Politics" Annas highlighted the need for women students to "discover their own voices in an expression [or] assertion" and to study "the stylistic strategies that various women essayists have used to deal with the problem of writing as women in an authentic female voice in a context that often does not value what women have to say" (362). Similarly, in "Composing as a Woman" Flynn introduced us to students like Kathy, for whom "other voices and external truths were more powerful than her own." Flynn writes, "She was clearly moving toward the development of an authentic voice and a way of knowing that integrates intuition with authoritative knowledge" (429). As these articles suggested, attention to voice in writing seemed to be a way that teachers could help students (especially women students) feel authoritative, empowered—"integrated."

While my personal experience with voice certainly isn't everyone's, I do know that many academics have had similar encounters with the metaphor. Through conversations with other composition specialists over the years, for example, I've learned that many of them write fiction and poetry; those who identify themselves as feminists often have strong backgrounds or interests in women's literature. For many of these scholars, voice (its meaning, pedagogical applications, and perceived usefulness) is necessarily multifaceted. Further, like mine, their experiences suggest how thoroughly voice has permeated academic culture. With respect to feminists, in particular, it's not just composition experts who have embraced voice as a metaphor; feminists in literature, law, linguistics, and psychology have employed the term too. In fact, the metaphorical power of voice, highlighted by such well-known academic titles as Carol Gilligan's *In a Different Voice,* has been recognized throughout the feminist community, as discourse aimed at wider, more popular female audiences suggests. I'm thinking here of Nancy Mairs's *Voice Lessons,* which links the pursuit of a "writing voice" to explorations of gender and able-bodiedness, and Marlene Schiwy's *A Voice of Her Own: Women and the Journal Writing Journey,* composed "with the belief that journal writing can help us . . . hear ourselves and each other into speech; and to discover, to express, and to embody this voice on the individual and cultural levels" (23). Finally, I want to suggest that voice has been embraced by so many women, in so many areas, because it makes sense to so many of us. There is no other metaphor that seems to capture the connections between speaking, writing, bodily expression, and subjectivity so well.

Of course, tradition and prevalence are not good reasons to keep doing *anything,* which is why our use of voice has been challenged in recent years. Because of its connection with self-expression, with genres that have been labeled self-expressive, and with words like *identity, ownership, authentic, real,* and *true,* "voice" has been thoroughly implicated in postmodern critiques of humanism. From a postmodern perspective, using words that have been associated with a unified, stable self, identifiable outside of language and community, is naive at best, dangerous at worst. Indeed, according to Darsie Bowden, it is highly un-feminist. About voice as a metaphor, she has this to say: "[V]oice is a pivotal metaphor for a tradition that has systematically privileged what is Western, what is white, and what is male, and . . . in using voice to articulate a struggle for the accretion of status and authority, marginalized groups, including women, are subscribing not only to the same language as the patriarchal system that they have struggled against but, as a necessary consequence, to the same value systems and ideology as well" (100).

Rather ironically (in light of postmodern thought) voice has fallen out of metaphorical favor for another reason: its own identity is shifting, unstable. As my historical account shows, voice means something different in different contexts. Within composition and rhetoric alone it has taken on a variety of meanings—some of them more text-based (e.g., style, tone); some more reader-based (e.g., resonance); and some more writer-based (e.g., identity, subjectivity, ownership, confidence, muse). Carl Leggo's essay on the concept offers ninety-nine questions about voice and twenty-six possible definitions. At one point in the essay, Leggo explains: "As a poet and a teacher, I am constantly reminded that language is a slippery affair. So often (most of the time? all of the time?) I am only partially successful in using words to understand and make sense and communicate. Still I continue to try. Again and again I have advised my students in both high school and university classes: Write in your own voices, your personal, authentic, sincere voices. But I am not at all sure that I know what I mean by *voice*" (145).

Peter Elbow's treatment of the term is similarly complex in "What Do We Mean When We Talk about Voice in Texts?" As a preface to his multilayered discussion of voice, Elbow writes: "The term has been used in such a loose and celebratory way as to mean almost anything. It's become a kind of warm fuzzy word: people say that writing has voice if they like it or think it is good or has some virtue that is hard to pin down" (2). The slipperiness suggested by Leggo and Elbow is reflected in more recent essays in which writers use the term *voice* only after painstakingly defining it for readers. "What kind of voice are we talking about here?" Jane Danielewicz asks in the introduction of her recent exploration of how to best "empower" student writers. Outlining and then drawing upon categories developed by Elbow, she writes, "It is resonant voice I wish to talk about here—voice linked to self, the kind of voice [bell] hooks describes as 'talking back'" (25). Importantly, instead of celebrating the multiplicity, many scholars have lamented it. As a colleague of mine said recently, "No one knows what it means anymore; that's a real problem."

Because voice as a metaphor has been called into question, many of us have grown reluctant to use it. This is especially the case, I think, for those of us who are just beginning our academic careers (e.g., teaching assistants, assistant professors) and are nervous about sounding too uninformed, romantic, or essentialist. We fall back on tidier terms like *style, tone,* and *ethos* that preceded *voice*—or we try out other terms that seem more theoretically, more politically sound. In her book, for instance, Bowden offers a few alternatives, including *dance, embrace,* and *web.* By using other words in place of *voice*—words that are more familiar, more current, more apparently appropriate—we gain quite a bit. We avoid the headache of messy definitions; we give patriarchy a momentary slip; we side-step (again, just for a moment, I think) challenges over self, identity, and authority. But I'd like to suggest that by abandoning voice as a metaphor we lose some things too. And what we lose is of no little importance to our students and to feminism.

First, because voice is a patriarchal metaphor (and I would agree with Bowden that it is), it brings with it a certain amount of cultural clout, a certain degree of power—just as words like *author* and *owner* bring. Women who employ the metaphor—who "speak up" in class discussions, who "talk back" in their writing, who proclaim, after years of struggling to express themselves, "Now I have found my voice"—these women take part in that power to some extent, experiencing, as bell hooks suggests, a "rite of passage where one moves from being an object to a subject" within the culture (12). I have seen it happen countless times in my classes and in classes I have observed. During the dissertation study mentioned in my introduction, for example,[1] women students regularly and quite explicitly connected the concept of *voice* to personal and social power. One young woman, Carrie, had this to say about her paper recounting events leading up to her decision to be a vegetarian: "The voice I describe [in the paper] is the one that enables me to be confident in my writing and successful in life."[2] In the paper itself, after illustrating struggles with parents, friends, and a track coach over her decision, she proclaims, "Yes, I AM A VEGETARIAN, A VEGAN. I'll announce it to the world. Call it whatever you want. I am proud of my choice, my *voice*" (my emphasis). Perhaps more importantly, during a subsequent class conversation about feminism, Carrie described how opportunities to express her voice in class discussions and papers prompted her to be more assertive outside of class. Instead of putting up with condescending comments from customers at the bar she tended, for instance, she began to challenge them. As she explained, "Everyone calls me cutie or sweetie. And I tell them, my name's not sweetie; it's Carrie. I tell them all the time. And so now I've started calling them sweetie back!"

Certainly, the multiple meanings associated with voice make communication with students, with one another, more challenging. When I encourage students to "trust your voices" as they pursue a research project, for example, I cannot guarantee that they will automatically know what I mean in this instance: that they should be wary of abandoning their own opinions and ideas in favor of published insights. Yet, poststructuralist theory suggests that no matter which words I use to convey my intentions, I cannot be sure that what I mean will match up with the meaning formed in my listener/reader's mind. As Terry Eagleton depicts this theoretical perspective, "Meaning is not immediately *present* in a sign. . . . [I]t cannot be easily nailed down" (128). Like poststructuralist thought more generally, feminist theories have encouraged me to resist the urge to "nail down" meaning or to simplify my discourse by abandoning complex, polymorphous forms. In fact, as a young feminist I was compelled by feminist scholars across the disciplines to reject tidy definitions, neat distinctions, little boxes that we, as a *patriarchal* society, tend to want to fit things into. With respect to language, for instance, theologian Mary Daly highlighted for me the inherent complexity in words and how such complexity (the "deep resonances") is ironed out to perpetuate "patriarchal patterns" (3–4). Concerned by the drive among contemporary scientists (and some feminist theorists) for theoretical and methodological coherence, philosopher Sandra Harding showed me that "stable and coherent theories are not always the ones to be most highly desired," that "instabilities and incoherences" can lead to important "understandings" (244). And in response to historical suggestions that biological sex can be easily delineated, linguist/philosopher Luce Irigaray illustrated the "multiplicity" of women's selves and their "desire." So, in important ways, the voice metaphor reflects the flux and fluidity that poststructuralism has presumed—and feminists have embraced—for years.

Of course, some might argue—and rightly so—that theories about language and knowledge do not always translate well to the practical, everyday realm. What makes sense, theoretically, may not help us to live our increasingly complicated lives, may not help us assist our students to deal with complexities they face as students and citizens. In addition, as composition theorists such as Lester Faigley and Andrea Lunsford have pointed out, the cultural and institutional values that shape our teaching contexts are in many ways at odds with the postmodern values we may embrace as theorists. Indeed, Lunsford prompts us to wonder if accommodating notions of multiplicity and fluidity are even possible when "our institutions are so firmly committed" (71) to individuality, unification, and stability. I would like to suggest, though, that if we offer space for our students to think outside of familiar structures, we will see that they can develop and articulate a sense that meanings shift according to context, that the match between signified and signifier is at best inexact. Further, with a little encouragement, they will become comfortable moving back and forth from one meaning to another—and in so doing will gain a fuller appreciation for the creative power of language and the many possibilities for themselves as language users.

In the class I studied, for instance, students demonstrated this kind of flexibility. Tracy typically used voice as a marker for group identity (women), yet at times she used the term to refer to something more personal, individual. Similarly, Jane alternated between a more singular, unified idea of voice and a more multifaceted conception. In a class discussion exploring the meaning of academic discourse, for example, Jane used voice to represent her "real self": "There's this format we have and I have my ideas and they're not going into that form, so I try to fit them into that form and it snowballs. . . . I produce something that I know I can write better, but I don't know how to do it because it's not in my voice. . . . It's not me." Though Jane further pursued a connection between voice and self in a paper on alternative academic forms, she complicated the connection by presenting herself as one of many selves (daughter, student, waitperson)—all of which were "her," but some of which seemed more "real," depending on the circumstance. As she ponders toward the end of the paper, "I cannot find any voice that would/can fully express myself . . . So, is language deceiving?" Importantly, much like the women interviewed by Mary Field Belenky, Blythe McVicker Clinchy, Nancy Rule Goldberger, and Jill Mattuck Tarule in the late 1970s, students in this class "repeatedly used the metaphor of voice to depict their intellectual and ethical development" (18)—without being prompted to do so. While the professor used the term *voice* at different times throughout the semester, she was careful not to define or present it in absolute terms. Instead, she assigned texts that employed voice in various ways, hoping that students would feel free to use the metaphor in a manner that made sense to them personally.

In similar fashion, many students in my recent graduate seminar in composition theory appeared to recognize, if not appreciate, the slipperiness of the voice metaphor. Before moving into a discussion of voice as a "key word" in composition (Harris ix), I asked students to spend some time free-writing definitions of the term. Kathy wrote about how some of her professors teach that voice "is malleable, that it changes to suit situations," while others offer a more static notion of voice: "that we all have *a* voice, and that this voice is a unique part of our own writing." She went on to explain, "I have always thought that there must be a little of both of these viewpoints involved with what voice is." Capturing the "both/and" flavor of Kathy's definition, Brenda employed the metaphor of a quilt to illustrate how voice can have both cultural and individual resonances: "Although [the writer] is influenced by everything she has ever read, seen and heard, her voice is what she thinks about what she knows expressed in a way she has developed herself from pieces of all that input from other sources and experiences. Voice can be compared to a scrap quilt I might make from a collection of tiny pieces of fabric saved over time and gathered from other people's collections of fabric. I did not personally choose all these fabrics, but I can put them together in a pattern that is uniquely mine."

And Cheryl, revealing a comparable sense of complexity, offered that voice "has the quality of being elusive and intrusive" at the same time. "When it's there, it's there. And, when you try to place it, it avoids you like the plague." Indeed, in contrast to many professional scholars I have known, these students seemed entirely at ease with the prospect of using voice in multiple ways and, thus, imagining their relationship to writing and reading (those media that allow for the expression of voice) variously. Practicing poststructuralists in their own right, what these students didn't need was a lecture on how voice is no longer a useful metaphor because it conjures up images of real selves and unified truths. What they needed was to be made conscious of the ways they were employing the term, for the multiple meanings they had already encountered to be highlighted, explicated, and analyzed—through free-writing exercises like the one mentioned earlier, as well as published discussions depicting its many potentialities.

Finally, in addition to giving up the cultural power and linguistic possibilities associated with voice, by abandoning the metaphor we lose an important link between speaking and other forms of expression. Other words, other metaphors, simply don't highlight the connection between the silencing of women's public (and private) speech and constraints on their written words and bodily expression or movement. And such connections have been the hallmark of feminism and the concern of countless individual feminists—from Tillie Olson, who characterized artistic constraints on women with the phrase "Shut up, you're only a girl" (27); to Adrienne Rich, who urged us to remember that "every mind resides in a body" (245); to Hélène Cixous, who warned in her treatise on women's writing, "Censor the body and you censor breath and speech at the same time" (880). Many of us know deeply, personally, how our physical, bodily experiences have *everything* to do with our ability to speak and write. We understand how often the women who have trouble expressing themselves in our classes are the same women who write about physical restrictions or abuse, rape, anorexia, and suicide. Discussing the writing blocks she has witnessed among her students, for example, Pamela Annas tells of the woman "stuck for two weeks on the same assignment," who submitted "a powerfully written account of how her father had molested her from age eleven to fourteen and had beaten her up when she tried to speak about it to her mother." Annas goes on to explain how the student traced "her particular form of silence—a polished, distant, ironic style"—to that time in her life (367). More recently, a young woman in a developmental writing course I taught last fall drew an especially strong connection between silence and physical and emotional abuse. In a literacy narrative designed to help students explore their particular writing histories, this student related her deep fear of writing to an episode in her life when an abusive stepfather found her journal documenting the abuse. She explains how upon discovering the journal he went into a violent rage: "He tried to suffocate me. He ripped my journal, threw it in the garbage and said I was never allowed to write in a journal again." In fact, the physical consequences of women's speech have a long history, as Susan Brownmiller illustrates in her 1984 bestseller, *Femininity.* In a section depicting common punishments for women who "disrupted the peace of the neighborhood" in earlier times, she describes the use of ducking stools, iron muzzles, and whipping posts. Of the muzzle, in particular, she writes: "An iron muzzle with a triangular bit that fitted the mouth . . . was another device to silence an idle tongue during the Middle Ages. Locked into the branks, an offender was chained to a post or led through town for all to witness her shame" (112–13).

While some of the alternative metaphors forwarded by theorists like Bowden (e.g., *dance, embrace*) emphasize a bodily connection, they seem restrictive in other ways. Most obviously, they don't capture the connections between speaking and writing that are so crucial. In Bowden's case, the limitation is intentional. Her claim that voice is a worn-out metaphor rests in large part on its associations with oral literacy traditions. From her perspective, voice as a metaphor is problematic because, historically, it has reflected a cultural emphasis on *presence* (of author, of self), which, as theorists like Jacques Derrida point out, is only a convenient "illusion" (34). Of course, presence—as it has been reflected in historical "master narratives" that focus on men's experiences and perspectives—has been the focus of feminist critiques as well.[3] Still, many feminists wonder if discarding the notion of presence altogether is helpful to the countless number of people whose values, voices, and bodies have been ignored, whose worth and potential have been discounted, whose only hope for more equitable treatment is to vigorously assert their presence in spheres where they have been too-long absent. Seyla Benhabib asks, for example, how we can even contemplate the idea of "female emancipation" without concepts such as "selfhood," "agency," and "autonomy"—all of which rest on the foundation of "presence" (21). Discussing women of color specifically, Gloria Anzaldua suggests that absence is just what a patriarchal culture wants: "The white man speaks: *Perhaps if you scrape the dark off your face. Maybe if you bleach your bones. Stop speaking in tongues, stop writing left-handed. Don't cultivate your colored skins nor tongues of fire if you want to make it in a right-handed world*" (166).

Further, these alternative metaphors seem incapable of capturing the range of emotions and experiences that many women desperately need to express. Expressing one's identity or desire often involves a deep release of anger that the terms *dance* and *embrace* simply cannot fully accommodate, in our culture, at the present time. Unlike the word *voice,* which has come to signify expression of a range of attitudes and emotions, *dance* and *embrace* carry everyday connotations that are quite positive. Though Bowden rightly suggests that these terms are etymologically complex, that they *can* involve distance, "move[s] apart" as well as connection (117), for most people they imply a unity, a reaching out, a desire to connect with someone toward some positive end. Many women have been attempting such unity and connection too willingly, far too often throughout their lives—and that, I would argue, is their problem.

The critiques of presence, of authenticity and truth that underlie recent dissatisfaction with voice as a metaphor have been crucial to feminism—and to rhetoric and composition, as a whole. From them we have learned to be less quick to generalize, to speak for others, to assume that the self presented in a student's paper, in a colleague's presentation, in a friend's letter is the only self there is, that one person's story is everyone's. Yet, uncritical application of postmodern ideas may undercut our ability to offer the *experience* of freedom and power (as limited as it may be) to our students. Speaking of the concept of a generalizable "female experience," for example, Diana Fuss suggests that although we (as theorists, researchers, teachers) understand that "truth clearly does not equate with experience," the "fiction that they are the same" can inspire otherwise reticent students to speak, to feel "empowered" (117–19). Surely, many of us have, like Fuss, witnessed the power of shared experience in our classrooms—those moments when students tell their stories *as if* they are expressing the thoughts and feelings of *all* eighteen-year-olds, *all* women, *all* African Americans, *as if* they are part of something much larger than themselves, a group of people who experience the world the same way they do, who understand them immediately, who speak their language. Though we may *want* to stop our students and explain the dangers of generalizing, of "speaking for"—and sometimes do—there are times when the theories that make sense to us outside the classroom just don't seem appropriate or useful. As Lad Tobin writes about critiques of more "positivist" notions of literacy and learning, "As a product of contemporary critical theory, these critiques make some sense to me. As a classroom teacher, though, I have my doubts, for while positivist notions of agency, authorship, voice, and self may be philosophically naive, they can still be pedagogically powerful" (15).

Like Fuss and Tobin, I think we can hold on to all that we've learned from postmodern theory without discarding concepts and metaphors that have been helpful to so many of us and to so many of our students. There are ways that we can use voice responsibly, by celebrating and highlighting its multiple meanings, by using it to imply a sense of ownership or identity without denying the influence of culture on the development of this sense. In fact, many scholars within composition and rhetoric have already taken on the challenging work of redefining voice in ways that acknowledge both the liberating potential of expressing one's "true self" and the empowering effect of recognizing multiple discursive "selves." Utilizing the "both/and" logic informing much contemporary feminist work, Randall Freisinger, for example, encourages us to see a "dialogic" relationship between romantic and postmodern perspectives on truth, self, and voice. "We find our voice," he explains, "among the voices of others, in a dialogic relation with them" (271). Similarly, Frank Farmer relies on Vygotsky and Bakhtin to illustrate how seemingly incompatible theoretical standpoints on voice can be negotiated "from a dialogic perspective" (305). Rather than seeing voice as something singular found within the self, for instance, we might more profitably view it as an effect of the self's orchestration of the many voices, the many perspectives encountered in daily life (308). And Jacqueline Jones Royster suggests that while we may at times identify ourselves in "singular" ways (e.g., as an African American scholar, as a woman), we nonetheless have many voices, each of which is "authentic." Perhaps more importantly, she suggests that voice is not just a visual or oral "phenomenon" but a "thing heard, perceived, and reconstructed" (30), thus highlighting the role or responsibility of another party in what appears to be an individual expression or articulation.

The metaphors we use, whether for teaching, writing, or living, are necessarily complex. As linguists George Lakoff and Mark Johnson explain, metaphors, by their very nature, "highlight" some aspects of a concept and "hide" others. Further, what is highlighted or hidden at any given time is dependent on context. This is why a metaphor like voice can successfully imply both the stable, enduring qualities and the endlessly changing nature of the self(s) and truth(s) we experience. And this is why voice can be used to restrict (e.g., to reinforce the notions of essentialism, the emphases on "presence" that have constrained women) or to liberate (e.g., to suggest a stable subject position from which to assert one's opinions, desires). Maybe this is the true power of voice—that it reveals the hazy boundary between constraint and freedom for us and for our students. Maybe this—instead of the word itself—is the source of our discomfort.

Notes

1. In the fall of 1997 I observed an upper-level composition course called Feminist Expository Writing at the University of Louisville, where I completed my doctoral work. The study was the subject of my dissertation, *Re-Writing the Academy: Issues of Voice, Identity, and Authority in the Feminist Composition Class.*

2. Carrie is a pseudonym, as are all other names used to refer to students in this essay. All quoted material is used by permission of students. Carrie's description of her paper comes from a reflective memo submitted with her revision.

3. See, for example, *Speculum of the Other Woman,* by Luce Irigaray, trans. Gillian C. Gill (Ithaca, NY: Cornell UP, 1985).

Works Cited

Annas, Pamela J. "Style as Politics: A Feminist Approach to the Teaching of Writing." *College English* 47 (1985): 360–71.

Anzaldua, Gloria. "Speaking in Tongues: A Letter to 3rd World Women Writers." *This Bridge Called My Back: Writings by Radical Women of Color.* Ed. Cherríe Moraga and Gloria Anzaldua. NY: Kitchen Table, Women of Color Press, 1983. 165–73.

Belenky, Mary Field, Blythe McVicker Clinchy, Nancy Rule Goldberger, and Jill Mattuck Tarule. *Women's Ways of Knowing: The Development of Self, Voice, and Mind.* New York: Basic Books, 1986.

Benhabib, Seyla. "Feminism and Postmodernism: An Uneasy Alliance." *Feminist Contentions: A Philosophical Exchange.* Seyla Benhabib, Judith Butler, Drucilla Cornell, and Nancy Fraser, eds. New York: Routledge, 1995.

Bolker, Joan. "Teaching Griselda to Write." *College English* 40 (April 1979): 906–08.

Bowden, Darsie. *The Mythology of Voice.* Portsmouth, NH: Boynton/Cook, 1999.

Brownmiller, Susan. *Femininity.* New York: Linden/Simon and Schuster, 1984.

Cixous, Helene. "The Laugh of the Medusa." Trans. Keith Cohen and Paula Cohen. *Signs* 1 (1976): 875–93.

Daly, Mary (with Jane Caputi). *Websters' First New Intergalactic Wickedary of the English Language.* New York: HarperCollins, 1987.

Danielewicz, Jane. "Developing Voice in the Writing Classroom." *Dialogue: A Journal for Writing Specialists* 3.1 (Spring 1997): 23–40.

Eagleton, Terry. *Literary Theory: An Introduction.* Minneapolis: U of Minnesota P, 1983.

Elbow, Peter. "What Do We Mean When We Talk about Voice in Texts?" *Voices on Voice: Perspectives, Definitions, Inquiry.* Ed. Kathleen Blake Yancey. Urbana, IL: National Council of Teachers of English, 1994. 1–35.

Eliot, T. S. "Tradition and the Individual Talent." *Selected Essays.* 1932. New York: Harcourt, Brace and World, 1960. 3–11.

Faigley, Lester. *Fragments of Rationality: Postmodernity and the Subject of Composition.* Pittsburgh: U of Pittsburgh P, 1992.

Farmer, Frank. "Voice Reprised: Three Etudes for a Dialogic Understanding." *Rhetoric Review* 13.2 (Spring 1995): 304–20.

Flynn, Elizabeth. "Composing as a Woman." *College Composition and Communication* 39 (1988): 423–35.

Forché, Carolyn. *The Country Between Us.* New York: Harper and Row, 1981.

Freisinger, Randall R. "Voicing the Self: Toward a Pedagogy of Resistance in a Postmodern Age." Yancey 242–74.

Fuss, Diana. *Essentially Speaking: Feminism, Nature, and Difference.* New York: Routledge, 1989.

Gilbert, Sandra, and Susan Gubar. *The Madwoman in the Attic: The Woman Writer and the Nineteenth-Century Literary Imagination.* New Haven: Yale UP, 1979.

Gilligan, Carol. *In a Different Voice: Psychological Theory and Women's Development.* Cambridge, MA: Harvard UP, 1982.

Harding, Sandra. *The Science Question in Feminism.* Ithaca, NY: Cornell UP, 1986.

Harris, Joseph. *A Teaching Subject: Composition since 1966.* Upper Saddle River, NJ: Prentice Hall, 1997.

hooks, bell. *Talking Back: Thinking Feminist, Thinking Black.* Boston: South End Press, 1989.

Irigaray, Luce. *This Sex Which is Not One.* Trans. Catherine Porter with Carolyn Burke. Ithaca, NY: Cornell UP, 1985.

Lakoff, George, and Mark Johnson. *Metaphors We Live By.* Chicago: U of Chicago P, 1980.

Leggo, Carl. "Questions I Need to Ask before I Advise My Students to Write in Their Own Voices." *Rhetoric Review* 10.1 (Fall 1991): 143–52.

Lunsford, Andrea. "Intellectual Property, Concepts of Selfhood, and the Teaching of Writing." *Journal of Basic Writing* 11.2 (1992): 61–73.

Mairs, Nancy. *Voice Lessons: On Becoming a (Woman) Writer.* Boston: Beacon Press, 1994.

Miller, Jane. *American Odalisque: Poems.* Port Townsend, WA: Copper Canyon Press, 1987.

Olson, Tillie. *Silences.* 1965. New York: Delta/Seymour Lawrence, 1989.

Rich, Adrienne. "Taking Women Students Seriously." *On Lies, Secrets, and Silence: Selected Prose, 1966–1978.* New York: W. W. Norton, 1979. 237–45.

Royster, Jacqueline Jones. "When the First Voice You Hear Is Not Your Own." *College Composition and Communication* 47.1 (February 1996): 29–40.

Schiwy, Marlene A. *A Voice of Her Own: Women and the Journal Writing Journey.* New York: Simon and Schuster, 1996.

Showalter, Elaine. *Sister's Choice: Tradition and Change in American Women's Writing.* 1991. Oxford: Oxford UP, 1994.

Tobin, Lad. "Process Pedagogy." *A Guide to Composition Pedagogies.* Ed. Gary Tate, Amy Rupiper, and Kurt Schick. Oxford: Oxford UP, 2001. 1–18.

10

Pedagogy and Public Engagement

The Uses of Women's Rhetorics

Kate Ronald and Joy Ritchie

> "Maggie can't appreciate these quilts!" she said. "She'd probably be backward enough to put them to everyday use."
>
> "She can always make some more," I said. "Maggie knows how to quilt."
>
> Alice Walker, "Everyday Use"

This essay analyzes how we have put women's rhetorics to use in order to teach both writers and teachers of writing. In particular, we examine the uses of women's rhetorics in reconfiguring rhetorical theory and practice, pedagogies of writing, and rhetorics of public engagement. Alice Walker, whose work we believe constitutes rhetorical theory, insists on the ethical responsibility to address the exigencies of women's lives through speech and writing and to recognize the interconnection between language and action. We bring women's rhetorics into the classroom in order to encourage students to use rhetoric in response to the exigencies of their own academic and personal contexts. By "use" we mean more than assigning women's rhetorics as reading material, although certainly that act alone has changed the rhetorical landscape, and we do not want to diminish the tremendous work of recovery and "regendering" that has paved the way for us, now, to ask more pointed and pragmatic questions about how women's rhetorics should change rhetorical stances and writing strategies. We are interested in exploring the potential that women's rhetorics hold for revising our teaching not just of this emerging tradition but of rhetoric, writing, and literacy as well. In other words, we expect that studying women's rhetorics should make a difference, that it should change practice, and that it should change the consequences of our practices—for us and for our students.[1]

These premises informed both of the classes we report on here: a graduate seminar called "Women's Rhetorics and Feminist Pedagogies" and an undergraduate/graduate course titled "The Rhetoric of Women Writers." We have taught both of these courses several times over the last eight years (in fact, together we designed the "Rhetoric of Women Writers" course at the University of Nebraska in the early 1990s).[2] In both courses we ask students to read from the emerging history of women's rhetorics, to use rhetorical analysis in order to understand these writers' contexts and strategies, and to apply what they've learned from their reading and reflection to their own contexts and purposes, including their own teaching.

It's that last part—the application of learning, the "so what?" question—that provides the impulse of this essay. In both courses, in addition to scholarly, analytical papers, we ask students to engage in some form of rhetorical action. When we teach this course for graduate students in rhetoric and composition—most of them teaching assistants assigned to first-year composition and most of them seeking professorships in the field—we focus the "action" on the public space of the classroom. One major assignment asks these students how they will use their learning about rhetorical women to inform their teaching of writing. At the undergraduate level, we ask students to invent, draft, revise, and deliver rhetorical acts that, as one of Joy's students says, actually "do" something rather than simply "say" something. Teaching these courses with a focus on action has raised a number of questions for us about encouraging students to engage in public rhetorical acts, including the issue of "everyday use": What difference does it make to their public and academic lives to have studied rhetoric by women? What "usable past" can we identify and enact from studying our heritage in women's rhetorics? How do students draw on or "use" the rhetoric of women writers for their own rhetorical purposes? And what are the consequences for their sense of agency and authority as rhetors and as teachers?

One of our basic goals has been to help students see that scholarship and reflection should have consequences in practice, or action. We push students in both classes to extrapolate what they learn from reading women's rhetorics toward their own practice—either as rhetors in public forums or as teachers of rhetoric in their own classrooms. We encourage them to move beyond the more initial—although necessary—responses we find some students have as they read women's rhetorics, often for the first time: "Look how skillful these women were as rhetoricians. What courageous women they were. How inspiring. More people should know about this heritage." Although one of the happy outcomes of recovering women's rhetorics should be inspiration and celebration, we've come to believe that once the celebration is over, the work must begin. We have found this work—moving from admiration to analysis to action—complicated and difficult, requiring conscious care about the relationships between practice and theory, reflection and action, and between heritage and "use."

Walker's short story "Everyday Use" explores questions of heritage as two sisters struggle over their conceptions of what it actually means to honor their African American history. One wants her mother's and grandmother's quilts for display; the other believes that using them is the best homage she can pay to the past. Our argument, too, takes us into questions of heritage, particularly the rhetorical history that informs our teaching of rhetoric and writing. The narrator of Walker's story argues for use when she says of her grandmother's quilts: "God knows I been saving 'em for long enough with nobody using 'em." She complains about her sister's impulse simply to "'Hang them,' she said. As if that was the only thing you *could* do with them" (2372). The renaissance of women's rhetorics we are witnessing and creating in composition has brought women's public voices, long silenced and invisible, out of storage. Now that women's rhetorics have been recovered and reclaimed, we think we should analyze the ways we can make use of them. We want to insist that there are more things to do with women's rhetorics than collect, analyze, display, and admire them; so we want to push toward the implications for our everyday work—the ways we invite, train, and challenge students to enter public and academic spaces. Moreover, we suggest that using women's rhetorics in our classrooms leads to "making more" rhetorics.

"Explicit Moves": Women's Rhetorics as Pedagogy

> While functioning as models, these feminist theories of rhetoric also open up new spaces in rhetorical history, theory, and pedagogy . . . What makes such considerations of theory and pedagogy so exciting to us and so confusing to our students is that the results of our considerations differ wildly. I believe that it is time to take responsibility for

our excitement and not leave making sense of our differences only to students.

Krista Ratcliffe, *Anglo-American Feminist Challenges to the Rhetorical Tradition*

In the graduate course that we have both taught on women's rhetorics, we ask the "so what?" question this way: how can recovery work and rhetorical rereadings influence the teaching of writing itself—not simply the pedagogy of a writing classroom, or its readings, or its social/cultural/political agendas, but the writing taught and practiced there? Can we extrapolate, to use Krista Ratcliffe's term, a practice of composition from the rhetorics of women writers? Since we have developed composition from the male rhetorical tradition, can we use women's disruption, accommodation, interruption, extension, and reimagining of that tradition to design or describe a different way of writing that does not come directly from the patriarchy? And that does not serve its ends?

In *Anglo-American Feminist Challenges to the Rhetorical Tradition,* Krista Ratcliffe seeks to "extrapolate" feminist theories of rhetoric from the writing of Virginia Woolf, Mary Daly, and Adrienne Rich. She moves from her rereading of the three authors toward "inconclusive musings" about what questions these feminist rhetors might lead us to ask about/within/against traditional rhetorical history and composition practice based in that tradition. Ratcliffe's questions seem to us an excellent start on the kind of thinking we're encouraging graduate student teachers to engage in. For example, from Woolf she extrapolates the exercise of asking students to define their own Angel in the House and consider its impact on their writing; she considers asking students to imitate Daly's play on language and definition, to make language more visible in terms of how it constructs categories; from Rich she suggests writing exercises that identify and compare the politics of location from which students and authors have spoken.

We have only touched on the uses Ratcliffe's work suggests; our point is that we and our students took this challenge seriously. Yet the move toward "use" remains fraught with traps like essentialism, dualism, and rigidity. For the rest of this essay we will demonstrate how difficult we find this work, but we will also show how important we believe it is to take this next integrative step. We will begin with the rather embarrassing first steps. Here's a partial list of what Kate's seminar came up with at midterm in an attempt to define "women's rhetorics": *personal, dialogic/conversational, nonlinear, truth-telling, redefining and reinventing terms, blurring boundaries, urgent, narrative, experiential, multiple,* and even *cannot be defined.* That last item probably comes closest to accuracy; we're sure readers will see how problematic this list immediately becomes, how unsatisfying, even un-useful it remains for thinking specifically about how to use women's rhetoric for the teaching of writing. Some of the characteristics here—although certainly apt descriptions of much of women's rhetorics—risk essentializing women's rhetoric into a false seamlessness or ghetto-izing women's writing into narrative, personal, or emotional corners. Yet other items on the list—*concerned with material conditions, writing the body, asserting the right to speak, subverting authority*—showed some promise for making the translation from analysis or admiration of women's rhetorics to pedagogical practice in the writing classroom. Other useful lists of the characteristics of women's writing helped the class extrapolate a theory and practice of composition. Cheryl Glenn's "regendering" of the rhetorical tradition describes at least these: a rhetoric of theology, a rhetoric of autobiography, a rhetoric of silence, of translation. As they read further in the history of women's rhetorics, Kate's class came up with more rhetorics: a rhetoric of naming (Ida B. Wells); of defiance (Zora Neale Hurston); of conversation (Margaret Fuller); of materiality (Virginia Woolf); of the body (Dorothy Allison). These lists were useful, especially in countering the rhetoric of logic, agonistic argument, and authority that the class had learned from the male rhetorical tradition.

In their seminar papers and in their course journals, students had a chance to write more fully about the connections between women's rhetoric and the pedagogy of writing. We present some of their conclusions below in order to illustrate the challenges and difficulties in this journey from practice to theory and then to "use."

Heidi suggests in one of her last reading journals that overt attention to context and exigency might be a theory she could extrapolate from the practices of women rhetors she had read:

> What I've gained in collaborating with the authors we've read and with the people in this class is greater sensitivity to what's beneath the words—what's being presented as well as what's being left out; who's doing the speaking/writing, who's not; who's being included, who's been excluded/made invisible; what's the history, the context? Or, in Dorothy Allison's words, what do I know for sure? So maybe that's also what I can pass on to my students—a willingness to look seriously beneath the words, their own and those of others, rather than taking the words as pure truth from an authoritative source without question or

> critical thought. And as we do this together, with our students and each other, we become more effective rhetors—and also better people.
>
> Heidi, journal, April 22, 1999

We think Heidi is suggesting more than a close reading or critique of language here, certainly part of most writing and reading classes. First, she describes her own stance as "collaborator" with the women she's reading and the class she's reading with, a rhetorical context that seems to us thoroughly pedagogical. By insisting that we "do this together,"[3] she seems to be suggesting that she's learning how to teach more carefully the contexts of language and the power relationships within them that ensure silence for some.

Certainly reading women like Ida B. Wells and Margaret Fell makes students more attentive to the constraints and exigencies of any rhetorical situation. Jennifer goes a bit further to suggest this attention must be explicit:

> In this treatise, Wollstonecraft makes particular rhetorical moves, motivated by explicit logic and reason. For instance, she says, "But I wish to speak the simple language of truth, and rather to address the head than the heart." Now, this could be interpreted as the author's reproduction of the values of her time, values which "uphold" the "masculine" qualities of the mind at the expense of "feminine" qualities of the heart. Instead of this rather reductive reasoning, why don't I read this line as: OK, Wollstonecraft knows what she is up against when she is writing this. Consequently, she is deliberately and explicitly embracing the values of the dominant culture not to support these values but to get her message across. Thus, Wollstonecraft's overt emphasis on the rational and logical is deliberate and overt and perhaps this is the feminist move. Doing what you do and knowing WHY you are doing it and perhaps, acknowledging this in your writing, in your reading, and in your speaking. Maybe this is what a feminist classroom should be about, in fact: deliberation and explicitness about moves and motivations.
>
> Jennifer, journal, February 11, 1999

Jennifer argues that attention to context is not enough; we should be helping students understand specific rhetorical "moves" and strategies. Moreover, we should be helping them (and ourselves) find ways to be more overt about rhetorical strategies and choices. The key line here for us is "acknowledging this in your writing": would a pedagogy of writing drawn from Wollstonecraft teach writers literally to stop and point to their rhetorical choices? Would students learn, then, to add commentary to their narratives and arguments that name their agendas? Or perhaps Jennifer is pointing toward taking more overt ethical stances in writing and speaking, acknowledging issues of power and authority, and naming, as Audre Lorde says, what one cannot yet say.

Kate's students kept ethical questions about the purposes for teaching and writing clearly in mind as they tried to formulate a composition pedagogy based in their reading of women's rhetorics. Lisa turns from her admiration of Ida B. Wells to the beginnings of a theory for teaching writing as an instrument of both success and subversion:

> A phrase in "Lynch Laws in All its Phases" has been at the front of my mind all week: " . . . I could no longer hold my peace, and I feel, yes I am sure, that if it had to be done over again (provided no one else was the loser save myself) I would do and say the very same again." To have the feeling that what you are doing is right must be the most gratifying feeling, and one I think I forget in my teaching and scholarship . . . We take a critical approach to teaching composition because we believe in challenging racism, classism, sexism and other forms of oppression. Equally, we believe in teaching writing so that students can succeed in their pursuits because writing is useful to a person spiritually and culturally—and they can use it to subvert oppression. But what I often forget is that it is also the right thing to do. I think it is right to teach how to use language so that it doesn't harm others.
>
> Lisa, journal, February 18, 1999

Here, Lisa describes the kind of class where undergraduate students, like Joy's, would struggle with how, when, where, and whether to "write as if their lives depended on it" (Rich, "What Is Found There" 255). But Lisa also points to one of the main difficulties graduate students encountered when trying to articulate a composition pedagogy for their own students out of women's rhetorics: the problem of teaching so that students can both "succeed" and "subvert." Many of the writers we study in both our classes offer stunning examples of using what Lorde would call the "master's tools" in order to challenge and disrupt patriarchal structures and stances. But how does one teach this fine line between safety and risk? Kay describes this double bind quite forcefully: "I feel like I have to be SO careful in continually telling my students that it is OK sometimes to subvert the status quo and sometimes it is just plain dangerous or dumb. THEY have to decide" (Kay, journal, March 18, 1999).

Given this tension between accommodation and resistance, many of Kate's students turned to close reading of particular women rhetors in order to search for rhetorical strategies—formal, stylistic, and ethical—that they might then teach to their writing students, who also face the exigencies of writing without power or voice. Erin used Toni Morrison's "Nobel Lecture" to think about how she teaches language in her first-year composition classes:

> To view language as connective and creative, as well as destructive and oppressive is so important. I spend a unit in 111 on the inferences one can make from types of language. We learn how language can serve to distance the speaker/writer/reader from events and evoke prejudices and alliances. It's a great unit, one I'm really proud of. But it only shows how divisive language can be. I'm excited to show the positive power of it too by using Morrison's speech. How we can create things "together." How we can counteract the destructive power of language. A lot of my students feel helpless after the unit. They think they can never say anything that isn't connected to a wider idea, to politics. That's the point. But I think what could help them feel more in control of their words are examples like Morrison's and Lorde's. I don't want to see another group of students throw up their hands in the air and concede to the dominant paradigm. I want them to see the gaps—the spaces in between—and understand that they can make them bigger. They can shift the structure. Their voices—their thinking—count.
>
> Erin, journal, April 1, 1999

This theme of student writing "counting" clearly runs through both of the classes we're describing. And we've included so much of our own students' writing here precisely because we agree with Ratcliffe that it's our shared responsibility to make overt the connections between the readings we assign and the use students make of them. Stacy, in her final seminar project, took this challenge seriously as she tried to extrapolate from Audre Lorde some principles of rhetorical pedagogy:

> Probably the most important value I would carry from Lorde into my classroom is the necessity that both myself and my students feel a responsibility to speak out. I need to do more than have participation as part of their grade. I need to have my students consider the power—defensive and active—that exists in their voices. . . .

> Speaking out about emotion also enacts the power of the erotic. . . . The erotic also encourages excellence. Lorde states that once we have "experienced the fullness of this depth of feeling and recognized its power, in honor and self-respect we can require no less of ourselves" (*Sister* 54). This should not lead to unrealistic expectations but a value on "how acutely and fully we can feel in the doing" (54). To value the erotic in a classroom would mean that student and teacher alike would be striving to achieve that excellence, to find that passion—not just for ideas but for processes—in their work. . . . Another lesson of the erotic is to value the experiences of our bodies. In the classroom this means recognizing the validity of student experience and teaching students the importance of locating themselves in both their discussions and their writing. It means valuing emotion and the personal in writing and attempts to take language beyond the traditional forms dictated by "white fathers" to find ways to write the "emotional sentence." And in asking my students to value their own experiences and locations, it becomes vital also to recognize the locations of the audiences they are addressing.
>
> Stacy, "Looking in the Dragon's Eyes: Discovering Pedagogy in the Writings of Audre Lorde," May 6, 1999

Other students worried overtly about the overemphasis on personal experience and narrative form that seemed to be emerging as a possible trait or tenet of a composition pedagogy based in women's rhetorics. Kit tries to reclaim "experience" as a critical move, in the process defining "use" in more and more complicated ways:

> Also important for me is the idea of inductive reasoning, starting from particular women's experiences and then moving to the general and then cycling back to the particular. I think "experiential knowledge" has become rather taboo in composition studies. This is an anti-feminist move. We want students to locate themselves socially, we want them to think critically about how their social location affects their world-view, yet we don't want them to rely on experiential knowledge. Yet critical thinking is implicitly tied to a feminist use of experiential knowledge. For example, Rich says understanding our locatedness means, "The white middle class girls taught to trade obedience for privilege." This is a fabulous line. The inductive reasoning Rich calls for is more than "expressing" our experience; it is reflecting, ques-

tioning, and analyzing those experiences to understand the complexities and contradictions of experiential knowledge.

Kit, journal, March 4, 1999

Kit's redefinition of rhetorical ethos as a critical questioning of experience represents one key "use" of women's rhetorics for pedagogical practices.

Each of the students we've quoted here came a long way in thinking about the consequences of their study for their teaching. By the end of the course the class had revised, expanded, and distilled the original attempt to characterize "women's rhetorics" into this list of possible uses or consequences for the teaching of writing:

- Speaking out/claiming a voice
- Extreme care with definition and context, always "looking beneath the words"
- Deliberateness about moves and motivations
- Choosing language that does not harm others
- Valuing experience, but always locating, contextualizing, and naming the ideological structure of experience
- Including the personal in the public and academic
- Teaching the political/ideological nature of language; teaching the language of the patriarchy at the same time teaching ways to subvert that language, as well as why, when, and how it might be brave, risky, dangerous, cowardly, smart, or stupid to do so

In their journals, lists, and final course papers, Kate's students highlight several pedagogical issues/principles that also arise when we teach the "The Rhetoric of Women Writers." In the next section, we draw on students' writing from two recent courses Joy has taught to examine the consequences when we put into practice the principles that Kate's students extrapolated from their reading of women's rhetorics.

"Doing Something About It": Using Women's Rhetorics for Public Engagement

And, of course, I am afraid—you can hear it in my voice—because the transformation of silence into language and action is an act of self-revelation.

Audre Lorde, "The Transformation of Silence into Language and Action"

Lorde asserts the interdependency of language and action and the interconnection between writing, speaking, and women's agency and authority. When our students read Lorde, they are often inspired by her call to engage in the "transformation of silence into language and action."[4] As Kate's students suggest, our responsibility is to "make writing and speaking count" by providing students with opportunities to move from the passive desire to act toward rhetorical activism of their own, putting theory into practice. Rereading Adrienne Rich's writing as rhetorical theory, Krista Ratcliffe notes that Rich calls on women to refuse stasis and to take action via re-vision. Ethical action demands that women know their own locations, subjectivity, and the systems that silence women, as well as those that enable their speaking (108–11). One of the potential consequences of overcoming silence and moving from passivity to action is the emergence of women's authority and agency. As Kate's students suggest, the development of rhetorical ability, then, is linked to women's emergence as speaking subjects who claim authority and agency to act in the world. But that process of moving from silence to action entails more than a simple one-step awakening; it involves a long process of self and rhetorical analysis, questioning normative values, and full engagement in speaking and writing. This too is one of the pedagogical tenet's Kate's students derived from their study of women's rhetorics. Joy's students provide some insights into what students might learn and how they may act rhetorically as they make the personal and rhetorical shift from silence to language and action.

Joy's class invited students to apply the understanding they derived from their analysis of women rhetors to their own rhetorical practice within and beyond the classroom. In addition to a more formal rhetorical study, students engaged in a series of "rhetorical action" projects. First, each student was in charge of one written "discussion starter" to be posted on the electronic bulletin board two days before the class. Second, they each did an in-class ten-minute "declamation" (see Roskelly) about an issue or topic they felt deeply committed to. The in-class declamations and follow-up class and online discussions provided valuable practice for the third, more public-action rhetoric project that required students to use writing or speaking to facilitate their audience's engagement with a particular public issue. They developed a wide variety of projects, including oral testimony for the legislature and student government, a handbook on date rape with sororities as its audience, a grant proposal to fund a visiting writer on disability, a film festival and follow-up discussion on aggression and violence, and a Women's Week marathon reading to benefit Afghan women.

This structure served to implement some of the pedagogical principles that Kate's students extrapolated from their study of women's rhetorics by providing students with opportunities to (1) speak out/claim a voice; (2) attend to rhetorical contexts and exigencies, "Knowing what you're doing and why you're doing it and making it explicit," as Kate's student Jennifer says; (3) recognize the political/ideological nature of language; (4) include the personal in the academic, but attend to Kit's concern that students learn to examine and critique experience; and (5) engage ethically with differences/others, what Kate's students describe as "choosing language that does not harm others."

In addition to the action rhetoric projects, Joy assigned reading and analysis of women's rhetorics. Although, as we said earlier, we are concerned that students move beyond their initial admiring, celebratory, but passive response to women rhetoricians of the past, we do think this is a necessary and potentially useful response. The texts provided inspiration and models on which students could draw as they found ways to implement Kate's students' first tenet: to help students speak out and "claim a voice." We think there's more going on in this "inspiration" than just a superficial admiration. In describing African American women rhetors, Royster points out that women's rhetorical action in arguing against slavery, for the franchise, the right to education, or against lynching (all part of our students' reading) opens up a "space for action" for other women (28).

And it's not just in historical women rhetors that our students find this potential "space." Peers in class whom they "admire" also inspire them and provide models of rhetorical authority. In one of Joy's recent classes, for example, several women were already involved in social justice activism on campus and in the community. Their declamations—urging students to get involved with international students on campus who have a different perspective on the U.S. "war on terrorism," or inviting students to become part of the "allies against homophobia," or to attend a training session for community literacy workers—were eloquent and passionate. Casey, an undergraduate, wrote: "I've never been around such inspiring women. I admire Sarah so much for being willing to stand out there in that peace demonstration. I don't think I could do that" (blackboard response, February 7, 2002). Later in the semester Casey did participate in a large demonstration for GLBT (gay, lesbian, bisexual, and transgender) rights. As students like Casey move beyond passive admiration, they may discover models of authoritative selfhood and new emerging rhetorical identities in texts by women rhetors and also in their own classmates' rhetorical acts. This is an important elaboration of what Kate's students called "claiming a voice."

Kate's student Heidi argues that our pedagogy should teach more carefully the contexts and exigencies out of which rhetorical acts emerge. As Joy's students read and analyzed the dramatic and compelling arguments for women's right to speak that Christine de Pizan, Sor Juana Inez de la Cruz, Gloria Anzaldua, and others have made over the centuries, they considered how those writers addressed and invoked their audiences with particular attention to their constraints as well. This analysis helped them begin to identify the gendered nature of authority and power that has shaped women's rhetorical practices. Renee wrote about this complex negotiation of relationships in response to another student:

> I think what you say about Hortensia and her group seeking help first from women and secondly from the tribunal of the triumvirs is really important. I find it fascinating that Hortensia must acknowledge and then use to her benefit the fact that women are completely outside of the political arena—that they are "exempted by their sex among all mankind" (18). What a phrase! To be exempt from mankind—to be and not to be, I guess this is what she's arguing in the end. Hortensia's (and that of her cohorts') first instinct is to bring their demands to women who themselves are outside of the public/political domain but who may hold some influence though marriage. When this fails and the women make their way into the forum and "dare to hold a public meeting" (18), they use their exclusion (their exemptness) from voting, as the basis for their rationale not to be taxed.
>
> Renee, response to discussion starter, February 19, 2002

Building on this basic analysis of women's negotiation of rhetorical power, students could then analyze the gendered nature of rhetorical theory. In her discussion of Aspasia, Sor Juana Inez de la Cruz, and Adrienne Rich, Ginny considered the inadequacy of traditional rhetorical definitions of speaker-audience relationships.

> For . . . these women, there is a danger involved in being rhetorical, a danger that is specifically tied to their role in a patriarchal society. Thus, in contrast to the nongendered definition of audience Covino and Jolliffe provide . . . these women have to be very sensitive because of the gendered nature of their audience. . . . What I think is interesting about all of these writers in relation to the topic of audience and the rhetorical tradition is that they [highlight] differences. In these examples, gender, class, and culture all become a part of our thinking

> about what it means to address, invoke, and relate to an audience. . . . Sor Juana was Mexican, Adrienne Rich is Jewish and lesbian. How do these elements factor into women's rhetorical . . . practice?
>
> Ginny, response to discussion starter, January 24, 2002

Students also turned their attention to their own rhetorical contexts and the gendered rhetorical assumptions that may influence their own attitudes toward speaking and writing. Many students identified with Audre Lorde's words about being afraid, her fear of "contempt, of censure, or some judgment, or recognition, of challenge, of annihilation" ("Transformation" 21). Although they understood that Lorde wrote in response to the extreme exigency of breast cancer, they found her words helpful in acknowledging their own less dramatic fears about speaking in class, about allowing others to read their writing or openly disagreeing with or challenging others whether in classrooms or in public contexts.

When teachers invite students to examine their own rhetorical contexts and constraints and to speak out and claim a voice, as Kate's students suggest we should, we offer them opportunities to move from a passive desire to speak and act. But we also invite them into new rhetorical roles and identities. Ginny noted in her discussion prompt: "I think Adrienne Rich had it right when she said, 'The awakening of consciousness is not like the crossing of a frontier—one step and you are in another country' ("When We Dead Awaken" 48)." Rich argues that the movement from inaction to action requires a fundamental "re-visioning" of subjectivity that also requires an understanding of one's location within particular personal, cultural, and political realities ("Notes Toward a Politics of Location"). So in order to move from silence to action, students must have access to rhetorical spaces where they can examine their rhetorical and political locations and try out an authoritative rhetorical stance as they respond to and reconstruct their own compelling exigencies.

As Ginny suggests, though, the consequences may not be quick, dramatic, or necessarily those we would hope for. At the beginning of the semester, Casey could not imagine engaging in the sort of public activism that her classmate Sarah took part in during weekly peace demonstrations. It wasn't surprising, then, that Casey chose for her declamation a very "safe" subject—the importance of expanding parking for students on campus. But at the same time, she was beginning to plan her "action rhetoric project" for later in the semester. In it she collaborated with two other students to create a documentary video of a public demonstration, a "human chain" around the state capitol organized by the Nebraska Coalition for Justice and Equality, a group working for expanded GLBT rights. In her final reflection Casey described her experience:

> At the beginning of this semester I never would have gotten involved in something like this, but this class has helped me do new things. Working with Beth and Kelly helped me a lot . . . I was holding hands around the Capital with more than a thousand other people, gays and lesbians and straights. And I was proud to be there . . . inspired by the speeches and the interviews I did. . . . When I helped to edit all the video I realized how important it was that we show GLBT issues persuasively to people who wouldn't be there. . . . I wanted to create something I would feel proud to stand up for—not just something that would benefit me personally.
>
> Casey, final course assessment, May 1, 2002

Although Casey may have taken only the slightest step into "a new country" and a new rhetorical identity, Casey's action rhetoric project, and her collaboration with others, stretched her conception of her own potential as a rhetor.

In contrast, Gretchen, an articulate, active women's studies major before she began studying women's rhetoric, made use of her reading of women's rhetoric to examine and connect the personal and academic sources of authority she was developing as a rhetor:

> These activities of self-definition and public debate are central to my personal feminist thought, and are integral parts of my life intellectually and privately. I cannot, and believe that one should not, separate the intellectual from the verbal from the political from the emotional. June Jordan and Audre Lorde lived this way. They've given me a way to tailor my anger. . . . A major force that brought me to feminism (and to words and action) was watching my mother die of breast cancer and watching without understanding how she was treated by the American medical establishment. . . . The past few weeks since [midterm] have been taken up with more action-based rhetorical study as opposed to more of the critical analysis of texts earlier. I really appreciate the combination of these two. To ignore the theoretical analysis gives little foundation for action, and to ignore the action part allows no room for progress to be made in the textual. I cannot draw the lines

> from text to action for others, but I know that reading these women made me feel that I could make a difference. I can change the system.
>
> Gretchen, final course assessment, April 29, 1999

Gretchen suggests that the transformation from silence to action is not just a shift in how one "acts." Idealism and individual "will" may help, but action also requires a complex understanding of rhetorical exigencies, one's own sources of authority, and the interconnection between her academic and personal lives, between theory and personal experience.

Kate's students worried about how personal experience has been overemphasized and underconceptualized in writing classes and feminist pedagogy, but they also asserted another important tenet of a pedagogy extrapolated from women's rhetorics: include the personal in the academic, but also engage in the critical examination of experience. Gretchen exemplifies the ability to reflect critically on the implications of her experience. Kate's students' epistemological concerns also arose in Joy's class when students read Patricia Williams, Evelyn Fox Keller, and Helen Longino. In the following response, Amanda Gailey articulates the importance of weighing different sources of knowledge:

> In this week's reading, Patricia Williams asks us how we determine what evidence to believe and whose testimony counts. She does NOT suggest that evidence and testimony themselves are useless, that experience is all that counts. Throughout the essay she argues with the legal profession, which, like the scientific community that Longino critiques, is set up to disregard all voices but those firmly at the center of power. Both writers want to see their professional communities become more inclusive by inviting often-silent perspectives to the table. . . . I would extend Joy's questions "How do we know?" and "What's left out and erased?" and add "Why do we believe?" "What is the basis of our belief?" These are the questions we should be asking of ourselves in class, of these discussions, and of the writers we read, as well as all the other voices that are leaking in through the windows.
>
> Amanda, discussion starter, Feb. 19, 2002

Going public in their rhetorical acts challenged our students to ask the critical questions about their experience and values that Amanda articulates. And it may also lead them to consider the immediate consequences of speaking and writing publicly about their experiences and to reexamine the beliefs they hold—another of Kate's students' principles. In Joy's class, Gretchen and Tina spent the semester creating and managing a women's studies web site to respond to the repeated assertions in the campus newspaper that women's studies is a lesbian political movement, not an academic discipline. Their letters and the web site prompted some national attention, including a letter from Daphni Patai supporting the local newspaper columnist's views. Gretchen said at midterm that this left her exhilarated at times, but at other times she was discouraged and exhausted from the effort it took to craft careful responses. Scrawled at the top of her final course assessment was this additional note: "Joy, have you heard about J. F.'s latest allegations in the *Daily Nebraskan*? She's accusing Tina and me of slander and threatening to sue the University because we reprinted her letter in the Women Studies web site. I'm stressed. I'll call you." Joy and her students were immediately reminded that there are real consequences when teachers encourage students to write and speak publicly. As Kate's students suggest, we're obligated to "teach ways to subvert the language of patriarchy" but also "how it might be brave, risky, dangerous, cowardly, smart or stupid to do so."

So far we've chosen accounts that illustrate the positive potential of studying women's rhetorics. We illustrate the sense of agency and authority students may begin to develop as they make use of the space for rhetorical action the class provided, the analysis they develop of the gendered rhetorical contexts and exigencies that women face and the implications those hold for them as rhetors, and their ability to attend critically to the authority of various sources of evidence, including personal experience. But some students have a much more conflicted response to the writers we read in these classes: they are too inaccessible, too theoretical, too political, in some students' words, "too angry," or they represent views that are antithetical to students' beliefs. As a consequence, women's rhetoric may prompt action and resistance of a much different sort than we imagine. Lisa, for example, was a senior in English education, devoutly religious and frustrated in Joy's class. At midterm, she described her response this way:

> I signed up for this class because it fulfilled two requirements for my major. I came to it blind, but I didn't come in empty-handed. I brought in a lot of stereotypes of the feminist movement. I had the usual ideas that all feminists were abortion-loving, man-hating, gay agenda–promoting . . . and to be brutally honest, I did refer on several occasions to this class as "my feminazi class." I really had trouble with Adrienne Rich because she seemed angry.
>
> Lisa, midterm self-assessment narrative, March 3, 1999

Lisa felt that her values and experiences were challenged, even threatened in this course. Other students' action rhetoric projects—addressing homophobia on campus, calling women to "take back their bodies," or advocating for women's reproductive rights—corresponded with Joy's goal to engage students in critiquing, resisting, and speaking back to existing social constraints. But these goals were inconsistent with Lisa's values. Her final action rhetoric project was a presentation intended to resist and disrupt her classmates' beliefs in feminist and pro-choice thought. Students responded to her speech with icy silence and barely contained anger, especially because she ended by appropriating Audre Lorde's words on the necessity of breaking silences and of transforming silence into action.

It's difficult to claim that Lisa took any steps into Rich's "other country" or that she experienced any awakening of consciousness in the direction feminists have expected. But hers was as difficult a rhetorical project as any, because she was forced to negotiate issues of audience and authority with her professor and her fellow students, and in doing so she had to assert her own agency and authority. Further, Lisa's declamation enacts what Kate's students asserted as key tenets of a pedagogy based on women's rhetorics: students themselves "have to decide" on their own rhetorical choices; they must believe that "their writing counts"; and they must recognize and deal with the consequences of their rhetorical acts. Lisa's declamation, however resistant to the dominant discourse of the course, enacted these principles.

Kate's students called on teachers to help students be responsible ethical rhetoricians and to engage in dialogue around difference. Reading Sojourner Truth or Gloria Anzaldua or the racist comments of nineteenth-century suffragists certainly directs students' attention to ethics and difference. But we find that students are often more prepared to talk about ethics and difference in the abstract, or to do battle with university administrators, the governor, or "the patriarchy" than to engage in dialogue with fellow students whose perspectives differ from their own. The presence of Lisa and students like her in women's rhetoric classes often necessitates an equally compelling engagement with these issues. Kate's students called it "choosing language that does not harm others."

We think that tenet articulated by Kate's students needs further elaboration. Because women are socialized *not* to disagree or make trouble, we worry that women may see rhetoric that challenges or interrupts, or is passionate or angry, as "harmful," that conflict itself is harmful. As Susan Jarratt points out, conflict is often necessary if women are to learn to confront the unequal power relationships that are inherent in differences (115). Joy's students struggled to explore the conflicts that arose out of their differences and at the same time to practice making ethical rhetorical choices. In a discussion about Patricia Williams's essay "Crimes of Passion," Carolyn, a senior heading for law school, responded to Williams's brief comment about the importance of affirmative action by recounting an experience that one of her sorority sisters had as she applied to law schools. Her friend's experience provided her with evidence of the unfairness of affirmative action. She was denied admission to a prestigious program, while an African American student in the pre-law program was admitted even though her LSAT scores were lower and she was a "less disciplined" student. Carolyn's comment drew a blaze of counterarguments from some of the other members of the class, many of whom could barely contain their anger. The class ran thirty minutes overtime while Joy attempted to help students sort out the issues and to address the rhetorical as well as the emotional consequences of this discussion.

Carolyn's anti–affirmative action statements, like Lisa's resistance, demanded that we put to use all the principles Kate's students had articulated at the end of their seminar: "Extreme care with definition and context, deliberateness about moves and motivations, choosing language that does not harm others, and valuing experience, but always locating, contextualizing, and naming the ideological structure of experience." Joy's students were prompted to ask: How do we have a dialogue with those with whom we fundamentally disagree? Is it even possible when two groups hold such different beliefs about what counts as evidence? What is the place of anger and "preaching" in our discussions? How do we challenge each other and understand our differences while also "choosing language that does not harm others"?

The most effective strategy we know for helping students work toward a response to these questions is to make the rhetoric in our classes the subject of our analysis—to analyze and make explicit our own moves and motivations. Some students relish these very difficult and honest discussions; others find the open tension and conflict threatening. Consequently, Joy planned to begin the subsequent class with a discussion analyzing what had happened rhetorically in the previous class. But before class Carolyn asked to have the floor first for a spontaneous declamation. As she spoke to the class, she drew on her reading of women rhetors and her analysis of her own rhetoric to talk about how it felt to be attacked for her views, how she might have framed her remarks more effectively and evaluated her friend's experience more critically, and how others might have countered her view more constructively. With women's rhetoric as her warrant, Carolyn stood up and analyzed her own and others' rhetorical moves, ideological investments, and use of power. In doing so, she claimed her own authority to use the classroom as a public space, a site for rhetorical action.

This class reminded us that the possibilities for rhetorical action are everywhere. We have avoided defining the "public" of public engagement in our title. But we hope it is clear that we view the dichotomy between classroom and public space as false. The classroom is a public site of rhetorical action as demanding in the negotiation of power and differences as the world beyond it, and our rhetorical acts within it hold consequences for students that are as serious as speaking in a public hearing at the legislature, making a public argument for GLBT rights, or writing a column for the newspaper.

Renee articulated this expansive conception of the sites for public rhetorical action in her final course assessment:

> Chela Sandoval describes the struggle of the third world feminists to recognize their prejudices and understand their differences rather than to . . . let these differences ferment unacknowledged beneath the surface. But the ultimate goal of the struggle was and is unity—a realistic, vibrant, changing unity that could lead to "the advancement of global egalitarian social relations" (68). These understandings for me as a writer, rhetor, and especially as a teacher do have profound implications. . . . My own experiences have always led me to seek out ways that I am similar to others, particularly to students. . . . But now I feel sort of like the white women at the NWSA, trying to build a false unity, a false sense of security. . . . So my teaching philosophy evolves. Perhaps it goes back to . . . the notion that theory is transformative. Women's rhetorical theory is transformation. My own teaching practices need to do the difficult and hard work of exploring difference first. No final word then, as I will carry these notions into future classrooms . . . discussions with my husband, . . . with my brother, future research and personal writings.
>
> Renee, final course assessment, April 20, 2002

Renee affirms the multiple sites in which she may apply women's rhetorical principles—pedagogical, personal, and professional. Like Kate's students, she examines women's rhetorics and the uses to which they can and should be put to engage in more ethical relationships with others in our personal, academic, and public lives.

Like Renee, we avoid a summarizing final word because so many questions remain to explore. But we do know that one of the most important ethical relationships is between teachers and students. We are struck, finally, by how much pedagogy inheres in women's rhetorics, how throughout history, sometimes without even knowing it, women wrote and spoke in order to teach others how to do so—with responsibility and courage. Our students' work suggests, we believe, that a responsible reading of women's rhetorics should lead to more "rhetorics," particularly rhetorics of teaching—the "everyday" work we all share—and consequently to rhetorics of public participation, especially if, as so many of us seem to hope, this renaissance of recovery is to make a difference to our professional, pedagogical, and public lives. Beyond "adding women," then, or even beyond revisions of rhetorical history, important as both projects might be, we must encourage our students to use women rhetors as their teachers.

Notes

1. We have had Lynn Worsham's concerns over the "will to pedagogy" in our minds as we've talked about the courses we describe here and as we've drafted this chapter. In "Writing Against Writing: The Predicament of *Ecriture Féminine,*" in *Contending with Words,* Worsham questioned what she saw as our field's desire to turn every theory into a teaching strategy. She worried over the "pedagogical imperative" that she thought threatened to uncomplicate, water down, or regulate new theories and rhetorics, particularly French feminist thought. We share her concerns about making easy connections between women's rhetorics and teaching strategies. However, given our own teaching of rhetoric by women, we remain convinced that this emerging canon both demands and deserves a rethinking of writing and rhetorical pedagogy and, as Worsham says, the "ideological investments" those represent. Moreover, we always try in our teaching and writing to resist the dualism between pedagogy and theory. Our practice as teachers and students has larger implications beyond the assignments we give and the writing/speaking practices that our students engage in. In *Gender and Rhetorical Space in American Life, 1866–1920,* Nan Johnson also reminds us that we must also analyze "the institutional role that rhetorical pedagogies play in inscribing discursive practices that maintain rather than destabilize status-quo relationships of gender, race, and class" (1). Our own rhetorical pedagogies should be subject to the same scrutiny. We also write this article to analyze our rhetorical pedagogies in teaching women's rhetorics.

2. When we first designed both these courses in 1993, we asked students to read primary material such as Christine de Pizan's *Book of the City of Ladies,* Margaret Fell's *Women's Speaking Justified,* Margaret Fuller's *Summer on the Lakes,* Dorothy Allison's *Two or Three Things I Know for Sure,* Virginia Woolf's *Three Guineas,* and

Audre Lorde's *Sister Outsider,* along with articles about women's writing, such as Cheryl Glenn's "Author, Audience, and Autobiography: Rhetorical Technique in *The Book of Margery Kempe*" and Barbara Biesecker's "Coming to Terms with Recent Attempts to Write Women into the History of Rhetoric." In the mid-nineties, we were inspired by the groundbreaking work included in Andrea Lunsford's *Reclaiming Rhetorica,* Shirley Logan's *With Pen and Voice,* Krista Ratcliffe's *Anglo-American Feminist Challenges to the Rhetorical Traditions,* and Cheryl Glenn's *Rhetoric Retold: Regendering the Tradition from Antiquity through the Renaissance.* But these works had to be supplemented with the primary material analyzed and explored in this scholarship. We longed for a collection of primary material in women's rhetorics. From 1998 to 2001 we developed *Available Means: An Anthology of Women's Rhetorics,* which gathers seventy women rhetors, from Diotima to Gloria Steinem, together for the first time. The courses we report on here used material we were gathering for that anthology as their texts. In the most recent class included here, students read primary texts from *Available Means,* supplemented by Lunsford, Glenn, Logan, Royster, and others mentioned above.

3. Jennifer's language is particularly appropriate for this essay. We deeply thank the students in all the courses we discuss here for collaborating with us on these ideas and practices and for giving us permission to quote from their work.

4. The connection between language and action is a central feature of women's rhetorical theory. In *Traces of a Stream,* Jacqueline Jones Royster says of African American women rhetors: "Social advocacy and activism constitute, therefore, an important analytical value. Their essays offer us prime examples of the will and capacity to use literate resources in order to participate in public arenas, and also of the desire to generate, and not just participate in, sociopolitical action. Among African American women there is . . . evidence of an ancient and dusky commitment to language and action."

Works Cited

Biesecker, Barbara. "Coming to Terms with Recent Attempts to Write Women into the History of Rhetoric." *Philosophy and Rhetoric* 25 (1992): 140–61.

Glenn, Cheryl. "Author, Audience, and Autobiography: Rhetorical Technique in *The Book of Margery Kempe.*" *College English* 54 (1992): 540–53.

———. *Rhetoric Retold: Regendering the Tradition from Antiquity through the Renaissance.* Carbondale: Southern Illinois UP, 1998.

Johnson, Nan. *Gender and Rhetorical Space in American Life, 1866–1910.* Carbondale: Southern Illinois UP, 2002.

Logan, Shirley Wilson. *With Pen and Voice: A Critical Anthology of Nineteenth-Century African American Women.* Carbondale: Southern Illinois UP, 1995.

Lorde, Audre. "The Transformation of Silence into Language and Action." *The Cancer Journals.* 1980. San Francisco: Aunt Lute Books, 1997. 18–23.

———. "The Master's Tools Will Never Dismantle the Master's House." *Sister Outsider.* Freedom, CA: Crossing Press, 1984. 110–13.

Lunsford, Andrea, ed. *Reclaiming Rhetorica: Women in the Rhetorical Tradition.* Pittsburgh: U of Pittsburgh P, 1995.

Ratcliffe, Krista. *Anglo-American Feminist Challenges to the Rhetorical Tradition: Virginia Woolf, Mary Daly, Adrienne Rich.* Carbondale: Southern Illinois UP, 1995.

Rich, Adrienne. "Notes on a Politics of Location." *Blood, Bread, and Poetry, Selected Prose, 1979–1985.* New York: W. W. Norton, 1986. 210–31.

———. *What Is Found There: Notebooks on Poetry and Politics.* New York: Norton, 1993.

———. "When We Dead Awaken: Writing as Revision." *On Lies, Secrets, and Silences, Selected Prose, 1966–1978.* New York: W. W. Norton, 1979. 33–49.

Roskelly, Hephzibah. "Teaching Other Available Means: Women's Declamation." Paper presented at the Conference on College Composition and Communication, March 2001. Milwaukee, Wisconsin.

Royster, Jacqueline Jones. *Traces of a Stream: Literacy and Social Change among African American Women.* Pittsburgh: U of Pittsburgh P, 2000.

Walker, Alice. "Everyday Use." *The Norton Anthology of Literature by Women.* Ed. Sandra M. Gilbert and Susan Gubar. New York: W. W. Norton, 1985. 2366–74.

Worsham, Lynn. "Writing against Writing: The Predicament of *Ecriture Féminine* in Composition Studies." *Contending with Words: Composition and Rhetoric in a Postmodern Age.* Ed. Patricia Harkin and John Schilb. New York: MLA, 1991. 82–104.

11

Between Fiction and Real Life

The Reality of Our Work

Dorothy Allison

I had the most extraordinary experience this morning. I was on California time, and there were people banging on the door under the impression that I was going to get up at a reasonable hour. I was laying in bed with *USA Today* and *Time* magazine, and I had *Time* open to an article about *Boys Don't Cry,* the movie about Brandon Teena, which had fierce details about the young woman who managed to transform herself into Brandon and how difficult it was for her to go from the female to the male—that took four weeks. And the more difficult transition that she made to go from male to heterosexual female—that took *five* weeks. Right beside it I had the clipping that I had torn out of *USA Today* that has a picture of the next cover of *Rolling Stone,* on which Brad Pitt is laying in a bed in a dress. Then I had the book for the Rhetoric(s) and Feminism(s) conference, and I'm looking at these magazines and the *USA Today,* and I'm thinking, *I'm in the wrong planet. While I was not looking, while I was being busy, something happened and I have not figured it out.* I wouldn't date Brad Pitt in a damn dress. But you put a good boy in a nice dress, I'll watch him and I'll think about it; it'll be interesting. Why is it that I suspect that it takes them so much less than four weeks?

This morning I got to listen to a good friend of mine read from a novel that she is working on (Judith Katz) and to watch another dear friend squirm in her chair because I kept asking her why she hadn't finished her memoir. We got around to the issue of why write memoir and why write fiction. I am very clear; I write fiction because I am a born liar and because it's easier. It's *far* easier. I cannot always explain my life or the life of a teenage girl who wanted to be a boy. But if I can start a story in which that human being has genuine grief—"bitter grief, hunger, fear"—I can go someplace that I understand, I can make sense of a world that mostly doesn't make sense. I think it's because I have a tiny Southern mind. I do not understand large, Wittgenstein words. I read Judith Butler, but I'd rather watch her. And as I'm watching her, I'm tempted to write a novel about a ferociously smart young woman at an eastern college who's gonna do good and confound those sons of bitches using them big words—gonna take them big words and give them other meanings and not explain. It could be a damn funny novel; I just might write it. I might.

I believe that what I understand about the world, I understand because of good books and music—bad music. I understand the world because I read Marge Piercy and Audre Lorde and Barbara Kingsolver and Adrienne Rich. . . . Because I fought my way through my rage at some of the early feminists that I had fights with and read their books anyway. I forgave them for being tacky and small and classist when they would be bared souls on the page.

What I love, what I deeply love, about American feminist fiction writers is that though we can be small sometimes, we write large on the page. We can have disagreements about language, community organizing, housing crises, which computer we use, but write large on the page—books that honor the differences between us. I was raised a Baptist. This means that there are damn few Baptists on the planet that I can stand. But I read Barbara Kingsolver's *Poisonwood Bible* and imagine myself into that family in the Congo, and I *forgive* the minister that glared at my mama when I was eleven years old. *That* is what a feminist fiction writer can accomplish. I believe memoirs can accomplish something close to that. I believe memoir, like Mary Karr's *The Liars' Club* or even Kathryn Harrison's *The Kiss.* I believe memoir because it is so transgressive, because it says, "I'm not making this up." Also, it has that sense of possibility. But what I love in memoir is the poetry of human life—not always the details. That's why I write fiction. That's why I choose to be a liar: deliberate, provocative, *useful.*

How many people in this room remember Marge Piercy's poem, "To Be of Use"? I'm in the right place. I think I reproduced about a thousand copies of that poem. It was Tallahassee, Florida. The women's center was imploding. There was a course being taught at the University of Florida called "The Rhetorics of Women's Liberation." I found myself thinking about it intensely when I began to prepare for this gathering. It was taught by an extremely kindly elderly gentleman with white hair. I was prepared to organize a sit-in in his classroom because I was a radical, lesbian feminist—wearing a canvas jacket because leather mildewed in Florida. We were going to confront his antifeminist prejudices. But he wanted to talk about language. I brought him a copy of Marge Piercy's "To Be of Use," and he understood. Turned out he was a working-class boy from south Georgia who had gotten an education on money provided by the U.S. Army. He had a sense about what it meant to try to change the world, and he had fallen in love—*genuinely in love*—with the revolutionary language he found in the poems of Robin Morgan. Put that together: white-headed little boy from south Georgia on an army scholarship reads Robin Morgan.

"And did you like the part about the furry genitals?" I asked him.

"The monster," he said. "Damn, yes!"

Large. Bold. Large. Bold. I forgave him for being Baptist.

To be of use, to make a difference in the world, to tell a true story, to be real. I've got nieces growing up in South Carolina, west Alabama, and north Florida. They are growing up on a diet of television. They all want to be Ally McBeal. They want to have a soundtrack for their lives. They want to worry about nothing else but finding the perfect man to love them. They want to wear them short, skimpy skirts and high heels and dance through life with those big lips and bright lipstick. They write me about it; they call me up and they ask me if I've met people like that. But I'm a liar, so I say, "Yeah, sure. But you know you have to get a high school degree and a college education. Learn to talk right." That's what they don't tell you when you watch her on Monday night, when she's dancing along to that soundtrack of her life.

There's a disjunction in the real. The real is constructed; what you believe about who you are and who you can be. Sometimes, if you are the thirteen-year-old daughter of a munitions worker in central Florida, like my niece Rachael, your world is constructed by the belief that if you're *very lucky*, you'll get a high school diploma, a boy who's got a good job, and maybe you'll work on the line next to your mama and wire bombs and sell them to the U.S. Army. It is *real* that my niece imagines that she could do that, since one generation before her, her mama never graduated from high school, never believed that she could. Real, what's possible, what you think you can do, you get from what the world tells you about who you are: boy or girl, white trash or Minneapolis Jew. You are a reflection of what you think you can do. And if you read Barbara Kingsolver, Jane Hamilton, Dorothy Allison, Janet Weis—feminist writers who write real young girls trying to be happy with or without the benefit of a soundtrack—your imagination is a little bit larger than what you might get listening to country western music and prime-time television.

I believe that I am a political worker. I know, I know; I get paid. I *demand* that I get paid. But I believe that what I am doing in the process of interpreting the world for myself in writing fiction (and making sense of teenage boys who want to be teenage girls, who want to be teenage boys), what I am doing is widening the possibilities for real people—my nieces and my nephews and the child I have been mentoring since a car hit her a year and a half ago, who woke up with no memory of what was real or what wasn't, who thought the entire world was daytime television. I started interviewing her because I was writing a new novel about someone who had a brain accident and then recovers her memory. But I had to sit down with this child from Oakland who had spent seven months in a hospital bed watching daytime television. She knew her mama had a job; she knew she used to go to school. She listened to the radio, and I brought her books. I read them to her out loud, because brain injury occasionally will interfere with one's ability to understand rhetoric. We talked about what was possible. We talked about the difference between fiction and reality. At the same time, I was reading novels. One of the things that I do as a lesbian/feminist/political activist/writer is I volunteer to judge contests, judge grants, and write recommendations. So I read a lot of bad fiction. I was reading to her from quite a bit of bad fiction. Her ambition was to become a coroner; she's quite convinced that coroners wear short skirts and have a soundtrack. I think it was the novels I read to her. But I'm not good at mysteries.

I really do believe that I went to college because I had read *To Kill a Mockingbird.* I really do believe that I got my scholarship because I had read Flannery O'Connor. I really do believe that I did not go crazy in college because I had read James Baldwin. I really do believe that I graduated because I had read Tennessee Williams, and I knew that sometimes a glass of whiskey will get you through a final exam. I have shaped my own reality. I am a proselytizer. I am an evangelical proselytizer. I go out to high schools at Navajo reservations and inner-city colleges in north New York, up in East Harlem, and I talk to kids about the value of books, and I talk about how you can construct your life. It doesn't have to be what they told you. And I am fierce. I am knowledge damage.

I say to them, "Shit, honey. I grew up so poor we couldn't even *spell* 'poor.' I grew up scared and terrified and look where I am. Look at this shirt;

look at this. I got this silk blouse. I got this linen jacket. Look at me. Children, you can do this."

I run into blank-faced kids whose imaginations are shaped by paperbacks, country music, rock-and-roll, and daytime television. And I back up and we start over. Mostly what I start over with is making them write me the story of their lives. I say the thing I was always afraid to explain to the world is how ashamed I was of my people. Then I give them a little bit of information—usually it has to do with hospitals, jails, rolled pickup trucks, or policemen. You'd be amazed at how universal that concept is, the rhetoric of being arrested. It carries. They recognize it.

I'm rueful. I say, "The first woman I fell in love with did me really bad." I'm talking to seventeen-year-old girls and fifteen-year-old boys.

"Yeah, mama, man I was in love."

"Oh boy, was she a hole."

"Oh honey, was he mean to me."

I get them to write me bad poetry. I *make* them write bad poetry. I read them aloud some of my own bad poetry—I saved it; it's useful. In the course of telling them terrible stories about where I come from and how I became this articulate, rhetorical feminist, we begin to talk about the difference between our *real* lives—rolled pickup trucks, sheriffs, hospitals, broken bones, sex you didn't want or sex you did. And in the course of getting them to start making a few little paragraphs about that and opening up a few pieces of their lives, something extraordinary happens. I think of it as the hallowing of the story. I think of it as, quite literally, honoring the human. You know, you can lose that if you listen to too much easy-listening music, if you watch too many sitcom television shows, too many easy movies. You begin to forget that when cars roll over, real people are inside. That when you say the word "orphan," not just one person died. That damage hurts. That survival is astonishing. I get young people to think of themselves as being powerful, as being capable of revenge, vindication. And then I read them Marge Piercy. I read them "To Be of Use."

I say to them, "Maybe, just maybe, you'll write a book. Maybe you'll get published. Maybe nobody will read it, or they won't tell you if they did. But maybe the one person that needed to know will see it. You might make a difference. You might reach past your own life. I am alive because of Flannery O'Connor, and Harper Lee, and James Baldwin, and Tennessee Williams, and oh, God help me, because of Jon McDonnell and Mickey Spillane. And honey, people you don't want to read, because I didn't want to read them at the time. I am alive because I began to think about my life as a novel. You can rewrite a novel. You can drop some characters completely. You can change genders; you can erase or highlight. You can say *what it meant.* That's not rhetorical; that's life-changing."

The virtue of being a published feminist is that people invite you to proclaim on these subjects. You get to talk and lecture, harangue and demand; they pay you money. It's a good thing. They pay you something more important than money; they give you respect. The thing we forget about art, about writing, about dance, about fiction, about music—the creative arts are for some of us the only way we can imagine, the only gate out of the path we've been locked in. I think some of you know what I'm talking about. If your entire life feels defined, shaped, and limited by other people; if somebody else has been telling you who you are and what you mean—and telling you with the precision of a Baptist minister, circa 1958 (there are a few better ones these days), or by a scared schoolteacher who just doesn't want to deal and just wants you to be quiet and to go to your typing classes and not ask dangerous questions—if your concept of who you are has been shaped by limits that small and walls that high, to be told that you have power is extraordinary. But the thing is stepping outside the walls.

I was born poor. When I was thirteen years old, the thing I wanted most in the world to do and be was to be a history teacher. My idea of safety, power, meaning, and respect was to be a history teacher. I was unaware of the fact that history teachers are paid very little and not given a whole lot of respect. Where I stood looking, that looked so good. I wanted it so bad. And it looked so far from where I was. Do you know what my sisters wanted? (Besides the fact that my sister Barbara did in fact contemplate a career as a high-priced call girl. We all did. It looked like something that would be easy to do; how hard can it be? We were wrong about that one too!) We imagined that we could be country singers—or possibly rock stars. We didn't play guitar; we didn't learn to play guitar at all. When you're very poor, or in some category in which the world shuts you down completely, you believe in the magical. You believe that somehow it just doesn't matter that you don't play an instrument at all or that you don't have a voice. Magic will happen if you're in the right place. You can survive on that fantasy. There is a distinction that happens. For some of us, if you fall in love with an art—it doesn't have to be writing; it doesn't have to be music; it doesn't even have to be dance (I once dated an Olympic runner; all she had to do was get up in the morning and pump those muscles)—the gates out of the locked room that the world puts you into can be very different, but if you know yourself poor, if you know yourself (I'm gonna use it, get ready) white trash, you know yourself trash, you know yourself denied; the great way out is art, because you step outside class. Now, I am of the impression that a lot of people became university professors because they believed that it was a gate outside class. Professors and artists have some things in common—we all wear these jackets, we all got suitcases and ride on airplanes when we can, we go to conferences like this—you earn a little respect. We all have a safe category to inhabit. When you're young, and looking at it from the outside, that's all you see. You don't see the work; you don't see the meetings; you don't see the struggle for tenure; you don't see the struggle to get published. You just see the outside; you see the form. That's enough sometimes. Enough to go further, to go into it, to get a degree, to learn to write, to separate yourself from your experience and create fiction. You have to keep manufacturing reason to do this.

Now I know that very few of you will tell me that you became professors in order to be safe. But that may in fact be shaped by the fact that you didn't feel safe once you became professors. But I can tell you now that I became a writer in order to change the world. I became a writer in the early women's movement, at a point in time in which I was told this is how the world could be changed. I believed it. Absolutely. My concept of who I could be had been so shaped by books that this made sense to me. I was going to write the great American novel. My concept of the great American novel was twofold. One, it would earn me some respect, possibly cash, but definitely respect. With respect would come some degree of safety. Because the kind of American novel that I would write would redefine *who* and *what* me and my people were. Now, whether you and your people are white or black, Christian or Jew, Yankee or Southerner, you know what I'm talking about. Self-definition and fiction do not usually get put together, but they should. Because to write a great novel, to tell a great story, you really do have to step through the box that the world has put around you; you have to see it. You have to see what the world has defined you as. And you have to refute it in language that the world will understand. You have to make a person like yourself—or maybe you'll be a boy, or maybe you'll be twenty years older, or maybe you'll be nine or ten years or eleven—but in the creation of a character you will reveal yourself, you and your people, and who you see your people as. If you do it very *deeply*—as I heard Judith Katz say this morning—if you go deep enough into it, at some point you won't be safe. You will be absolutely *not* safe. At that point you'll have to take a leap of faith. At that point you'll have to repay your debt to every writer or artist or organizer that you ever saw, who fed you some piece of substance, to whom you owe a debt. You'll have to make that leap; be naked; say *yeah, I was raped, I was a child;* say *yeah, I don't trust nobody;* say *yeah, I really do hate you people.* You will have to show the scariest, most hateful, most painful part of your life—even if it's a fiction, honey. Most *deeply* if it is a fiction, because you will have fooled yourself into believing that the construction will protect you. Repaying the debt that kept you alive, you will make an art and you will take a leap. And, oh God, I hope that you get all the way over to the other side. Because some of us don't. Because some of us spend our lives trying to write the great American novel and fall short.

I think the thing that I most want you to know is that I believe that the leap itself is of use. An attempt to create that art is of essential use. Now, maybe no one will buy your book. Or your book will be published and no one will notice. Mostly that's what happens. Writers, particularly women writers—particularly feminist women writers in this country—fail more often than they succeed. Our books go out into the world with all of our love, all of our soul, with the enormous leap of the secrets we know about ourselves and our people. A few people love them and tell us so, but most people don't even know that they go out. Surely there are a few writers in this room that know what I am talking about. Maybe you'll get a letter. Maybe some little magazine in Ohio will review you. But mostly you make that leap and you create that art and you do it alone, in isolation. That wave that goes out from you doesn't feel like it ever comes back. I spent this summer on Sandra Cisneros's porch. She and I have been fighting this little problem of depression. It's called "write a great book; try to write another one." The thing we kept saying to one another was, "I wanna read your book."

"I wanna read *your* book."

"Let's just write it for each other."

We didn't want to be in that place where we had to send it out, and then feel like it didn't do everything that we wanted it to do.

I gave her a frayed old copy of "To Be of Use." I felt like a damn fool. We talked about what it meant. What it means very simply is that I am engaged in a work that many of you are engaged in. We are trying to remake the world in a real image. In a piece of real that we recognize, we understand, we want to change, but that we *know.* If we do this work and we send it out, it don't matter about awards, it don't matter about money, it don't matter about attention, it don't matter if we jumped and jumped short. The jump is the thing. This story is the thing—the rolled pickup truck, that child in Nebraska, the Navajo sixteen-year-old who sang me the most gorgeous song and swore that she'd never sing it to nobody else and twenty minutes later I heard her singing it to somebody else. The art, the creation *is* magic, *is* powerful, *does* make a difference. But I'll tell you what I tell everybody: "You show me yours, I'll show you mine."

Finally, I wanted to acknowledge the butch femme nature of this evening. I understood completely as soon as I saw the plenary book. I saw Judith Halberstam's picture just below mine. Seemed right—I am a little older than she is. I feel sometimes like my life is a paradigm. I feel sometimes like I move through my life like a feminist parable—like Jesus should come along and talk about me. You can take some of my ex-girlfriends and you've got wine and loaves, honey. You've got astonishment. I understand how this is constructed. I love the fact that you say "rhetoric(s)." I love that you say "feminism(s)." I love the wideness of the vision and the specificity of some of them workshops. You people are talking about books that I ain't got to yet—and I read a lot. I am grateful that this event is as queer as it is, as proud as it is, and as diverse, strong, and calculatedly disruptive as it is. I love this town. I have fallen on ice in February here. I just gave a deposition swearing that I did in fact read in Amazon bookstore twenty-five years ago as part of a lawsuit. You have here an astonishing community. You have things that you don't even know about. And twenty years ago you took my girlfriend in when she was still drinking, and you kept her drunk for a whole winter. She's desperate to come back; she's sober now, so she won't be half as good a time. But it was a women's community here, a feminist community, a queer community. And I have loved it always. I am very proud that you invited me.

I am writing a book about someone who loses her memory, who has to re-create the world in her own brain. I think that's what I do all the time anyway. I am making another jump. Should I start to fall short, I am expecting that some of you will stretch a hand out and yell real loud. That's as much as we can do for each other. Some of you in this room owe me books. You know who you are. The promises were made a long time ago. I have been out here alone for a while. Get to work. Thank you.

Works Cited

Harrison, Kathryn. *The Kiss.* New York: Random House, 1997.

Karr, Mary. *The Liar's Club: A Memoir.* New York: Viking, 1995.

Kingsolver, Barbara. *The Poisonwood Bible.* New York: HarperFlamingo, 1998.

Lee, Harper. *To Kill a Mockingbird.* Philadelphia: Lippincott, 1960.

Piercy, Marge. "To Be of Use." *Circles on the Water.* New York: Knopf, 1982.

Bibliography

Abbott, Christopher. *Julian of Norwich: Autobiography and Theology.* Cambridge: D. S. Brewer, 1999.

Alcoff, Linda. "Cultural Feminism vs. Poststructuralism: The Identity Crisis in Feminist Theory." *Signs: Journal of Women in Culture and Society* 13 (1988): 405–36.

Alcoff, Linda, and Eduardo Mendieta. *Identities: Race, Class, Gender, and Nationality.* Malden, MA: Blackwell, 2003.

Annas, Pamela J. "Style as Politics: A Feminist Approach to the Teaching of Writing." *College English* 47 (1985): 360–71.

Ardis, Ann L. *New Women, New Novels: Feminism and Early Modernism.* New Brunswick, NJ: Rutgers UP, 1990.

Arthur, Marilyn B. "Early Greece: The Origins of the Western Attitude toward Women. *Arethusa* 6 (1973): 7–58.

Baecker, Diann Lynn. "Rhetoric's Role in the Development of the Bourgeois Public Sphere: A Study of Women's Responses to Rhetorical Texts in Eighteenth-Century England." *DAI* 61, no. 07A (2000): 2691.

Baker, Houston A., Jr. *Workings of the Spirit: The Poetics of Afro-American Women's Writing.* Chicago: U of Chicago P, 1991.

Barratt, Alexandra. "Julian of Norwich and the Holy Spirit, 'Our Good Lord.'" *Mystics Quarterly* 28.2 (2002): 78–84.

Baumlin, James S., and Tita French Baumlin, eds. *Ethos: New Essays in Rhetorical and Critical Theory.* Dallas: Southern Methodist UP, 1994.

Belenky, Mary Field, Blythe McVicker Clinchy, Nancy Rule Goldberger, and Jill Mattuck Tarule, eds. *Women's Ways of Knowing: The Development of Self, Voice, and Mind.* New York: Basic Books, 1986.

Benhabib, Seyla, Judith Butler, Drucilla Cornell, and Nancy Fraser, eds. *Feminist Contentions.* New York: Routledge, 1995.

Biesecker, Barbara. "Coming to Terms with Recent Attempts to Write Women into the History of Rhetoric." *Philosophy and Rhetoric* 25 (1992): 140–61.

Bizzell, Patricia, and Bruce Herzberg. *The Rhetorical Tradition: Readings from Classical Times to the Present.* 2nd ed. Boston: Bedford/St. Martin's, 2001.

Bolker, Joan. "Teaching Griselda to Write." *College English* 40 (April 1979): 906–08.

Bordin, Ruth. *Frances Willard: A Biography.* Chapel Hill: U of North Carolina P, 1986.

Bridenthal, Renate, and Claudia Koonz. *Becoming Visible: Women in European History.* Boston: Houghton Mifflin, 1977.

Bridwell-Bowles, Lillian. "Discourse and Diversity: Experimental Writing within the Academy." *College Composition and Communication* 43 (1992): 349–68.

———. "Freedom, Form, Function: Varieties of Academic Discourse." *Women/Writing/Teaching.* Ed. Jan Zlotnik Schmidt. Albany: SUNY Press, 1998. 179–97.

———. "Master's Tools." *Narration as Knowledge: Tales of the Teaching Life.* Ed. Joseph Trimmer. Portsmouth, NH: Boynton/Cook, 1997. 142–51.

Bridwell-Bowles, Lillian, Kathleen Sheerin DeVore, and Holly Littlefield, eds. *Identity Matters: Rhetorics of Difference.* Upper Saddle River, NJ: Prentice Hall, 1998.

Brody, Miriam. *Manly Writing: Gender, Rhetoric, and the Rise of Composition.* Carbondale: Southern Illinois UP, 1993.

Brown, Wendy. "The Impossibility of Women's Studies." *differences* 9.3 (1997): 79–101.

Brownmiller, Susan. *Femininity.* New York: Linden/Simon and Schuster, 1984.

Butler, Judith. *Gender Trouble: Feminism and the Subversion of Identity.* New York: Routledge, 1990.

Campbell, JoAnn. *Toward a Feminist Rhetoric: The Writing of Gertrude Buck.* Pittsburgh: U of Pittsburgh P, 1996.

Campbell, Karlyn Kohrs. "Consciousness Raising: Linking Theory, Criticism, and Practice," *Rhetoric Society Quarterly* 32 (2002): 45–64.

———. *Man Cannot Speak for Her.* Vols. I and II. New York: Praeger, 1989.

Canfield, Gae Whitney. *Sarah Winnemucca of the Northern Paiutes.* Norman: U of Oklahoma P, 1983.

Cantarella, Eva. *Pandora's Daughters: The Role and Status of Women in Greek and Roman Antiquity.* Trans. Maureen B. Fant. Baltimore: Johns Hopkins UP, 1981.

Chicago, Judy, and Edward Lucie-Smith. *Women and Art: Contested Territory.* New York: Watson-Guptill, 1999.

Cixous, Hélène. "The Laugh of the Medusa." Trans. Keith Cohen and Paula Cohen. *Signs* 1 (1976): 875–93.

Clark, Suzanne. *Sentimental Modernism: Women Writers and the Revolution of the Word.* Bloomington: Indiana UP, 1991.

Clarke, Danielle, and Elizabeth Clarke, eds. *"This Double Voice": Gendered Writing in Early Modern England.* New York: St. Martin's, 2000.

Code, Lorraine. *What Can She Know? Feminist Theory and the Construction of Knowledge.* Ithaca, NY: Cornell UP, 1991.

Cohen, Monica F. *Professional Domesticity in the Victorian Novel: Women, Work, and Home.* Cambridge: Cambridge UP, 1998.

Connors, Robert J. "Frances Wright: First Civic Rhetor in America." *College English* 42 (1999): 30–57.

Cott, Nancy. *The Grounding of Modern Feminism.* New Haven, CT: Yale UP, 1987.

Cox, Virginia. "The Single Self: Feminist Thought and the Marriage Market in Early Modern Venice." *Renaissance Quarterly* 48 (1995): 513–81.

Cucullu, Lois. *Expert Modernists, Matricide, and Modern Culture: Woolf, Forster, Joyce.* London: Palgrave Macmillan, 2004.

———. "Retailing the Female Intellectual." *differences* 9.2 (1997): 25–68.

Daly, Mary (with Jane Caputi). *Websters' First New Intergalactic Wickedary of the English Language.* New York: HarperCollins, 1987.

Donawerth, Jane. "Conversation and the Boundaries of Public Discourse in Rhetorical Theory by Renaissance Women." *Rhetorica* 16.2 (Spring 1998): 181–99.

———. "Nineteenth-Century United States Conduct Book Rhetoric by Women." *Rhetoric Review* 21.1 (2002): 5–21.

———. "Poaching on Men's Philosophies of Rhetoric: Eighteenth- and Nineteenth-Century Rhetorical Theory by Women." *Philosophy and Rhetoric* 33.3 (2000): 155–62.

———, ed. *Rhetorical Theory by Women before 1900.* Lanham, MD: Rowman and Littlefield, 2002.

Dow, Bonnie J. "The 'Womanhood' Rationale in the Woman Suffrage Rhetoric of Frances E. Willard." *Southern Communication Journal* 56.4 (Summer 1991): 298–307.

Eger, Elizabeth, Charlotte Grant, Cliona O'Gallchoir, and Penny Warburton. *Women, Writing, and the Public Sphere, 1700–1800.* Cambridge: Cambridge UP, 2001.

Eldred, Janet Carey, and Peter Mortensen. *Imagining Rhetoric: Composing Women of the Early United States.* Pittsburgh: U of Pittsburgh P, 2002.

Ezell, Margaret. *Writing Women's Literary History.* Baltimore: Johns Hopkins UP, 1993.

Ferguson, Kathy E. *The Man Question: Visions of Subjectivity in Feminist Theory.* Berkeley: U of California P, 1993.

Fleckenstein, Kristie. "Resistance, Women, and Dismissing the 'I.'" *Rhetoric Review* 17 (1998): 107–25.

Flynn, Elizabeth. "Composing as a Woman." *College Composition and Communication* 39 (1988): 423–35.

Foss, Karen, Sonja Foss, and Cindy Griffin. *Feminist Rhetorical Theories.* Thousand Oaks, CA: Sage, 1999.

———. *Readings in Feminist Rhetorical Theory.* Thousand Oaks, CA: Sage, 2004.

Foster, Gwendolyn Audrey. *Troping the Body: Gender, Etiquette, and Performance.* Carbondale: Southern Illinois UP, 2000.

Fuss, Diana. *Essentially Speaking: Feminism, Nature, and Difference.* New York: Routledge, 1989.

Gallagher, Catherine. "A History of the Precedent: Rhetorics of Legitimation in Women's Writing." *Critical Inquiry* 26 (2000): 309–27.

Gannett, Cinthia. *Gender and the Journal: Diaries and Academic Discourse.* Albany: SUNY Press, 1992.

Gere, Anne Ruggles. *Intimate Practices: Literacy and Cultural Work in U.S. Women's Clubs, 1880–1920.* Urbana: U of Illinois P, 1997.

Gilbert, Sandra, and Susan Gubar. *The Madwoman in the Attic: The Woman Writer and the Nineteenth-Century Literary Imagination.* New Haven, CT: Yale UP, 1979.

Gilligan, Carol. *In a Different Voice: Psychological Theory and Women's Development.* Cambridge, MA: Harvard UP, 1982.

Ginzberg, Lori D. " 'The Hearts of Your Readers Will Shudder': Fanny Wright, Infidelity, and American Freethought." *American Quarterly* 46 (1994): 195–226.

Glenn, Cheryl. "Author, Audience, and Autobiography: Rhetorical Technique in *The Book of Margery Kempe.*" *College English* 54 (1992): 540–53.

———. *Rhetoric Retold: Regendering the Tradition from Antiquity through the Renaissance.* Carbondale: Southern Illinois UP, 1997.

Green, Rayna. "The Pocahontas Perplex: The Image of Indian Women in American Culture." *Works Massachusetts Review 16* (Autumn 1975).

Gubar, Susan. "What Ails Feminism?" *Critical Inquiry* 24 (1998): 878–902.

Gunew, Sneja, ed. *Feminist Knowledge: Critique and Construct.* London: Routledge, 1990.

Halsband, Robert. *The Life of Lady Mary Wortley Montagu.* Oxford: Clarendon, 1956.

Hamburger, Jeffrey F. *The Visual and the Visionary: Art and Female Spirituality in Late Medieval Germany.* New York: Zone Books, 1998.

Harding, Sandra. *The Science Question in Feminism.* Ithaca, NY: Cornell UP, 1986.

Harjo, Joy, and Gloria Bird, eds. *Reinventing the Enemy's Language: Contemporary Native Women's Writings of North America.* New York: W. W. Norton, 1997.

Heilbrun, Carolyn G. *Writing a Woman's Life.* New York: W. W. Norton, 1988.

Hekman, Susan J. *Gender and Knowledge: Elements of a Postmodern Feminism.* Boston: Northeastern UP, 1990.

Hobbs, Catherine, ed. *Nineteenth-Century Women Learn to Write.* Charlottesville: UP of Virginia, 1995.

hooks, bell. *Talking Back: Thinking Feminist, Thinking Black.* Boston: South End Press, 1989.

———. " 'When I Was a Young Soldier for the Revolution': Coming to Voice." *Land-*

mark Essays on Voice and Writing. Ed. Peter Elbow. Davis, CA: Hermagoras Press, 1994. 51–58.

Hull, Suzanne W. *Chaste, Silent & Obedient: English Books for Women, 1475–1640.* San Marino, CA: Huntington Library, 1982.

Hutchinson, Louise D. *Anna Julia Cooper: A Voice from the South.* Washington, DC: Smithsonian Institution Press, 1982.

Irigaray, Luce. *This Sex Which Is Not One.* Trans. Catherine Porter with Carolyn Burke. Ithaca, NY: Cornell UP, 1985.

Jarratt, Susan, and Lynn Worsham, eds. *Feminism and Composition Studies: In Other Words.* New York: Modern Language Association, 1998.

Jarratt, Susan, and Nedra Reynolds. "The Splitting Image: Contemporary Feminisms and the Ethics of Ethos." *Ethos: New Essays in Rhetorical and Critical Theory.* Ed. James S. Baumlin and Tita French Baumlin. Dallas: Southern Methodist UP, 1994. 37–63.

Johnson, Lynn Staley. "The Trope of the Scribe and the Question of Literary Authority in the Works of Julian of Norwich and Margery Kempe." *Speculum* 66.4 (1991): 820–38.

Johnson, Nan. *Gender and Rhetorical Space in American Life, 1866–1910.* Carbondale: Southern Illinois UP, 2002.

———. *Nineteenth-Century Rhetoric in North America.* Carbondale: Southern Illinois UP, 1991.

———. "Reigning in the Court of Silence: Women and Rhetorical Space in Postbellum America." *Philosophy and Rhetoric* 33.3 (2000): 221–43.

Justice, George L., and Nathan Tinker, eds. *Women's Writing and the Circulation of Ideas: Manuscript Publication in England, 1550–1800.* Cambridge: Cambridge UP, 2002.

Kates, Susan. "Subversive Feminism: The Politics of Correctness in Mary Augusta Jordan's *Correct Writing and Speaking* (1904)." *College Composition and Communication* 48 (December 1997): 501–17.

Kirsch, Gesa. *Women Writing the Academy: Audience, Authority, and Transformation.* Carbondale: Southern Illinois UP, 1993.

Kirsch, Gesa E., Faye Spencer Maor, Lance Massey, Lee Nickoson-Massey, Mary P. Sheridan-Rabideau, eds. *Feminism and Composition: A Critical Sourcebook.* Boston: Bedford/St. Martin's, 2003.

Kunze, Bonnelyn Young. *Margaret Fell and the Rise of Quakerism.* Stanford, CA: Stanford UP, 1994.

Labalme, Patricia H., ed. *Beyond Their Sex: Learned Women of the European Past.* New York: New York UP, 1980.

Lane, Margaret. *Frances Wright and the "Great Experiment."* Manchester, Eng.: Manchester UP, 1972.

Langland, Elizabeth. *Nobody's Angels: Middle-Class Women and Domestic Ideology in Victorian Culture.* Ithaca: Cornell UP, 1995.

Latz, Dorothy L. "The Writings of St. Angela Merici in the Light of Bonaventuran

Exemplarism: The Motherhood, Fatherhood, and Transcendence of God." *Mystics Quarterly* 10 (1984): 126–35.

Leech, Kenneth, and Benedicta Ward, eds. *Julian Reconsidered.* Oxford: Fairacres Press, 1988.

Leeman, Richard W., ed. *"Do Everything" Reform—The Oratory of Frances E. Willard.* Westport, CT: Greenwood Press, 1992.

Lemert, Charles, and Esme Bhan, eds. *The Voice of Anna Julia Cooper.* New York: Rowman and Littlefield, 1998.

Levin, Carole, and Patricia A. Sullivan, eds. *Political Rhetoric, Power, and Renaissance Women.* Albany: SUNY Press, 1995.

Levy, Anita. *Other Women: The Writing of Class, Race, and Gender, 1832–1898.* Princeton, NJ: Princeton UP, 1991.

Logan, Shirley W. *"We Are Coming": The Persuasive Discourse of Nineteenth-Century Black Women.* Carbondale: Southern Illinois UP, 1999.

Looser, Davoney. *British Women Writers and the Writing of History, 1670–1820.* Baltimore: Johns Hopkins UP, 2000.

Lorde, Audre. *Sister Outsider.* Freedom, CA: Crossing Press, 1984.

Lowndes, Mary. "Genius and Women Painters." *Common Cause* (Apr. 17, 1914), 31.

Lunsford, Andrea. "Medieval Women as Collaborative Writers." Paper presented at the Conference on College Composition and Communication. Minneapolis, April 2000.

——, ed. *Reclaiming Rhetorica: Women in the Rhetorical Tradition.* Pittsburgh: U of Pittsburgh P, 1995.

Maginnis, Sr. Monica. *Angela Merici and Her Teaching Idea.* New York: Longmans Green, 1927.

Mahl, Mary, and Helene Koon, eds. *The Female Spectator: English Women Writers before 1800.* Old Westbury, NY: Feminist Press, 1977.

Mairs, Nancy. *Voice Lessons: On Becoming a (Woman) Writer.* Boston: Beacon Press, 1994.

Mattingly, Carol. *Appropriate[ing] Dress: Women's Rhetorical Style in Nineteenth-Century America.* Carbondale: Southern Illinois UP, 2002.

——. *Well-Tempered Women: Nineteenth-Century Temperance Rhetoric.* Carbondale: Southern Illinois UP, 1998.

McAvoy, Liz Herbert. "Julian of Norwich and a Trinity of the Feminine." *Mystics Quarterly* 28.2 (2002): 68–77.

McEntire, Sandra J., ed. *Julian of Norwich: A Book of Essays.* New York: Garland, 1998.

McKeon, Michael. "Historicizing Patriarchy: The Emergence of Gender Difference in England, 1660–1760." *Eighteenth-Century Studies* 28.3 (Spring 1995): 295–321.

Meale, Carol, ed. *Women and Literature in Britain, c. 1150–1500.* Cambridge: Cambridge UP, 1993.

Miller, Hildy. "The Impact of Women's Studies on Rhetoric and Composition."

Transforming the Disciplines: A Women's Studies Primer. Ed. Elizabeth MacNabb, et al. New York: Haworth, 2001.

———. "Writing Aphrodite: Reclaiming the Archetypal Feminine Muse." *Archetypes, Creativity, and Writing.* Ed. Regina Foehr and John Hruschka. Portsmouth, NH: Boynton/Cook, forthcoming.

Miller, Susan. *Assuming the Positions: Cultural Pedagogy and the Politics of Commonplace Writing.* Pittsburgh: U of Pittsburgh P, 1998.

Moi, Toril. "Feminism's Apocalyptic Futures." *New Literary History* 31 (2000): 805–25.

———. *Sexual/Textual Politics: Feminist Literary Theory.* London: Methuen, 1985.

———. "What Ails Feminist Criticism? A Second Opinion." *Critical Inquiry* 25 (1999): 362–79.

Moran, Michael G., and Michelle Ballif, eds. *Twentieth-Century Rhetorics and Rhetoricians.* Westport, CT: Greenwood Press, 2000.

Moraga, Cherríe, and Gloria Anzaldua, eds. *This Bridge Called My Back: Writings by Radical Women of Color.* New York: Kitchen Table, Women of Color Press, 1983.

Morris, Celia [Eckhardt]. *Fanny Wright: Rebel in America.* Urbana: U of Illinois P, 1984.

Nicholson, Linda J., ed. *Feminism/Postmodernism.* New York: Routledge, 1990.

Olson, Tillie. *Silences.* 1965. New York: Delta/Seymour Lawrence, 1989.

Oravec, Christine. "Madwomen in the Balcony: The Female Audience, Fanny Wright, and the Rhetorical Criticism of Nineteenth-Century America." Unpublished manuscript, 1990. University of Utah.

Peterson, Carla. *"Doers of the Word": African-American Women Speakers and Writers in the North (1830–1880).* New York: Oxford UP, 1995.

Petroff, Alvilda, ed. *Medieval Women's Visionary Literature.* Oxford: Oxford UP, 1986.

Phelps, Louise, and Janet Emig, eds. *Feminine Principles and Women's Experience in American Composition and Rhetoric.* Pittsburgh: U of Pittsburgh P, 1995.

Poynton, Cate. *Language and Gender: Making the Difference.* Oxford: Oxford UP, 1989.

Ratcliffe, Krista. *Anglo-American Feminist Challenges to the Rhetorical Traditions: Virginia Woolf, Mary Daly, Adrienne Rich.* Carbondale: Southern Illinois UP, 1996.

Rich, Adrienne. "Notes on a Politics of Location." *Blood, Bread, and Poetry: Selected Prose, 1979–1985.* New York: W. W. Norton, 1986. 210–31.

———. *On Lies, Secrets, and Silences: Selected Prose, 1966–1978.* New York: W. W. Norton, 1979. 33–49.

Ritchie, Joy, and Kate Ronald, eds. *Available Means: An Anthology of Women's Rhetoric(s).* Pittsburgh: U of Pittsburgh P, 2001.

Rogers, Katharine M. *Feminism in Eighteenth-Century England.* Urbana: U of Illinois P, 1982.

Ross, Isabel. *Margaret Fell: Mother of Quakerism.* London: Longmans Green, 1949.

Royster, Jacqueline Jones. *Southern Horrors and Other Writings: The Anti-Lynching Campaign of Ida B. Wells, 1892–1900.* Boston: Bedford Books, 1997.

——. *Traces of a Stream: Literacy and Social Change among African American Women.* Pittsburgh: U of Pittsburgh P, 2000.

——. "When the First Voice You Hear Is Not Your Own." *College Composition and Communication* 47.1 (February 1996): 29–40.

Schiwy, Marlene A. *A Voice of Her Own: Women and the Journal Writing Journey.* New York: Simon and Schuster, 1996.

Schmertz, Johanna. "Constructing Essences: Ethos and the Postmodern Subject of Feminism." *Rhetoric Review* 18 (1999): 82–91.

Schultz, Lucille M. *The Young Composers: Composition's Beginnings in Nineteenth-Century Schools.* Carbondale: Southern Illinois UP, 1999.

Showalter, Elaine. *A Literature of Their Own: British Women Novelists from Brontë to Lessing.* Princeton, NJ: Princeton UP, 1989.

——. *Sister's Choice: Tradition and Change in American Women's Writing.* 1991. Oxford: Oxford UP, 1994.

Solomon, Barbara Miller. *In the Company of Educated Women: A History of Women and Higher Education in America.* New Haven, CT: Yale UP, 1985.

Solomon, Martha, ed. *A Voice of Their Own: The Woman Suffrage Press, 1840–1910.* Tuscaloosa: U of Alabama P, 1991.

Sutherland, Christine Mason, and Rebecca Sutcliffe, eds. *The Changing Tradition: Women in the History of Rhetoric.* Calgary: U of Calgary P, 1999.

Watson, Martha. *Lives of their Own: Rhetorical Dimensions in Autobiographies of Women Activists.* Columbia: U of South Carolina P, 1999.

Watson, Nicholas. "The Composition of Julian of Norwich's Revelation of Love." *Speculum* 68 (1993): 637–83.

Wertheimer, Molly Meijer, ed. *Listening to Their Voices: The Rhetorical Activities of Historical Women.* Columbia: U of South Carolina P, 1997.

Worsham, Lynn. "Writing against Writing: The Predicament of *Ecriture Féminine* in Composition Studies." *Contending with Words: Composition Studies in a Postmodern Age.* Ed. Patricia Harkin and John Schilb. New York: Modern Language Association, 1991. 82–104.

Contributors

Dorothy Allison writes fiction, nonfiction, poetry, and autobiography at the intersections of Southern and working-class literature from the perspective of a feminist and lesbian-feminist activist. She is best known for her books—*Bastard Out of Carolina, Cavedweller, Two or Three Things I Know for Sure,* and *Trash.* In addition, she teaches classes, workshops, and seminars at universities across the country.

Lillian Bridwell-Bowles, currently Professor of English and Director of Communication across the Curriculum at Louisiana State University, was previously Director of the Center for Interdisciplinary Studies of Writing at the University of Minnesota. A past Chair of the Conference on College Composition and Communication (CCCC), she has been actively publishing in rhetoric and composition for over twenty-five years, including early work such as *New Directions in Composition Research,* with Richard Beach (1984), and *Word Processors and the Writing Process,* with Donald Ross and Paula Nancarrow (1984). Her feminist rhetorical work includes "The Master's Tools," in *Narration as Knowledge* (Trimmer, 1997); her CCCC chair's address, "Freedom, Form, and Function: Varieties of Academic Discourse" (*CCC,* 1995); and "Discourse and Diversity," originally published in *CCC* (1992) and now reprinted in many anthologies; and a textbook, *Identity*

Matters: Rhetorics of Difference (1999), with Kathleen Sheerin Devore and Holly Littlefield.

Karlyn Kohrs Campbell is a pioneering figure in the development of feminist rhetoric within the fields of speech and communication studies. She is Professor and Chair of the Department of Communication Studies at the University of Minnesota. Among her many publications, she is the author of *Man Cannot Speak for Her: A Critical Study of Early Feminist Rhetoric,* Volumes I and II (1989), and editor of *Women Public Speakers in the United States, 1800–1925* (1993) and *Women Public Speakers in the United States, 1925–present* (1994). She has also edited *The Interplay of Influence: News, Advertising, Politics, and the Mass Media* (5th ed., 2001), with Kathleen Hall Jamieson; *Critiques of Contemporary Rhetoric* (1997), with Thomas Burkholder; and *The Rhetorical Act* (3d ed., 2003) with Susan Schultz Huxman.

Lois Cucullu is Associate Professor in the Department of English at the University of Minnesota. She has previously published on British and American feminist criticism, gender studies, modernism, and postcolonial studies. Her book *Expert Modernists, Matricide, and Modern Culture: Woolf, Forster, Joyce* was published by Palgrave Macmillan in 2004.

Julia Dietrich is Professor of English and Associate Dean for Undergraduate Education at the University of Louisville. Her research is in medieval rhetoric, especially argumentation, and its role in mediating social and cultural change.

Jane Donawerth, Professor of English and affiliate in Women's Studies at the University of Maryland, has won many teaching awards and has recently published *Rhetorical Theory by Women before 1900: An Anthology* and, with one of her students, *Selected Orations, Letters, and Dialogues by Madeleine De Scudéry.* Currently, she is working on a critical analysis of women's rhetorical theory through an NEH fellowship. She has also taught and published on Shakespeare, early modern women's writing, and science fiction by women.

Jane Gallop, Distinguished Professor of English and Comparative Literature at University of Wisconsin–Milwaukee, has published mainly in the areas of critical theory, feminist psychoanalysis, and French feminism. She has numerous publications, including her early book *The Daughter's Seduc-*

tion (Cornell UP, 1982) and her more recent books *Anecdotal Theory* (Duke UP, 2002) and *Living with the Camera* (Duke UP, 2003).

Yvonne Merrill is the Writing across the Curriculum (WAC) Coordinator for the University of Arizona Department of English. She has taught college writing from first-year composition to graduate and professional business and technical writing. Her research and writing focus on how perceptual reality is socially constructed through language, determining what we can know, and especially what historic women have been able to know. Her work combines rhetoric with philosophy, psychology, history, sociology, and linguistics. She is especially interested in how students continue to develop disciplinary literacy and become socialized in their academic disciplines.

Hildy Miller, Associate Professor of English and Director of Writing at Portland State University, teaches graduate courses in rhetoric and composition. Her research interests focus on the areas of cognition and visual literacy, feminist theory, and the history of women in rhetoric. She has published in *CCC* and other composition journals and is currently working on a book (with Cindy Moore) on professional development for English graduate students. Her feminist rhetorical work includes "Goddess Spirituality and Academic Knowledge-Making" in *The Academy and the Possibility of Belief* (Buley-Meissner et al., 2000); "The Impact of Women's Studies on Rhetoric and Composition" in *Transforming the Disciplines: A Women's Studies Primer* (MacNabb et al., 2001); and "Writing Aphrodite: Reclaiming the Archetypal Feminine Muse" in *Archetypes, Creativity, and Writing* (Foehr and Hruschka, forthcoming).

Cindy Moore is Assistant Professor of English at Eastern Kentucky University, where she teaches courses in writing and writing theory. Along with issues of voice, she has written about classroom practice, mentoring, and professional development. She is coeditor of *Practice in Context: Situating the Work of Writing Teachers* (NCTE) and *The Dissertation and the Discipline: Reinventing Composition Studies* (Boynton/Cook).

Malea Powell is a mixed-blood of Indiana Miami, Eastern Shawnee, and Euro-American ancestry. She is an Associate Professor of Writing, Rhetoric, and American Culture at Michigan State University, where she has spent the past year developing a PhD concentration in cultural rhetorics. She teaches graduate and undergraduate courses in writing, rhetoric, critical theory and

American Indian rhetorics. Her research focuses on examining the rhetorics of "survivance" used by nineteenth-century American Indian intellectuals, and has been published in *CCCC; Paradoxa; Race, Rhetoric & Composition; AltDis;* and other essay collections. She has recently edited *Of Color: Native American Literatures,* forthcoming from Prentice-Hall.

Joy Ritchie, Professor of English and Director of Women's Studies at University of Nebraska, Lincoln, teaches graduate and undergraduate courses in the areas of rhetoric and composition, literacy studies, women's literature, and women's studies. Her recent publications include *Teacher Narrative as Critical Inquiry: Rewriting the Script* (with David E. Wilson) published by Columbia University, Teachers College Press, (2000), *Available Means: An Anthology of Women's Rhetoric(s)* (with Kate Ronald), University of Pittsburgh Press (2001), along with articles in *CCC* and other composition and rhetoric journals.

Kate Ronald is the Roger and Joyce L. Howe Professor of English at Miami University in Oxford, Ohio. She teaches graduate and undergraduate courses in composition theory, history, and practice. Her areas of research include the history of rhetoric, writing across the curriculum, theory and practice of pedagogy, and studies of student and disciplinary writing. Recent publications include *Reason to Believe: Romanticism, Pragmatism, and the Teaching of Writing* (with Hephzibah Roskelly) (1998) and *Available Means: An Anthology of Women's Rhetoric(s)* (with Joy Ritchie), University of Pittsburgh Press (2001).

Elizabeth West, an Assistant Professor of English at Georgia State University, conducts research and teaches with a particular interest in intersections of gender, race, class and the spiritual in literary works. She has published essays and reviews in *MELUS, South Atlantic Review, South Central Review, Womanist,* and *CLA* as well as entries in the *Oxford Companion to African American Literature.* With a research fellowship from the American Association of University Women, she began her current book-length project that examines the evolution of African spirituality in black women's writings.

Index